Angular UI Development with PrimeNG

Build rich and compelling Angular web applications using PrimeNG

Sudheer Jonna
Oleg Varaksin

BIRMINGHAM - MUMBAI

Angular UI Development with PrimeNG

First published: July 2017

Production reference: 1250717

Published by Packt Publishing Ltd.
Livery Place
35 Livery Street
Birmingham
B3 2PB, UK.
ISBN 978-1-78829-957-2

www.packtpub.com

Credits

Authors
Sudheer Jonna
Oleg Varaksin

Reviewer
Aristides Villarreal Bravo

Commissioning Editor
Smeet Thakkar

Acquisition Editor
Reshma Raman

Content Development Editor
Jason Pereira

Technical Editor
Prajakta Mhatre

Copy Editor
Charlotte Carneiro

Project Coordinator
Sheejal Shah

Proofreader
Safis Editing

Indexer
Rekha Nair

Production Coordinator
Melwyn D'sa

Foreword

Angular is a sophisticated technology that aims to create a framework with multi-platform support, including web, mobile and desktop. When I heard the news about Angular 1 being rewritten for Angular 2, I got excited instantly, since it was an opportunity for us to develop a UI component suite that I was pretty sure would be a success similar to its predecessor.

Then at the beginning of 2016, with the early alpha releases of Angular, we started working on PrimeNG to bring our years of expertise in PrimeFaces, the most popular UI framework for JavaServer Faces to Angular. Initially, we hit some roadblocks in the technology that prevented us from developing what we had in mind; however, all of those were temporary and the more we worked with Angular, the more we started to realize its true potential. From the perspective of a UI component library, Angular gives us all the APIs we need to develop easy to use, customizable, and accessible components easily.

Currently, PrimeNG is the most complete UI solution for Angular web development, with over 70+ high quality components and over a hundred thousand download per month. PrimeNG aims to solve complex enterprise requirements and as a result, its feature set is way beyond other UI libraries. As with all other PrimeTek libraries, PrimeNG is open source under the MIT license, which enables us to combine the power of the open source community with professional services and add-ons.

The standard documentation along with the showcase are the core resources for PrimeNG; however, there are many cases that cannot be covered in the documentation, and *Angular UI Development with PrimeNG* fills this gap and offers practical examples to serve as a companion to enhance your PrimeNG experience. I have known the authors, Oleg and Sudheer, for a long time and they have years of expertise in Prime projects, such as PrimeFaces before, and now PrimeNG. Their extensive knowledge of PrimeNG that is documented in this book is the best complementary PrimeNG resource available.

Overall, Angular and PrimeNG are a great duo for any type of Angular web application and considering the fact that both are developed with high pace, we can expect greater benefits in the future.

Cagatay Civici

Founder and Creator of PrimeNG

About the Authors

Sudheer Jonna was born in Nellore, India. Currently, he works as a senior software engineer in Singapore. He completed his master's degree in computer applications from JNTU University. In the past few years, he has worked on building various Java and JavaScript web applications based on JSF, PrimeFaces, Struts, Spring, REST, jQuery, Angular, React, and VueJS. He has also worked on many JavaEE and API development technologies, such as JPA (Hibernate), EJB, GraphQL, and Sequelize.

He is the founder of GeekoTek company (`http://geekotek.com`) and is a longtime JSF and Prime products expert. He is also a project member of the PrimeFaces, PrimeFaces Extensions, and PrimeNG open source projects. He is the author of three other Packt books, titled *Learning PrimeFaces Extension Development*, *PrimeFaces BluePrints*, and *PrimeFaces Theme Development*. He has worked as a technical reviewer on a few books. He is a regular speaker, trainer, reviewer, blogger, organizer, and active member of public forums. He is interested in R&D on the latest technologies.

He shares his knowledge through his personal website, `http://sudheerjonna.com`. You can follow him on Twitter with the handle `@SudheerJonna`.

Oleg Varaksin is a senior software engineer living in the Black Forest, Germany. He is a graduate computer scientist who studied informatics at Russian and German universities. His main occupation and "daily bread" in the last few years has consisted of building various Java-and JavaScript-based web applications based on JSF, PrimeFaces, Spring, REST, JavaScript, jQuery, Angular, and HTML5. Currently, he is working at Swiss Federal Railways on a new ticket webshop.

Oleg is an experienced and passionate web developer and has been working with the Prime UI libraries from the beginning. He is also a well-known member of the PrimeFaces community, creator of the PrimeFaces Extensions project, and the author of the *PrimeFaces Cookbook*. Oleg loves JavaScript, new ECMAScript standards, TypeScript, Angular, PrimeNG, RxJS, and Redux architecture. He has a deep understanding of web usability and accessibility.

Oleg normally shares the knowledge he has acquired on his blog at `https://medium.com/@OlegVaraksin`. His Twitter handle is `@OlegVaraksin`.

About the Reviewer

Aristides Villarreal Bravo is a Java developer. He is a member of the NetBeans Dream Team and Java User Groups. He is also the developer of the jmoordb framework. He lives in Panamá.

He has organized and participated in various conferences and seminars related to Java, JavaEE, NetBeans, the NetBeans platform, free software, and mobile devices nationally and internationally.

He is a writer of tutorials and blogs about Java NetBeans, and web developers. He has participated in several interviews on sites such as NetBeans, NetBeans Dzone, and JavaHispano. He has also developed plugins for NetBeans.

He is the CEO of Javscaz Software Developers and has reviewed a number of books, such as *PrimeFaces Blueprints*, *Apache Hive Cookbook, Dart By Example*, and *Express.js Blueprints*, all by Packt.

I want to thank my parents and brothers for their unconditional support (Nivia, Aristides, Secundino, Victor).

www.PacktPub.com

For support files and downloads related to your book, please visit www.PacktPub.com. Did you know that Packt offers eBook versions of every book published, with PDF and ePub files available? You can upgrade to the eBook version at www.PacktPub.com and as a print book customer, you are entitled to a discount on the eBook copy. Get in touch with us at service@packtpub.com for more details.

At www.PacktPub.com, you can also read a collection of free technical articles, sign up for a range of free newsletters and receive exclusive discounts and offers on Packt books and eBooks.

https://www.packtpub.com/mapt

Get the most in-demand software skills with Mapt. Mapt gives you full access to all Packt books and video courses, as well as industry-leading tools to help you plan your personal development and advance your career.

Why subscribe?

- Fully searchable across every book published by Packt
- Copy and paste, print, and bookmark content
- On demand and accessible via a web browser

Customer Feedback

Thanks for purchasing this Packt book. At Packt, quality is at the heart of our editorial process. To help us improve, please leave us an honest review on this book's Amazon page at www.amazon.com/dp/1788299574.

If you'd like to join our team of regular reviewers, you can e-mail us at customerreviews@packtpub.com. We award our regular reviewers with free eBooks and videos in exchange for their valuable feedback. Help us be relentless in improving our products!

Table of Contents

Preface

PrimeNG is a leading UI component library for Angular single page applications with 80+ rich UI components. PrimeNG has had huge success in the Angular world due to its active development over a short space of time. It is a rapidly evolving library, which is aligned with the last Angular release. Unlike this competitors, PrimeNG was created with enterprise applications in mind. This book provides a headstart for readers who want to develop real-time single page applications using this popular development stack.

This book consists of ten chapters and starts with a short introduction to single page applications. TypeScript and Angular fundamentals are important first steps for the PrimeNG topics that follow. Later, it discusses how to set up and configure a PrimeNG application in different ways for a kick-start. Once the environment is ready, then it is time to learn PrimeNG development, starting with the concept of theming and responsive layouts. Readers will learn enhanced Input, Select, and Button components, followed by various Panel, DataIteration, Overlays, Messages, and Menu components. The validation of form elements will not be missed out. An extra chapter demonstrates how to create map and chart components for real-world applications. Apart from the built-in UI components and their features, readers will see how to customize components as per their requirements.

Miscellaneous use cases are discussed in a separate chapter. Just to name a few: file uploading, drag and drop, blocking page pieces during AJAX calls, CRUD sample implementation, and more. This chapter goes beyond common topics, implements a custom component, and discusses a popular form of state management with @ngrx/store. The final chapter describes unit and end-to-end testing. To make sure Angular and PrimeNG development is flawless, full-fledged testing frameworks will be explained with systematic examples. Tips for speeding up unit testing and debugging Angular applications round out this book.

The book also focuses on how to avoid some common pitfalls, and shows best practices with tips and tricks for efficient Angular and PrimeNG development. At the end of this book, readers will know the ins and outs of how to use PrimeNG in Angular applications and get ready to create real-world Angular applications using rich PrimeNG components.

What this book covers

Chapter 1, *Getting Started with Angular and PrimeNG*, gives you the knowledge you need to dive into the next chapters. The chapter gives an overview of the TypeScript and Angular constructs used in this book. It is not possible to explain numerous features in detail. Instead, we will concentrate on the most important key concepts such as types, template syntax, decorators, component communication scenarios, modularity, and lifecycle hooks. After that, this chapter will introduce PrimeNG, which consists of rich UI components for Angular 2+, and show three possible project setups using SystemJS and Webpack loaders, as well as Angular CLI, a command-line tool for blazing fast Angular development.

Chapter 2, *Theming Concepts and Layouts*, introduces PrimeNG themes and the concepts involved. Readers will learn about the theming of PrimeNG components. The difference between structural and skinning CSS, the recommended project structure when working with SASS, installing and customizing PrimeNG themes and creating new themes will all be detailed. A discussions of two variants of responsive layouts, PrimeNG's own grid system, and Bootstrap's flexbox grid, finish this chapter.

Chapter 3, *Enhanced Inputs and Selects*, explains how to work with the input and select components available in PrimeNG. Such components are the main parts of every web application. PrimeNG provides nearly 20 components for data input that extend the native HTML elements with user-friendly interfaces, skinning capabilities, validation, and many other useful features.

Chapter 4, *Button and Panel Components*, covers various buttons such as radio, split, toggle, and select buttons, and Panel components, such as Toolbar, Accordion, FieldSet, and tabbed view. Panel components act as container components, which allow the grouping of other components. Various settings to configure Panel components are detailed in this chapter.

Chapter 5, *Data Iteration Components*, covers basic and advanced features to visualize data with the data iteration components provided by PrimeNG, including DataTable, DataList, PickList, OrderList, Tree, and TreeTable. The features discussed include sorting, pagination, filtering, lazy loading, and single and multiple selections. Advanced data visualization with the Schedule and DataScroller components will be demonstrated as well.

Chapter 6, *Amazing Overlays and Messages*, demonstrates a range of variations in content, displaying in modal or non-modal overlays such as Dialog, LightBox, and Overlay panel. The user does not leave the page flow when the content is displayed in the mentioned Overlays. An Overlay component overlays other components on a page. PrimeNG also offers notification components to show any messages or advisory information. Those components will be described as well.

Chapter 7, *Endless Menu Variations*, explains several menu variations. PrimeNG's menus fulfill all major requirements. They come with various facets--static, dynamic, tiered, hybrid, iPod-styled, and so on, and leave nothing to be desired. Readers will see a lot of recipes that discuss menu structure, configuration options, customizations, and integration with other components.

Chapter 8, *Creating Charts and Maps*, covers the ways to create visual charts with PrimeNG's extensive charting features and maps based on Google Maps. PrimeNG offers basic and advanced charting with its easy-to-use and user-friendly charting infrastructure. Besides standard charts, the chapter shows a special organization chart for visualizing hierarchical data. Throughout the chapter, mapping abilities such as drawing polylines, polygons, handling markers, and events will be explained as well.

Chapter 9, *Miscellaneous Use Cases and Best Practices*, introduces more interesting features of the PrimeNG library. You will learn about file uploading, drag and drop capabilities, displaying collections of images, practical CRUD implementation, deferred page loading, blocking page pieces, displaying a confirmation dialog with guarded routes, and more. An extra section will go through the complete process of building reusable components and developing a custom wizard component. After reading this chapter, readers will be aware of state-of-the-art state management with @ngrx/store and will see the benefits of Redux architecture.

Chapter 10, *Creating Robust Applications*, describes unit and end-to-end testing. The chapter begins with setting up a test environment with Jasmine and Karma. To make sure Angular and PrimeNG development is flawless, full-fledged testing frameworks will be explained with systematic examples. Tips for speeding up testing and debugging Angular applications end this chapter.

What you need for this book

This book will guide you through the installation of all the tools that you need to follow the examples. You will need to install npm to effectively run the code samples present in this book.

Who this book is for

This book is for everybody who would like to learn to create modern Angular-based single page applications using the PrimeNG component library. This book is a good choice for beginner to advanced users who are serious about learning modern Angular applications. The prerequisites for this book are some basic knowledge of Angular 2+, as well as TypeScript and CSS skills.

Conventions

In this book, you will find a number of text styles that distinguish between different kinds of information. Here are some examples of these styles and an explanation of their meaning. Code words in text, database table names, folder names, filenames, file extensions, pathnames, dummy URLs, user input, and Twitter handles are shown as follows: "Interfaces begin with the keyword `interface`."

A block of code is set as follows:

```
let x: [string, number];
x = ["age", 40]; // ok
x = [40, "age"] ; // error
```

Any command-line input or output is written as follows:

```
npm install -g typescript
```

New terms and **important words** are shown in bold. Words that you see on the screen, for example, in menus or dialog boxes, appear in the text like this: "File upload also provides a simpler UI with just one button **Choose**."

Warnings or important notes appear like this.

Tips and tricks appear like this.

Reader feedback

Feedback from our readers is always welcome. Let us know what you think about this book-what you liked or disliked. Reader feedback is important for us as it helps us develop titles that you will really get the most out of. To send us general feedback, simply e-mail feedback@packtpub.com, and mention the book's title in the subject of your message. If there is a topic that you have expertise in and you are interested in either writing or contributing to a book, see our author guide at www.packtpub.com/authors.

Customer support

Now that you are the proud owner of a Packt book, we have a number of things to help you to get the most from your purchase.

Downloading the example code

You can download the example code files for this book from your account at http://www.packtpub.com. If you purchased this book elsewhere, you can visit http://www.packtpub.com/support and register to have the files e-mailed directly to you. You can download the code files by following these steps:

1. Log in or register to our website using your e-mail address and password.
2. Hover the mouse pointer on the **SUPPORT** tab at the top.
3. Click on **Code Downloads & Errata**.
4. Enter the name of the book in the **Search** box.
5. Select the book for which you're looking to download the code files.
6. Choose from the drop-down menu where you purchased this book from.
7. Click on **Code Download**.

Once the file is downloaded, please make sure that you unzip or extract the folder using the latest version of:

- WinRAR / 7-Zip for Windows
- Zipeg / iZip / UnRarX for Mac
- 7-Zip / PeaZip for Linux

The code bundle for the book is also hosted on GitHub:

- `https://github.com/ova2/angular-development-with-primeng`. Every chapter has section-driven sub-folders with README files that contain all required instructions on how to run a demo applications. All demo applications in the book were developed with Angular 4 and PrimeNG 4.
- `https://github.com/PacktPublishing/Angular-UI-Development-with-Prime NG`.

We also have other code bundles from our rich catalog of books and videos available at `htt ps://github.com/PacktPublishing/`. Check them out!

Downloading the color images of this book

We also provide you with a PDF file that has color images of the screenshots/diagrams used in this book. The color images will help you better understand the changes in the output. You can download this file from `https://www.packtpub.com/sites/default/files/downloads/LearningAngularUIDevelop mentwithPrimeNG_ColorImages.pdf`.

Errata

Although we have taken every care to ensure the accuracy of our content, mistakes do happen. If you find a mistake in one of our books-maybe a mistake in the text or the code-we would be grateful if you could report this to us. By doing so, you can save other readers from frustration and help us improve subsequent versions of this book. If you find any errata, please report them by visiting `http://www.packtpub.com/submit-errata`, selecting your book, clicking on the **Errata Submission Form** link, and entering the details of your errata. Once your errata are verified, your submission will be accepted and the errata will be uploaded to our website or added to any list of existing errata under the Errata section of that title.

To view the previously submitted errata, go to `https://www.packtpub.com/books/conten t/support` and enter the name of the book in the search field. The required information will appear under the **Errata** section.

Piracy

Piracy of copyrighted material on the Internet is an ongoing problem across all media. At Packt, we take the protection of our copyright and licenses very seriously. If you come across any illegal copies of our works in any form on the internet, please provide us with the location address or website name immediately so that we can pursue a remedy.

Please contact us at copyright@packtpub.com with a link to the suspected pirated material.

We appreciate your help in protecting our authors and our ability to bring you valuable content.

Questions

If you have a problem with any aspect of this book, you can contact us at questions@packtpub.com, and we will do our best to address the problem.

1
Getting Started with Angular and PrimeNG

This book presupposes some basic knowledge of TypeScript and Angular 2. Anyway, we would like to give the readers an overview of the most important TypeScript and Angular key concepts used in this book. We will summarize TypeScript and Angular features and present them in understandable, simple, but deeply explained portions. At the time of writing the book, the current TypeScript and Angular Versions are 2.3.x and 4.2.x, respectively. Readers will also meet the PrimeNG UI library for the first time and gain experience with project setups in three various ways. At the end of this chapter, readers will be able to run the first Angular- and PrimeNG-based web application.

In this chapter, we will cover the following topics:

- TypeScript fundamentals
- Advanced types, decorators, and compiler options
- Angular cheat sheet - overview of key concepts
- Angular modularity and lifecycle hooks
- Running PrimeNG with SystemJS
- Setting up PrimeNG project with Webpack
- Setting up PrimeNG project with Angular CLI

TypeScript fundamentals

Angular 2 and higher is built with features of ECMAScript 2015/2016 and TypeScript. The new ECMAScript standards target evergreen browsers and helps to write more powerful, clean, and concise code. You can also use these features in any other less modern browsers with Polyfills such as `core-js` (`https://github.com/zloirock/core-js`). But, why do we need to use TypeScript?

TypeScript (`http://www.typescriptlang.org`) is a typed language and a super set of JavaScript developed by Microsoft. One can say that TypeScript is an advanced JavaScript with optional static typing. TypeScript code is not processed by browsers, it has to be translated into JavaScript by means of a TypeScript compiler. This translation is called *compilation* or *transpilation*. The TypeScript compiler transpiles `.ts` files into `.js` files. The main advantages of TypeScript are as follows:

- Types help you find and fix a lot of errors during development time. That means, you have less errors at runtime.
- Many modern ECMAScript features are supported out of the box. More features are expected according to the roadmap (`https://github.com/Microsoft/TypeScript/wiki/Roadmap`).
- Great tooling and IDE support with IntelliSense makes the coding a pleasure.
- It is easier to maintain and refactor a TypeScript application than one written in untyped JavaScript.
- Developers feel comfortable with TypeScript due to object-oriented programming patterns, such as interfaces, classes, enums, generics, and so on.
- Last but not least, Angular 2+ and PrimeNG are written in TypeScript.

It is also important to keep the following points in mind:

- The Typescript Language Specification says, *every JavaScript program is also a TypeScript program*. Hence, a migration from JavaScript to TypeScript code is easily done.
- TypeScript compiler emits output even when any errors are reported. In the next section, *Advanced types, decorators, and compiler options*, we will see how we can forbid emitting JavaScript on errors.

What is the best way to learn the TypeScript language? There is an official handbook on the TypeScript's homepage, which is aligned with the last released version. Hands-on learning is possible with the TypeScript playground (`http://www.typescriptlang.org/play`), which compiles on-the-fly TypeScript code entered in a browser and shows it side by side with the generated JavaScript code:

```
Using Generics              ▼    TypeScript  Share  Options                              Run  JavaScript
 1 class Greeter<T> {                             1 var Greeter = (function () {
 2     greeting: T;                                2     function Greeter(message) {
 3     constructor(message: T) {                   3         this.greeting = message;
 4         this.greeting = message;                4     }
 5     }                                           5     Greeter.prototype.greet = function () {
 6     greet() {                                   6         return this.greeting;
 7         return this.greeting;                   7     };
 8     }                                           8     return Greeter;
 9 }                                               9 }());
10                                                10 var greeter = new Greeter("Hello, world");
11 let greeter = new Greeter<string>("Hello, world");  11
```

Alternatively, you can install the TypeScript globally by typing the following command in the command line:

```
npm install -g typescript
```

Global installation means, the TypeScript compiler `tsc` can be reached and used in any of your projects. Installed Node.js and npm are presupposed. Node.js is the JavaScript runtime environment (`https://nodejs.org`). npm is the package manager. It is shipped with Node.js, but can be installed separately as well. After that, you can transpile one or more `.ts` files into `.js` files by typing the following command:

```
tsc some.ts another.ts
```

This will result in two files, `some.js` and `another.js`.

Basic types

TypeScript exposes the basic types, as well as a couple of extra types. Let's explore the type system with these examples.

- `Boolean`: The type is a primitive JavaScript boolean:

  ```
  let success: boolean = true;
  ```

- `Number`: The type is a primitive JavaScript number:

  ```
  let count: number = 20;
  ```

- `String`: The type is a primitive JavaScript string:

  ```
  let message: string = "Hello world";
  ```

- `Array`: The type is an array of value. There are two equivalent notations:

```
let ages: number[] = [31, 20, 65];
let ages: Array<number> = [31, 20, 65];
```

- `Tuple`: The type represents a heterogeneous array of values. `Tuple` enables storing multiple fields of different types:

```
let x: [string, number];
x = ["age", 40];      // ok
x = [40, "age"] ;     // error
```

- `Any`: The type is *anything*. It is useful when you need to describe the type of variables that you do not know at the time of writing your application. You can assign a value of arbitrary type to a variable of type `any`. A value of type `any` in turn can be assigned to a variable of arbitrary type:

```
let some: any = "some";
some = 10000;
some = false;

let success: boolean = some;
let count: number = some;
let message: string = some;
```

- `Void`: The type represents the absence of having an `any` type. This type is normally used as the return type of functions:

```
function doSomething(): void {
   // do something
}
```

- `Nullable`: These types denote two specific types, `null` and `undefined` that are valid values of every type. That means, they can be assigned to any other type. It is not always desired. TypeScript offers a possibility to change this default behavior by setting the compiler options `strictNullChecks` to `true`. Now, you have to include the `Nullable` types explicitly using a union type (explained later on), otherwise, you will get an error:

```
let x: string = "foo";
x = null;      // error
let y: string | null = "foo";
y = null;      // ok
```

Sometimes, you would like to tell compiler that you know the type better than it does and it should trust you. For instance, imagine a situation where you receive data over HTTP and know exactly the structure of the received data. The compiler doesn't know such structure of course. In this case, you want to turn off the type checking when assigning the data to a variable. It is possible with so called **type assertions**. A type assertion is like a type cast in other languages, but without the checking of data. You can do that either with *angle bracket* or the `as` syntax.

```
let element = <HTMLCanvasElement> document.getElementById('canvas');
let element = document.getElementById('canvas') as HTMLCanvasElement;
```

Interfaces, classes, and enums

An *interface* is a way to take a particular structure/shape and give it a name so that we can reference it later as a type. It defines a contract within our code. Interfaces begin with the keyword `interface`. Let's take an example:

```
interface Person {
    name: string
    children?: number
    isMarried(): boolean
    (): void
}
```

The specified interface `Person` has the following:

- The `name` property of type `string`.
- The optional property `children` of type `number`. Optional properties are denoted by a question mark and can be omitted.
- The `isMarried` method that returns a `boolean` value.
- Anonymous (unnamed) method that returns nothing.

Typescript allows you to use the syntax `[index: type]` to specify a `string` or `number` type based collection of key/value pairs. Interfaces perfectly fit such data structures. For example, consider the following syntax:

```
interface Dictionary {
    [index: number]: string
}
```

An interface is only used by TypeScript compiler at compile time, and is then removed. Interfaces don't end up in the final JavaScript output. General, no types appear in the output. You can see that in the TypeScript playground mentioned earlier.

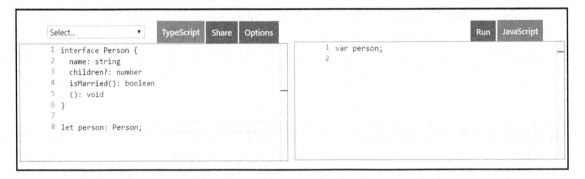

Beside interfaces, there are *classes* that describe objects. A class acts as a template for instantiating specific objects. The syntax for TypeScript's classes is almost identical to that of native classes in ECMAScript 2015 with some handy additions. In TypeScript, you can use `public`, `private`, `protected`, and `readonly` access modifiers:

```
class Dog {
    private name: string;    // can only be accessed within this class
    readonly owner: string = "Max";    // can not be modified
    constructor(name: string) {this.name = name;}
    protected sayBark() { }
}

let dog = new Dog("Sam");
dog.sayBark();  // compiler error because method 'sayBark' is protected and
                // only accessible within class 'Dog' and its subclasses.
```

Members with omitted modifiers are `public` by default. If a property or method is declared with the `static` keyword, there is no need to create an instance to access them.

A class can be abstract, that means, it may not be instantiated directly. Abstract classes begin with the keyword `abstract`. A class can implement an interface as well as extend another class. We can achieve that using the `implements` and `extends` keywords, respectively. If a class implements some interface, it must adopt all properties from this interface; otherwise, you will get an error about missing properties:

```
interface Animal {
    name: string;
}
```

```
class Dog implements Animal {
  name: string;
  // do specific things
}

class Sheepdog extends Dog {
  // do specific things
}
```

 Derived classes that contain constructor functions must call `super()`. The `super()` call executes the constructor function on the base class.

It is possible to declare a `constructor` parameter with a modifier. As result, a member will be created and initialized in one place:

```
class Dog {
  constructor(private name: string) { }

  // you can now access the property name by this.name
}
```

 This shortened syntax is often used in Angular when we inject services into components. Angular's services are normally declared in the component's constructor with the `private` modifier.

The last basic type to be mentioned here is *enum*. Enums allow us to define a set of named constants. Enum members have numeric values associated with them (started with 0):

```
enum Color {
  Red,
  Green,
  Blue
}

var color = Color.Red;     // color has value 0
```

Functions

Parameters and return values in the function signature can be typed too. Types protects you against JavaScript errors during function execution because the compiler warns you punctually at build time when the wrong types are used:

```
function add(x: number, y: number): number {
    return x + y;
}
```

Function type is a way to declare the type of a function. To explicitly declare a function type, you should use the keywords `var` or `let`, a variable name, a colon, a parameter list, a fat arrow `=>`, and the function's return type:

```
var fetchName: (division: Division, customer: Customer) => string;
```

Now, you must provide an implementation of this declaration:

```
fetchName = function (division: Division, customer: Customer): string {
    // do something
}
```

This technique is especially useful for callbacks. Imagine a filter function which filters arrays by some criterion. An exact criterion can be encapsulated in the passed in callback function that acts as predicate:

```
function filter(arr: number[], callback: (item: number) => boolean):
number[] {
    let result: number[] = [];
    for (let i = 0; i < arr.length; i++) {
        if (callback(arr[i])) {
            result.push(arr[i]);
        }
    }
    return result;
}
```

A possible function call with a specific callback could appear as follows:

```
let result = filter([1, 2, 3, 4], (item: number) => item > 3);
```

In TypeScript, every function parameter is assumed to be required. There are two ways to mark a parameter as optional (optional parameters can be omitted when calling the function).

- Use a question mark after the parameter name:

```
function doSomething(param1: string, param2?: string) {
    // ...
}
```

- Use the parameter's default value (ECMAScript 2015 feature), which gets applied when no value is provided:

```
function doSomething(param1: string, param2 = "some value") {
    // ...
}
```

Now, you are able to call this function with just one value.

```
doSomething("just one value");
```

Generics

In TypeScript, you can define generic functions, interfaces, and classes like in other programming languages. A generic function has type parameters listed in angle brackets:

```
function reverseAndMerge<T>(arr1: T[], arr2: T[]): T[] {
    return arr1.reverse().concat(arr2.reverse());
}

let arr1: number[] = [1, 2, 3];
let arr2: number[] = [4, 5, 6];
let arr = reverseAndMerge(arr1, arr2);
```

Such generic functions can be defined with generic interfaces as well. The function signature for `reverseAndMerge` is compatible with the following generic interface:

```
interface GenericArrayFn<T> {
    (arr1: T[], arr2: T[]): T[];
}

let arr: GenericArrayFn<number> = reverseAndMerge;
```

Note that the generic type parameter list in angle brackets follows the name of the function and interface. This is also true for classes:

```
class GenericValue<T> {
    constructor(private value: T) { }
    increment: (x: T) => T;
    decrement: (x: T) => T;
```

```
}

let genericValue = new GenericValue<number>(5);
genericValue.increment = function (x) {return ++x;};
genericValue.decrement = function (x) {return --x;};
```

Modules

ECMAScript 2015 has introduced built-in modules. The features of modules are as follows:

- Each module is defined in its own file.
- Functions or variables defined in a module are not visible outside unless you explicitly export them.
- You can place the export keyword in front of any variable, function, or class declaration to export it from the module.
- You can use the import keyword to consume the exported variable, function, or class declaration.
- Modules are singletons. Only a single instance of a module exists, even if it was imported multiple times.

Some exporting possibilities are listed here:

```
// export data
export let color: string = "red";

// export function
export function sum(num1: number, num2: number) {
  return num1 + num1;
}

// export class
export class Rectangle {
  constructor(private length: number, private width: number) { }
}
```

You can declare a variable, function, or class and export it later. You can also use the as keyword to rename exports. A new name is the name used for importing:

```
class Rectangle {
  constructor(private height: number, private width: number) { }
}

export {Rectangle as rect};
```

Once you have a module with exports, you can access its functionality in another module using the `import` keyword:

```
import {sum} from "./lib.js";
import {Rect, Circle} from "./lib.js";

let sum = sum(1, 2);
let rect = new Rect(10, 20);
```

There is a special case that allows you to import the entire module as a single object. All exported variables, functions, and classes are available on that object as properties:

```
import * as lib from "./lib.js";

let sum = lib.sum(1, 2);
```

Imports can be renamed with the `as` keyword and used under the new name:

```
import {sum as add} from "./lib.js";

let sum = add(1, 2);
```

Advanced types, decorators, and compiler options

TypeScript has more types and advanced constructs such as decorators and type definition files. This chapter gives an overview on advanced topics and shows how to customize the compiler configuration.

Union types and type aliases

A *union type* describes a value that can be one of many types. The vertical bar | is used as separator for each type the value can have. For instance, `number | string` is the type of a value that can be a number or string. For such values, we can only access members that are common to all types in the union. The following code works because the `length` property exists on both strings and arrays:

```
var value: string | string[] = 'some';
let length = value.length;
```

The next code snippet gives an error because the `model` property does not exist on the `Bike` type:

```
interface Bike {
  gears: number;
}

interface Car {
  gears: number;
  model: string;
}

var transport: Bike | Car = {gears: 1};
transport.model = "Audi";    // compiler error
```

Type alias is used as alternative name for the existing type or combination of types. It doesn't create a new type. A type alias begins with the `type` keyword.

```
type PrimitiveArray = Array<string|number|boolean>;
type Callback = () => number;
type PrimitiveArrayOrCallback = PrimitiveArray | Callback;
```

Type aliases can be used for better code readability, for example, in the function parameter list.

```
function doSomething(n: PrimitiveArrayOrCallback): number {
  ...
}
```

Type aliases can also be generic and make tricky types, which can not be made with interfaces.

Type inference

Type inference is used when the type is not provided explicitly. For instance in the following statements:

```
var x = "hello";
var y = 99;
```

These don't have explicit type annotations. TypeScript can infer that x is a string and y is a number. As you see, the type can be omitted if the compiler is able to infer it. TypeScript improves the type inference continuously. It tries to guess a best common type when elements of several types are present in an array. The type of the following variable `animal`, where `Sheepdog extends Dog`, is `Dog[]`:

```
let animal = [new Dog(), new Sheepdog()];
```

The best common type of the next array is `(Dog | Fish)[]` because the class `Fish` doesn't extend to any other class:

```
class Fish {
    kind: string;
}

let animal = [new Dog(), new Sheepdog(), new Fish()];
```

Type inference is also used for functions. In the next example, the compiler can figure out the types of the function's parameter (`string`) and the return value (`boolean`):

```
let isEmpty: (param: string) => boolean;
isEmpty = function(x) {return x === null || x.length === 0};
```

Decorators

Decorators were proposed in ECMAScript 2016 (`https://github.com/wycats/javascript-decorators`). They are similar to Java annotations--they also add metadata to class declaration, method, property, and the function's parameter, but they are more powerful. They add new behaviors to their targets. With decorators, we can run arbitrary code before, after, or around the target execution, like in aspect-oriented programming, or even replace the target with a new definition. In TypeScript, you can decorate constructors, methods, properties, and parameters. Every decorator begins with the @ character followed by the name of the decorator.

How does it work under the hood that takes its target as argument? Let's implement a classic example with a logging functionality. We would like to implement a method decorator @log. A method decorator accepts three arguments: an instance of the class on which the method is defined, a key for the property, and the property descriptor (`https://developer.mozilla.org/en/docs/Web/JavaScript/Reference/Global_Objects/Object/defineProperty`).

If the method decorator returns a value, it will be used as a new property descriptor for this method:

```
const log = (target: Object, key: string | symbol, descriptor:
PropertyDescriptor) => {
  // save a reference to the original method
  var originalMethod = descriptor.value;
  // replace the original function
  descriptor.value = function(...args: any[]) {
    console.log("Arguments: ", args.join(", "));
    const result = originalMethod.apply(target, args);
    console.log("Result: ", result);
    return result;
  }
  return descriptor;
}

class Rectangle {
  @log
  area(height: number, width: number) {
    return height * width;
  }
}

let rect = new Rectangle();
let area = rect.area(2, 3);
```

This decorator logs received arguments and return values. Decorators can be composed and customized with parameters too. You can write the following, for instance:

```
class Rectangle {
  @log("debug")
  @persist("localStorage")
  area(height: number, width: number) {
    return height * width;
  }
}
```

Angular offers different types of decorators that are used for dependency injection or adding metadata information at compilation time:

- Class decorators such as @NgModule, @Component, and @Injectable
- Property decorators such as @Input and @Output
- Method decorators such as @HostListener
- Parameter decorators such as @Inject

TypeScript compiler is able to emit some design-time type metadata for decorators. To access this information, we have to install a Polyfill called `reflect-metadata`:

```
npm install reflect-metadata --save
```

Now we can access, for example, the type of the property (`key`) on the `target` object as follows:

```
let typeOfKey = Reflect.getMetadata("design:type", target, key);
```

Refer to the official TypeScript documentation to learn more about decorators and reflect metadata API (`http://www.typescriptlang.org/docs/handbook/decorators.html`).

In TypeScript, Angular applications, decorators are enabled by setting the compiler options `emitDecoratorMetadata` and `experimentalDecorators` to `true` (compiler options are described later on).

Type definition files

JavaScript programs written in native JavaScript don't have any type information. If you add a JavaScript library such as jQuery or Lodash to your TypeScript-based application and try to use it, the TypeScript compiler can find any type information and warn you with compilation errors. Compile-time safety, type checking, and context-aware code completion get lost. That is where *type definition files* come into play.

Type definition files provide type information for JavaScript code that is not statically typed. Type definition files ends with `.d.ts` and only contain definitions which are not emitted by TypeScript. The `declare` keyword is used to add types to JavaScript code that exists somewhere. Let's take an example. TypeScript is shipped with the `lib.d.ts` library describing ECMAScript API. This type definition file is used automatically by the TypeScript compiler. The following declaration is defined in this file without implementation details:

```
declare function parseInt(s: string, radix?: number): number;
```

Now, when you use the `parseInt` function in your code, the TypeScript compiler ensures that your code uses the correct types and IDEs show context-sensitive hints when you're writing code. Type definition files can be installed as dependencies under the `node_modules/@types` directory by typing the following command:

```
npm install @types/<library name> --save-dev
```

A concrete example for jQuery library is:

npm install @types/jquery --save-dev

 In Angular, all type definition files are bundled with Angular npm packages and located under `node_modules/@angular`. There is no need to install such files separately like we did for jQuery. TypeScript finds them automatically.

Most of the time, you have the compile target ES5 (generated JavaScript version, which is widely supported), but want to use some ES6 (ECMAScript 2015) features by adding Polyfills. In this case, you must tell the compiler that it should look for extended definitions in the `lib.es6.d.ts` or `lib.es2015.d.ts` file. This can be achieved in compiler options by setting the following:

```
"lib": ["es2015", "dom"]
```

Compiler options

Typically, the first step in a new TypeScript project is to add in a `tsconfig.json` file. This file defines the project and compiler settings, for instance, files and libraries to be included in the compilation, output structure, module code generation, and so on. A typical configuration in `tsconfig.json` for Angular 2+ projects looks like the following:

```
{
  "compilerOptions": {
    "target": "es5",
    "module": "es2015",
    "moduleResolution": "node",
    "noImplicitAny": true,
    "sourceMap": true,
    "emitDecoratorMetadata": true,
    "experimentalDecorators": true,
    "outDir": "dist",
    "lib": ["es2015", "dom"]
  },
  "types": ["node"],
```

```
        "exclude": ["node_modules", "dist"]
    }
```

The listed compiler settings are described as follows. A full list of all options is available at the TypeScript documentation page (`https://www.typescriptlang.org/docs/handbook/compiler-options.html`).

Option	Type	Default	Description
target	string	ES3	This specifies ECMAScript target version: ES3, ES5, ES2015, ES2016, and ES2017.
module	string	ES6 if target is "ES6" and CommonJS otherwise	This specifies the format of module code generation: None, CommonJS, AMD, System, UMD, ES6, or ES2015.
moduleResolution	string	Classic if module is "AMD," System, ES6, and Node otherwise	This determines how modules get resolved. Either Node for Node.js style resolution or Classic.
noImplicitAny	boolean	false	This raises errors on expressions and declarations with an implied any type.
sourceMap	boolean	false	This generates the corresponding .map file. This is useful if you want to debug original files.
emitDecoratorMetadata	boolean	false	This emits design type metadata for decorated declarations in source. You have to set this value to true if you want to develop web applications with Angular.

`experimentalDecorators`	`boolean`	`false`	This enables experimental support for ECMAScript decorators. You have to set this value to `true` if you want to develop web applications with Angular.
`outDir`	`string`	`-`	This is the output directory for compiled files.
`lib`	`string[]`	Refer to the documentation for more information.	This is the list of library files to be included in the compilation. Refer to the documentation for more information.
`types`	`string[]`	`-`	This is the list of names of type definitions to include.
`exclude`	`string[]`	`-`	This is the list of (sub) directories excluded from the compilation.

You can stop the compiler from emitting JavaScript on errors by setting the `--noEmitOnError` option to `true`.

Angular cheat sheet - overview of key concepts

Angular 2 introduces completely new concepts for building web applications. The new Angular platform is complex. It is not possible to explain numerous Angular features in detail. Instead, we will concentrate on the most important key concepts such as dependency injection, components, and communication between them, built-in directives, services, template syntax, forms, and routing.

Components, services, and dependency injection

Normally, you write Angular applications by composing HTML templates with the Angular-specific markup and component classes to manage those templates. A **component** is simply a TypeScript class annotated with @Component. The @Component decorator is used to define the associated metadata. It expects an object with the following most used properties:

- selector: This is the name of the HTML tag representing this component
- template: This is an inline-defined template with HTML/Angular markup for the view
- templateUrl: This is the path to an external file where the template resides
- styles: An inline-defined styles to be applied to this component's view
- styleUrls: An array of paths to external files with styles to be applied to this component's view
- providers: An array of providers available to this component and its children
- exportAs: This is the name under which the component instance is exported in a template
- changeDetection: This is the change detection strategy used by this component
- encapsulation: This is the style encapsulation strategy used by this component

A component class interacts with the view through an API of properties and methods. Component classes should delegate complex tasks to services where the business logic resides. **Services** are just classes that Angular instantiates and then injects into components. If you register services at the root component level, they act as singletons and share data across multiple components. In the next section, *Angular modularity and lifecycle hooks*, we will see how to register services. The following example demonstrates how to use components and services. We will write a service class ProductService and then specify an argument of type ProductService in the constructor of ProductComponent. Angular will automatically inject that service into the component:

```
import {Injectable, Component} from '@angular/core';

@Injectable()
export class ProductService {
  products: Product[];

  getProducts(): Array<Product> {
    // retrieve products from somewhere...
    return products;
  }
}
```

```
    }

@Component({
  selector: 'product-count',
  template: `<h2 class="count">Found {{products.length}} products</h2>`,
  styles: [`
    h2.count {
      height: 80px;
      width: 400px;
    }
  `]
})
export default class ProductComponent {
  products: Product[] = [];

  constructor(productService: ProductService) {
    this.products = productService.getProducts();
  }
}
```

 Notice that we applied the @Injectable() decorator to the service class. This is necessary for emitting metadata that Angular needs to inject other dependencies into this service. Using @Injectable is a good programming style even if you don't inject other services into your service.

It is good to know what an item in the providers array looks like. An item is an object with the provide property (symbol used for dependency injection) and one of the three properties useClass, useFactory, or useValue that provide implementation details:

```
{provide: MyService, useClass: MyMockService}
{provide: MyService, useFactory: () => {return new MyMockService()}}
{provide: MyValue, useValue: 50}
```

Templates and bindings

A template tells Angular how to render the component's view. Templates are HTML snippets with the specific Angular's template syntax, such as interpolation, property, attribute, and event bindings, built-in directives, and pipes to mention just a few. We will give you a quick overview of the template syntax starting with interpolation. **Interpolation** is used to evaluate expressions in double curly braces. The evaluated expression is then converted to a string. The expression can contain any mathematical calculations, component's properties and methods, and many more:

```
<p>Selected car is {{currentCar.model}}</p>
```

Angular evaluates template expressions after every change detection cycle. Change detection cycles are triggered by many asynchronous activities such as HTTP responses, key and mouse events, and many more. The next fundamental template syntax is related to various bindings. *Property binding* sets an element property to a component property value. The element property is defined in square brackets:

```
<img [src]="imageUrl">
<button [disabled]="formValid">Submit</button>
```

Here, `imageUrl` and `formValid` are a component's properties. Note that this is a *one-way* binding because the data flow occurs in one direction, from the component's properties into target element properties. *Attribute binding* allows us to set an attribute. This kind of binding is used when there is no element property to bind. The attribute binding uses square brackets too. The attribute name itself is prefixed with `attr.`, for example, consider ARIA attributes for web accessibility:

```
<button [attr.aria-expanded]="expanded" [attr.aria-controls]="controls">
  Click me
</button>
```

User interactions result in a data flow from an element to a component. In Angular, we can listen for certain key, mouse, and touch events by means of *event binding*. The event binding syntax consists of a target event name within parentheses on the left and a quoted template statement on the right. In particular, you can call a component's method. In the next code snippet, the `onSave()` method is called on a click:

```
<button (click)="onSave()">Save</button>
```

The method (generally template statement) gets a parameter--an event object named `$event`. For native HTML elements and events, `$event` is a DOM event object:

```
<input [value]="name" (input)="name=$event.target.value">
```

Two-way binding is possible as well. The `[(value)]` syntax combines the brackets of property binding with the parentheses of event binding. Angular's directive `NgModel` is best suited for the two-way binding on native or custom input elements. Consider the following sample:

```
<input [(ngModel)]="username">
```

Is equivalent to:

```
<input [value]="username" (input)="username=$event.target.value">
```

Two-way binding in a nutshell: a property gets displayed and updated at the same time when the user makes changes. A *template reference variable* is another example of handy template syntax. You can declare a variable with the hash symbol (#) on any DOM element and reference this variable anywhere in the template. The next example shows the `username` variable declared on an `input` element. This reference variable is consumed on a button--it is used to get an input value for the `onclick` handler:

```
<input #username>
<button (click)="submit(username.value)">Ok</button>
```

A template reference variable can also be set to a directive. A typical example is the `NgForm` directive which provides useful details about the `form` elements. You can, for example, disable the submit button if the form is not valid (required fields are not filled in and so on):

```
<form #someForm="ngForm">
  <input name="name" required [(ngModel)]="name">
  ...
  <button type="submit" [disabled]="!someForm.form.valid">Ok</button>
</form>
```

Last but not least, the *pipe* operator (|). It is used for the transformation of the expression's result. The pipe operator passes the result of an expression on the left to a pipe function on the right. For example, the pipe `date` formats JavaScript `Date` object according to the specified format (`https://angular.io/docs/ts/latest/api/common/index/DatePipe-pipe.html`):

```
Release date: {{releaseDate | date: 'longDate'}}
// Output: "August 30, 2017"
```

Multiple chained pipes can be applied as well.

Built-in directives

Angular has a lot of built-in directives: `ngIf`, `ngFor`, `ngSwitch`, `ngClass`, and `ngStyle`. The first three directives are so called *structural directives*, which are used to transform the DOM's structure. Structural directives start with an asterisk (*). The last two directives manipulate the CSS classes and styles dynamically. Let's explain the directives in the examples.

The `ngIf` directive adds and removes elements in the DOM, based on the Boolean result of an expression. In the next code snippet, `<h2>ngIf</h2>` is removed when the `show` property evaluates to `false` and gets recreated otherwise:

```
<div *ngIf="show">
  <h2>ngIf</h2>
</div>
```

Angular 4 has introduced a new `else` clause with the reference name for a template defined by `ng-template`. The content within `ng-template` is shown when the `ngIf` condition evaluates to `false`:

```
<div *ngIf="showAngular; else showWorld">
  Hello Angular
</div>
<ng-template #showWorld>
  Hello World
</ng-template>
```

`ngFor` outputs a list of elements by iterating over an array. In the next code snippet, we iterate over the `people` array and store each item in a template variable called `person`. This variable can be then accessed within the template:

```
<ui>
  <li *ngFor="let person of people">
    {{person.name}}
  </li>
</ui>
```

`ngSwitch` conditionally swaps the contents dependent on condition. In the next code snippet, `ngSwitch` is bound to the `choice` property. If `ngSwitchCase` matches the value of this property, the corresponding HTML element is displayed. If no matching exists, the element associated with `ngSwitchDefault` is displayed:

```
<div [ngSwitch]="choice">
  <h2 *ngSwitchCase="'one'">One</h3>
  <h2 *ngSwitchCase="'two'">Two</h3>
  <h2 *ngSwitchDefault>Many</h3>
</div>
```

`ngClass` adds and removes CSS classes on an element. The directive should receive an object with class names as keys and expressions as values that evaluate to `true` or `false`. If the value is `true`, the associated class is added to the element. Otherwise, if `false`, the class is removed from the element:

```
<div [ngClass]="{selected: isSelected, disabled: isDisabled}">
```

`ngStyle` adds and removes inline styles on an element. The directive should receive an object with style names as keys and expressions as values that evaluate to style values. A key can have an optional `.<unit>` suffix (for example, `top.px`):

```
<div [ngStyle]="{'color': 'red', 'font-weight': 'bold', 'border-top':
borderTop}">
```

In order to be able to use built-in directives in templates, you have to import `CommonModule` from `@angular/common` and add it to the root module of your application. Angular's modules are explained in the next chapter.

Communication between components

Components can communicate with each other in a loosely coupled manner. There are various ways Angular's components can share data, including the following:

- Passing data from parent to child using `@Input()`
- Passing data from child to parent using `@Output()`
- Using services for data sharing
- Calling `ViewChild`, `ViewChildren`, `ContentChild`, and `ContentChildren`
- Interacting with the child component using a local variable

We will only describe the first three ways. A component can declare input and output properties. To pass the data from a parent to a child component, the parent binds the values to the input properties of the child. The child's input property should be decorated with `@Input()`. Let's create `TodoChildComponent`:

```
@Component({
  selector: 'todo-child',
  template: `<h2>{{todo.title}}</h2>`
})
export class TodoChildComponent {
  @Input() todo: Todo;
}
```

Now, the parent component can use `todo-child` in its template and bind the parent's `todo` object to the child's `todo` property. The child's property is exposed as usual in square brackets:

```
<todo-child [todo]="todo"></todo-child>
```

If a component needs to pass the data to its parent, it emits custom events via the output property. The parent can create a listener to a particular component's event. Let's see that in action. The child component `ConfirmationChildComponent` exposes an `EventEmitter` property decorated with `@Output()` to emit events when the user clicks on buttons:

```
@Component({
  selector: 'confirmation-child',
  template: `
    <button (click)="accept(true)">Ok</button>
    <button (click)="accept(false)">Cancel</button>
  `
})
export class ConfirmationChildComponent {
  @Output() onAccept = new EventEmitter<boolean>();

  accept(accepted: boolean) {
    this.onAccept.emit(accepted);
  }
}
```

The parent subscribes an event handler to that event property and reacts to the emitted event:

```
@Component({
  selector: 'confirmation-parent',
  template: `
    Accepted: {{accepted}}
    <confirmation-child (onAccept)="onAccept($event)"></confirmation-child>
  `
})
export class ConfirmationParentComponent {
  accepted: boolean = false;

  onAccept(accepted: boolean) {
    this.accepted = accepted;
  }
}
```

A bi-directional communication is possible via services. Angular leverages RxJS library (htt ps://github.com/Reactive-Extensions/RxJS) for asynchronous and event-based communication between several parts of an application as well as between an application and remote backend. The key concepts in the asynchronous and event-based communication are `Observer` and `Observable`. They provide a generalized mechanism for push-based notification, also known as the observer design pattern. `Observable` represents an object that sends notifications, and `Observer` represents an object that receives them.

Angular implements this design pattern everywhere. For example, Angular's Http service returns an Observable object:

```
constructor(private http: Http) {}

getCars(): Obvervable<Car[]> {
  return this.http.get("../data/cars.json")
    .map(response => response.json().data as Car[]);
}
```

In case of the inter-component communication, an instance of the Subject class can be used. This class inherits both Observable and Observer. That means it acts as a message bus. Let's implement TodoService that allows us to emit and receive Todo objects:

```
@Injectable()
export class TodoService {
  private subject = new Subject();

  toggle(todo: Todo) {
    this.subject.next(todo);
  }

  subscribe(onNext, onError, onComplete) {
    this.subject.subscribe(onNext, onError, onComplete);
  }
}
```

Components can use this service in the following way:

```
export class TodoComponent {
  constructor(private todosService: TodosService) {}
  toggle(todo: Todo) {
    this.todosService.toggle(todo);
  }
}

export class TodosComponent {
  constructor(private todosService: TodosService) {
    todosService.subscribe(
      function(todo: Todo) { // TodoComponent sent todo object },
      function(e: Error) { // error occurs },
      function() { // completed }
    );
  }
}
```

Forms

Forms are the main building blocks in every web application. Angular offers two approaches to build forms: *template-driven forms* and *reactive forms*. This section gives you a short overview of template-driven forms.

Reactive forms are suitable when you need to create dynamic forms programmatically in the component's class. Refer to the official Angular documentation to learn reactive forms (https://angular.io/docs/ts/la test/guide/reactive-forms.html).

We already mentioned two directives: NgForm and NgModel. The first directive creates a FormGroup instance and binds it to a form in order to track aggregate form value and validation status. The second one creates a FormControl instance and binds it to the corresponding form element. The FormControl instance tracks the value and the status of the form element. Each input element should have a name property that is required to register the FormControl by the FormGroup under the name you assigned to the name attribute. How to deal with this tracked data? You can export the NgForm and NgModel directives into local template variables such as #f="ngForm" and #i="ngModel", respectively. Here, f and i are local template variables that give you access to the value and status of FormGroup and FormControl, respectively. This is possible because the properties from FormGroup and FormControl are duplicated on the directives themselves. With this knowledge in hand, you can now check if the whole form or a particular form element:

- Is valid (valid and invalid properties)
- Has been visited (touched and untouched properties)
- Has some changed value (dirty and pristine properties)

The next example illustrates the basic concept:

```
<form #f="ngForm" (ngSubmit)="onSubmit(f)" novalidate>
  <label for="name">Name</label>
  <input type="text" id=name" name="name" required
         [(ngModel)]="name" #i="ngModel">
  <div [hidden]="i.valid || i.pristine">
    Name is required
  </div>
  <button>Submit</button>
</form>

// Output values and states
Input value: {{i.value}}
```

```
Is input valid? {{i.valid}}
Input visited? {{i.touched}}
Input value changed? {{i.dirty}}
Form input values: {{f.value | json}}
Is form valid? {{f.valid}}
Form visited? {{f.touched}}
Form input values changed? {{f.dirty}}
```

The `NgModel` directive also updates the corresponding `form` element with specific CSS classes that reflect the element's state. The following classes are added/removed dependent on the current state:

State	Class if true	Class if false
Element has been visited	`ng-touched`	`ng-untouched`
Element's value has changed	`ng-dirty`	`ng-pristine`
Element's value is valid	`ng-valid`	`ng-invalid`

This is handy for styling. For example, in case of validation errors, you can set red borders around input elements:

```
input.ng-dirty.ng-invalid {
  border: solid 1px red;
}
```

Routing

Angular's `router` module allows you to configure navigation in a single page application without a full page reload. The router can display different views (compiled component templates) within a special tag called `<router-outlet>`. During navigation, one view will be replaced by another one. A simple routing configuration looks as follows:

```
const router: Routes = [
  {path: '', redirectTo: 'home', pathMatch: 'full'},
  {path: 'home', component: HomeComponent},
  {path: 'books', component: BooksComponent}
];
```

When you navigate to the web context root, you will be redirected to /home. As a reaction to that, the view of the HomeComponent will be displayed in <router-outlet>. It is obvious that a direct navigation to /home displays the same view. A navigation to /books displays the view of BooksComponent. Such router configuration should be converted to an Angular's module by RouterModule.forRoot:

```
const routes: ModuleWithProviders = RouterModule.forRoot(router);
```

This is then imported in a root module class. In addition to the root module, an Angular application can consist of a lot of feature or lazy-loaded modules. Such separate modules can have their own router configurations which should be converted to Angular's modules with RouterModule.forChild(router). The next section, *Angular modularity and lifecycle hooks*, discusses modules in detail. Angular offers two strategies for implementing client-side navigation:

- HashLocationStrategy: This strategy adds a hash sign (#) to the base URL. Everything after this sign represents a hash fragment of the browser's URL. The hash fragment identifies the route. For example, http://somehost.de:8080/#/books. Changing the route doesn't cause a server-side request. Instead, the Angular application navigates to a new route and view. This strategy works with all browsers.
- PathLocationStrategy: This strategy is based on the **History API** and only works in browsers that support HTML5. This is the default location strategy.

The details are to be mentioned here. If you want to use the HashLocationStrategy, you have to import two classes, LocationStrategy and HashLocationStrategy from '@angular/common' and configure providers as follows:

```
providers: [{provide: LocationStrategy, useClass: HashLocationStrategy}]
```

Providers are described in the next section, *Angular modularity and lifecycle hooks*. The PathLocationStrategy class requires a configuration of the base URL for the entire application. The best practice is to import APP_BASE_HREF constant from '@angular/common' and use it as a provider in order to configure the base URL:

```
providers: [{provide: APP_BASE_HREF, useValue: '/'}]
```

How to trigger a navigation? You can achieve that in two ways, either by a link with a `routerLink` property, which specifies an array consisting of route (path) and optional parameters:

```
<a [routerLink]="['/']">Home</a>
<a [routerLink]="['/books']">Books</a>

<router-outlet></router-outlet>
```

Or programmatically, by invoking the `navigate` method on Angular's `Router` service:

```
import {Router} from '@angular/router';

...

export class HomeComponent {
  constructor(private router: Router) { }

  gotoBooks() {
    this.router.navigate(['/books']);
  }
}
```

You can also pass parameters to a route. Placeholders for parameters start with a colon (`:`):

```
const router: Routes = [
  ...
  {path: 'books/:id', component: BookComponent}
];
```

Now, when navigating to a book with real parameters, for example, programmatically as `this.router.navigate(['/books/2'])`, the real parameter can be accessed by `ActivatedRoute`:

```
import {ActivatedRoute} from '@angular/router';

...

export class BooksComponent {
  book: string;
  constructor(private route: ActivatedRoute) {
    this.book = route.snapshot.params['id'];
  }
}
```

The router outlet can be named as well:

```
<router-outlet name="author"></router-outlet>
```

The associated configuration should contain the `outlet` property with the name of the router outlet:

```
{path: 'author', component: AuthorComponent, outlet: 'author'}
```

Angular modularity and lifecycle hooks

Angular modularity with NgModules provides a great way to organize the code in a web application. Many third-party libraries, such as PrimeNG, Angular Material, Ionic, are distributed as NgModules. *Lifecycle hooks* allow us to perform custom logic at component level at a well-defined time. This section covers these major concepts in detail.

Modules and bootstrapping

Angular modules make it possible to consolidate components, directives, services, pipes, and many more into cohesive blocks of functionality. Angular's code is modularized. Every module has its own functionality. There are `FormsModule`, `HttpModule`, `RouterModule`, and many other modules as well. What does a module look like? A module is a class annotated with the `@NgModule` decorator (imported from `@angular/core`). `@NgModule` takes a configuration object that tells Angular how to compile and run the module code. The most significant properties of the the configuration object are:

- `declarations`: The array with components, directives, and pipes, which are implemented in that module and belong to that module.
- `imports`: The array with dependencies in form of other modules which need to be made available to that module.
- `exports`: The array of components, directives, and pipes to be exported and permitted to be imported by another modules. The rest is private. This is the module's public API and similar to how the `export` keyword works in ECMAScript modules.
- `providers`: This is the array of services (service classes, factories, or values), which are available in that module. Providers are parts of the module and can be injected into components (inclusive sub-components), directives, and pipes defined within the module.

- `bootstrap`: Every Angular application has at least one module--the root module. The `bootstrap` property is only used in the root module and contains the component which should be instantiated first when bootstrapping the application.
- `entryComponents`: This is the array of components that Angular generates component factories for. Normally, you need to register a component as an entry component when it is intended to be created dynamically at runtime. Such components can not be figured out automatically by Angular at template compilation time.

A typical module configuration for any separate example in this book looks something like this:

```
import {NgModule} from '@angular/core';
import {BrowserModule} from '@angular/platform-browser';
import {BrowserAnimationsModule} from '@angular/platform-
browser/animations';
import {FormsModule} from '@angular/forms';
import {APP_BASE_HREF} from '@angular/common';

// PrimeNG modules needed in this example
import {ButtonModule} from 'primeng/components/button/button';
import {InputTextModule} from 'primeng/components/inputtext/inputtext';

import {AppComponent} from './app.component';
import {SectionComponent} from './section/section.component';
import {routes} from './app-routing.module';

@NgModule({
    imports: [BrowserModule, BrowserAnimationsModule, FormsModule,
              routes, ButtonModule, InputTextModule],
    declarations: [AppComponent, SectionComponent],
    providers: [{provide: APP_BASE_HREF, useValue: '/'}],
    bootstrap: [AppComponent]
})
export class AppModule { }
```

BrowserModule is needed to get access to the browser-specific renderers and Angular standard directives such as `ngIf` and `ngFor`. Don't import BrowserModule in any other modules except the root module. Feature modules and lazy-loaded modules should import `CommonModule` instead.

The following is an example of how to bootstrap an Angular application in the JIT mode (just in time compilation):

```
import {platformBrowserDynamic} from '@angular/platform-browser-dynamic';
import {AppModule} from './app';

platformBrowserDynamic().bootstrapModule(AppModule);
```

In the **ahead-of-time** mode (**AOT** compilation), you need to provide a factory class. To generate the factory class, you must run the ngc compiler instead of the TypeScript tsc compiler. In the last two sections of this chapter, you will see how to use AOT with Webpack and Angular CLI. The bootstrapping code in the AOT mode looks like the following:

```
import {platformBrowser} from '@angular/platform-browser';
import {AppModuleNgFactory} from './app.ngfactory';

platformBrowser().bootstrapModuleFactory(AppModuleNgFactory);
```

 Templates with bindings written in Angular need to be compiled. With AOT, the compiler runs once at build time. With JIT, it runs every time at runtime. Browsers load a pre-compiled version of the application much faster and there is no need to download the Angular compiler if the app is already compiled.

Modules can also be lazy loaded when they get requested (on demand). This approach reduces the size of web resources loaded on initial page display. The page appears faster. If you want to enable lazy loading, you have to configure the router to load the module lazy. All you need is a path object with a loadChildren property, which points to the path and name of the lazy loaded module:

```
{path: "section", loadChildren: "app/section/section.module#SectionModule"}
```

Note that the value of loadChildren property is a string. Furthermore, the module importing this router configuration should not declare the lazy loaded module as dependency in the imports property of the configuration object.

Lifecycle hooks

Angular components come with lifecycle hooks, which get executed at specific times in the component's life. For this purpose, Angular offers different interfaces. Each interface has a method of the same name as the interface name with the prefix ng. Each method is executed when the corresponding lifecycle event occurs. They are also called lifecycle hook methods. Angular calls the lifecycle hook methods in the following sequence after the constructor has been called:

The lifecycle hook method	Purpose and timing
ngOnChanges	This is called whenever one or more data-bound input properties change. This method is called on initial changes (before ngOnInit) and any other subsequent changes. This method has one parameter--an object with keys of type string and values of type SimpleChange. The keys are the component's property names. The SimpleChange object contains current and previous values. A usage example is shown next.
ngOnInit	This is called once, after the first ngOnChanges. Note that the constructor of a component should only be used for dependency injection because data-bound input values are not yet set in the constructor. Everything else should be moved to the ngOnInit hook. A usage example is shown next.
ngDoCheck	This is called during every change detection run. It is a good place for custom logic, which allows us to do a fine-grained check of which property on our object changed.
ngAfterContentInit	This is called once, after Angular puts external content into the component's view. A placeholder for any external content is marked with the ngContent directive (the ng-content tag). A usage example of the ngContent directive is demonstrated afterwards.
ngAfterContentChecked	This is called after Angular checks the content put into the component's view.
ngAfterViewInit	This is called once, after Angular initializes the component's and child's views.
ngAfterViewChecked	This is called after Angular checks the component's views and child views.

ngOnDestroy	This is called just before Angular destroys the component's instance. This happens when you remove the component with built-in structural directives such as `ngIf`, `ngFor`, `ngSwitch`, or when you navigate to another view. This is a good place for cleanup operations such as unsubscribing observables, detaching event handlers, canceling interval timers, and so on.

Let's see an example of how to use `ngOnInit` and `ngOnChanges`:

```
import {Component, OnInit, OnChanges, SimpleChange} from '@angular/core';

@Component({
  selector: 'greeting-component',
  template: `<h1>Hello {{text}}</h1>`
})
export class GreetingComponent implements OnInit, OnChanges {
  @Input text: string;

  constructor() { }

  ngOnInit() {
    text = "Angular";
  }

  ngOnChanges(changes: {[propertyName: string]: SimpleChange}) {
    console.log(changes.text);
    // changes = {'text': {currentValue: 'World', previousValue: {}}}
    // changes = {'text': {currentValue: 'Angular',
                    previousValue: 'World'}}
  }
}
```

Usage in HTML:

```
<greeting-component [text]="World"></greeting-component>
```

Let's now see how to use the `ngContent` directive:

```
export @Component({
  selector: 'greeting-component',
  template: `<div><ng-content></ng-content> {{text}}</div>`
})
class GreetingComponent {
  @Input text: string;
}
```

Usage in HTML:

```
<greeting-component [text]="World"><b>Hello</b></greeting-component>
```

After the component's initialization, the following hook methods get always executed on every change detection run: `ngDoCheck` -> `ngAfterContentChecked` -> `ngAfterViewChecked` -> `ngOnChanges`.

Running PrimeNG with SystemJS

PrimeNG (`https://www.primefaces.org/primeng`) is an open source library of rich UI components for Angular 2+. PrimeNG is derived from PrimeFaces--the most popular **JavaServer Faces (JSF)** component suite. If you know PrimeFaces, you will feel at home with PrimeNG due to similar API. Currently, PrimeNG has 80+ visually stunning widgets that are easy to use. They are divided into several groups such as input and select components, buttons, data iteration components, panels, overlays, menus, charts, messages, multimedia, drag-and-drop, and miscellaneous. There are also 22+ free and premium themes.

PrimeNG fits perfectly with the mobile and desktop development because it is a responsive and touch optimized framework. PrimeNG showcase is a good place to play with the components, try them in action, study documentation, and code snippets. Anyway, we need a systematic approach for getting started with PrimeNG. This is what this book tries to convey. In this chapter, we will set up and run PrimeNG with SystemJS (`https://github.com/systemjs/systemjs`)--universal module loader supporting various module formats. SystemJS is a good choice for learning purposes if you want to try TypeScript, Angular, PrimeNG code snippets, or write small applications in Plunker (`https://plnkr.co`) because it can load your files, transpile them (if needed) and resolve module dependencies on-the-fly. In the real applications, you should choose Webpack or Angular CLI-based setups that have more power and advanced configurations. They also bundle your application in order to reduce the amount of HTTP requests. Those setups will be discussed in the next two sections.

The SystemJS configuration for Angular

First of all, you need to install Node.js and npm, which we already mentioned in the *TypeScript fundamentals you need to know* section. Why do we need npm? In HTML and SystemJS configuration, we could reference all dependencies from `https://unpkg.com`. But, we prefer to install all dependencies locally so that IDEs are fine with autocompletion. For instance, to install SystemJS, you have to run the following command in a console of your choice:

```
npm install systemjs --save
```

For readers, we created a complete demo seed project where all dependencies are listed in the `package.json` file.

The complete seed project with PrimeNG and SystemJS is available on GitHub at `https://github.com/ova2/angular-development-with-primeng/tree /master/chapter1/primeng-systemjs-setup`.

All dependencies in the seed project can be installed by running `npm install` in the project root. If you explore the `index.html` file, you can see that the SystemJS library is included in the `<head>` tag. After that, it becomes available as a global `System` object, which exposes two static methods: `System.import()` and `System.config()`. The first method is used to load a module. It accepts one argument--a module name, which can be either a file path or a logical name mapped to the file path. The second method is used for setting configuration. It accepts a configuration object as an argument. Normally, the configuration is placed within the `systemjs.config.js` file. Complete scripts to be included in `index.html` are TypeScript compiler, Polyfills, and SystemJS related files. The bootstrapping occurs by executing `System.import('app')`:

```html
<script src="../node_modules/typescript/lib/typescript.js"></script>
<script src="../node_modules/core-js/client/shim.min.js"></script>
<script src="../node_modules/zone.js/dist/zone.js"></script>
<script src="../node_modules/systemjs/dist/system.src.js"></script>
<script src="../systemjs.config.js"></script>

<script>
  System.import('app').catch(function (err) {
    console.error(err);
  });
</script>
```

An excerpt from the configuration object for Angular projects is listed here:

```
System.config({
  transpiler: 'typescript',
  typescriptOptions: {
    "target": "es5",
    "module": "commonjs",
    "moduleResolution": "node",
    "sourceMap": true,
    "emitDecoratorMetadata": true,
    "experimentalDecorators": true
  },
  map: {
    '@angular/animations':
      'node_modules/@angular/animations/bundles/animations.umd.min.js',
    '@angular/common':
      'node_modules/@angular/common/bundles/common.umd.min.js',
    '@angular/compiler':
      'node_modules/@angular/compiler/bundles/compiler.umd.min.js',
    '@angular/core':
      'node_modules/@angular/core/bundles/core.umd.min.js',
    '@angular/forms':
      'node_modules/@angular/forms/bundles/forms.umd.min.js',
    ...
    'rxjs': 'node_modules/rxjs',
    'app': 'src'
  },
  meta: {
    '@angular/*': {'format': 'cjs'}
  },
  packages: {
    'app': {
      main: 'main',
      defaultExtension: 'ts'
    },
    'rxjs': {main: 'Rx'}
  }
});
```

A brief explanation gives an overview of the most important configuration options:

- The `transpiler` option specifies a transpiler for TypeScript files. Possible values are `typescript`, `babel`, and `traceur`. The transpilation happens in browser on-the-fly.
- The `typescriptOptions` option sets the TypeScript compiler options.

- The `map` option creates aliases for module names. When you import a module, the module name is replaced by an associated value according to the mapping. In the configuration, all entry points for Angular files are in UMD format.
- The `packages` option sets meta information for imported modules. For example, you can set the main entry point of the module. Furthermore, you can specify default file extensions to be able to omit them when importing.

Adding PrimeNG dependencies

Every project using PrimeNG needs the locally installed library. You can achieve this by running the following command:

```
npm install primeng --save
```

As a result, PrimeNG is installed in your project root under the `node_modules` folder as well as added in `package.json` as a dependency. Here again, you can skip this step if you use the seed project hosted on GitHub--just run `npm install`. The next step is to add two new entries to the SystemJS configuration file. For shorter `import` statements, it is recommended to map `primeng` to `node_modules/primeng`. PrimeNG components are distributed as CommonJS modules ending with `.js`. That means we should set the default extension too:

```
System.config({
  ...
  map: {
    ...
    'primeng': 'node_modules/primeng'
  },
  packages: {
    'primeng': {
      defaultExtension: 'js'
    },
    ...
  }
});
```

Now, you are able to import PrimeNG modules from `primeng/primeng`. For instance, write this line to import `AccordionModule` and `MenuItem`:

```
import {AccordionModule, MenuItem} from 'primeng/primeng';
```

This way of importing is not recommended in production because all other available components will be loaded as well. Instead of that, only import what you need using a specific component path:

```
import {AccordionModule} from 'primeng/components/accordion/accordion';
import {MenuItem} from 'primeng/components/common/api';
```

In the demo application, we will only use `ButtonModule` and `InputTextModule` so that we need to import them as follows:

```
import {ButtonModule} from 'primeng/components/button/button';
import {InputTextModule} from 'primeng/components/inputtext/inputtext';
```

The demo project we want to create consists of application code and assets. A detailed description of every file would go beyond the scope of this book. We will only show the project structure:

```
▼ primeng-systemjs-setup
   ▶ node_modules library root
   ▼ src
      ▼ app
         ▼ section
              section.component.css
              section.component.html
              section.component.ts
           app.component.css
           app.component.html
           app.component.ts
           app.module.ts
           app-routing.module.ts
      ▼ assets
         ▼ icons
            ▼ css
                 font-awesome.min.css
            ▶ fonts
         index.html
         main.ts
      .gitignore
      package.json
      README.md
      systemjs.config.js
      tsconfig.json
      tslint.json
```

A typically PrimeNG application needs a theme. We would like to take the *Bootstrap* theme. The file `index.html` must have three CSS dependencies included within the `<head>` tag-- the theme, the PrimeNG file, and the FontAwesome file for SVG icons (`http://fontawesome.io`):

```
<link rel="stylesheet" type="text/css"
      href="../node_modules/primeng/resources/themes/bootstrap/theme.css"/>
<link rel="stylesheet" type="text/css"
      href="../node_modules/primeng/resources/primeng.min.css"/>
<link rel="stylesheet" type="text/css"
      href="src/assets/icons/css/font-awesome.min.css"/>
```

All FontAwesome files were placed under `src/assets/icons`. Mostly PrimeNG components are native, but there is a list of components with third-party dependencies. These are explained in the following table:

Component	Dependency
Schedule	FullCalendar and Moment.js
Editor	Quill editor
GMap	Google Maps
Charts	Charts.js
Captcha	Google Recaptcha

Exact links to those dependencies will be shown later in concrete examples. For now, we have finished our setup. Let's start our first application by running `npm start` in the project root.

The application gets launched in browser with two PrimeNG components, as shown in the following screenshot. As you can see, a lot of single web resources (CSS and JS files) are being loaded in the browser:

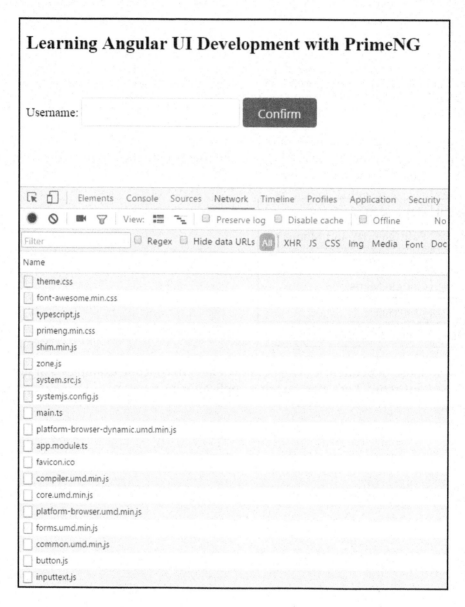

Setting up PrimeNG project with Webpack

Webpack (`https://webpack.js.org`) is a de facto standard bundler for single-page applications. It analyzes dependencies between JavaScript modules, assets (styles, icons, and images) as well as other files in your application and bundles everything together. In Webpack, everything is a module . You can, for example, import a CSS file like a JavaScript file using `require('./myfile.css')` or `import './myfile.css'`.

Webpack can figure out the right processing strategy for imported files by means of the file extension and associated loader. It is not always reasonable to build one big bundle file. Webpack has various plugins to split your code and generate multiple bundle files. It can also load parts of your application asynchronously on demand (lazy loading). All these features make it a power tool. In this section, we will give a high-level overview of Webpack 2 core concepts and show essential steps for creating a Webpack-based Angular, PrimeNG application.

 The complete seed project with PrimeNG and Webpack is available on GitHub at
`https://github.com/ova2/angular-development-with-primeng/tree/master/chapter1/primeng-webpack-setup`.
The project structure was kept the same as in the SystemJS-based setup.

Entry point and output

JavaScript and other files imported into each other are closely interwoven. Webpack creates a graph of all such dependencies. The starting point of this graph is called *entry point*. An entry point tells Webpack where to start to resolve all dependencies and creates a bundle. Entry points are created in the Webpack configuration file using the `entry` property. In the seed project on GitHub, we have two configuration files, one for the development mode (`webpack.dev.js`) and one for the production (`webpack.prod.js`) mode, each with two entry points.

In the development mode, we use the main entry point for JIT compilation. The `main.jit.ts` file contains quite normally bootstrapping code. The second entry point combines files from `core-js` (Polyfills for modern ECMAScript features) and `zone.js` (the basis for Angular's change detection):

```
entry: {
  'main': './main.jit.ts',
  'polyfill': './polyfill.ts'
}
```

In the production mode, we use the main entry point for AOT compilation. JIT and AOT were mentioned in the *Angular modularity and lifecycle hooks* section:

```
entry: {
  'main': './main.aot.ts',
  'polyfill': './polyfill.ts'
}
```

The `output` property tells Webpack where to bundle your application. You can use placeholders such as `[name]` and `[chunkhash]` to define what the names of output files look like. The `[name]` placeholder will be replaced by the name defined in the `entry` property. The `[chunkhash]` placeholder will be replaced by the hash of the file content at project build time. The `chunkFilename` option determines the names of on-demand (lazy) loaded chunks--files loaded by `System.import()`. In the development mode, we don't use `[chunkhash]` because of performance issues during hash generation:

```
output: {
  filename: '[name].js',
  chunkFilename: '[name].js'
}
```

The `[chunkhash]` placeholder is used in the production mode to achieve so called *long term caching*--every file gets cached in the browser and will be automatically invalidated and reloaded when the hash changes:

```
output: {
  filename: '[name].[chunkhash].js',
  chunkFilename: '[name].[chunkhash].js'
}
```

 A hash in the filename changes every compilation when the file content is changed. That means, files with hashes in names can not be included manually in the HTML file (`index.html`). `HtmlWebpackPlugin` (https ://github.com/jantimon/html-webpack-plugin) helps us to include generated bundles with `<script>` or `<link>` tags in the HTML. The seed project makes use of this plugin.

Loaders and plugins

Webpack only understands JavaScript files as modules. Every other file (`.css`, `.scss`, `.json`, `.jpg`, and many more) can be transformed into a module while importing. *Loaders* transform these files and add them to the dependency graph. Loader configuration should be done under `module.rules`. There are two main options in the loader configuration:

- The `test` property with a regular expression for testing files the loader should be applied to
- `loader` or `use` property with the concrete loader name

```
module: {
  rules: [
    {test: /.json$/, loader: 'json-loader'},
    {test: /.html$/, loader: 'raw-loader'},
    ...
  ]
}
```

Note that loaders should be registered in `package.json` so that they can be installed under `node_modules`. Webpack homepage has a good overview of some popular loaders (`https://webpack.js.org/loaders`). For TypeScript files, it is recommended to use the following sequence of loaders in the development mode:

```
{test: /.ts$/, loaders: ['awesome-typescript-loader', 'angular2-template-loader']}
```

Multiple loaders are applied from right to left. The `angular2-template-loader` searches for `templateUrl` and `styleUrls` declarations and inlines HTML and styles inside of the `@Component` decorator. The `awesome-typescript-loader` is mostly for speeding up the compilation process. For AOT compilation (production mode), another configuration is required:

```
{test: /.ts$/, loader: '@ngtools/webpack'}
```

Webpack has not only loaders, but also *plugins* which take responsibility for custom tasks beyond loaders. Custom tasks could be the compression of assets, extraction of CSS into a separate file, generation of a source map, definition of constants configured at compile time, and so on. One of the helpful plugins used in the seed project is the `CommonsChunkPlugin`. It generates chunks of common modules shared between entry points and splits them into separate bundles. This results in page speed optimizations as the browser can quickly serve the shared code from cache. In the seed project, we moved Webpack's runtime code to a separate `manifest` file in order to support long-term caching. This will avoid hash recreation for vendor files when only application files are changed:

```
plugins: [
  new CommonsChunkPlugin({
    name: 'manifest',
    minChunks: Infinity
  }),
  ...
]
```

As you can see, configuration of plugins is done in the `plugins` option. There are two plugins for production configuration yet to be mentioned here. The `AotPlugin` enables AOT compilation. It needs to know the path of `tsconfig.json` and the path with module class used for bootstrapping:

```
new AotPlugin({
  tsConfigPath: './tsconfig.json',
  entryModule: path.resolve(__dirname, '..') +
               '/src/app/app.module#AppModule'
})
```

`UglifyJsPlugin` is used for code minification:

```
new UglifyJsPlugin({
  compress: {
    dead_code: true,
    unused: true,
    warnings: false,
    screw_ie8: true
  },
  ...
})
```

Adding PrimeNG, CSS, and SASS

It's time to finish the setup. First, make sure that you have PrimeNG and FontAwesome dependencies in the `package.json` file. For example:

```
"primeng": "~2.0.2",
"font-awesome": "~4.7.0"
```

Second, bundle all CSS files into one file. This task is accomplished by `ExtractTextPlugin`, which is needed for loaders and plugin configuration:

```
{test: /.css$/, loader: ExtractTextPlugin.extract({
    fallback: "style-loader",
    use: "css-loader"
  })
},
{test: /.scss/, loader: ExtractTextPlugin.extract({
    fallback: "style-loader",
    use: ['css-loader', 'sass-loader']
  }),
  exclude: /^_.*.scss/
}
...
```

```
plugins: [
  new ExtractTextPlugin({
    filename: "[name].css"  // file name of the bundle
  }),
  ...
]
```

 For production, you should set the filename to
"[name].[chunkhash].css". The bundled CSS file gets automatically
included into index.html by HtmlWebpackPlugin.

We prefer not to use styleUrls in the components. The seed project imports a CSS und
SASS files in one place--inside of main.scss file located under src/assets/css:

```
// vendor files (imported from node_modules)
@import "~primeng/resources/themes/bootstrap/theme.css";
@import "~primeng/resources/primeng.min.css";
@import "~font-awesome/css/font-awesome.min.css";

// base project stuff (common settings)
@import "global";

// specific styles for components
@import "../../app/app.component";
@import "../../app/section/section.component";
```

Note that the tilde ~ points to the node_modules. More precisely the Sass preprocessor
interprets it as the node_modules folder. Sass is explained in Chapter 2, *Theming Concepts
and Layouts*. The main.scss file should be imported in the entry points main.jit.ts and
main.aot.ts:

```
import './assets/css/main.scss';
```

Webpack takes care of the rest. There are more goodies from Webpack--a development
server with live reloading webpack-dev-server (https://webpack.js.org/configurati
on/dev-server). It detects changes made to files and recompiles automatically. You can
start it with npm start or npm run start:prod. These commands represent npm scripts:

```
"start": webpack-dev-server --config config/webpack.dev.js --inline --open
"start:prod": webpack-dev-server --config config/webpack.prod.js --inline -
-open
```

When running `webpack-dev-server`, the compiled output is served from memory. This means, the application being served is not located on disk in the `dist` folder.

That's all. More configuration options for unit and end-to-end testing will be added in `Chapter 10`, *Creating Robust Applications*.

Setting up PrimeNG project with Angular CLI

Angular CLI (`https://cli.angular.io`) is a comfortable tool to create, run, and test Angular applications out of the box. It generates the code in no time. We will describe some useful commands and show you how to integrate PrimeNG with Angular CLI. First, the tool should be installed globally:

```
npm install -g @angular/cli
```

When it is installed, every command can be executed in the console with prepended `ng`. For instance, to create a new project, run `ng new [projectname] [options]`. Let's create one. Navigate to a directory that will be the parent directory of your project and run the following command:

```
ng new primeng-angularcli-setup --style=scss
```

This command will create an Angular 4 project within the folder `primeng-angularcli-setup`. The option `--style` sets a CSS preprocessor. Here, we want to use SASS files and need a Sass preprocessor. The preprocessor compiles SASS files whenever we make changes. You don't need to set a preprocessor if you only have CSS files.

The complete preconfigured seed project with PrimeNG and Angular CLI is available on GitHub at `https://github.com/ova2/angular-development-with-primeng/tree/master/chapter1/primeng-angularcli-setup`.

The created project has the following top directories and files:

Directory/file	Short description
e2e	Folder with e2e tests (`.e2e-spec.ts` files) and page objects (`.po.ts` files).
src	Source code folder where the application code should be written.

`.angular-cli.json`	Set up configuration file. PrimeNG dependencies can be listed here.
`karma.conf.js`	Karma configuration file for unit testing.
`protractor.conf.js`	Protractor configuration file for e2e testing.
`package.json`	Standard file for package management of npm-based projects.
`tsconfig.json`	Settings for TypeScript compiler.
`tslint.json`	Settings for TSLint.

You can now start the application by typing the following:

ng serve

This command will run a local server at `http://localhost:4200` by default. You will see the text **app works!** in the browser. The `ng serve` command uses `webpack-dev-server` internally. The server is running in the watch mode. It refreshes the page automatically when any changes occur. There are a lot of configuration options. You can, for example, set a custom port by the `--port` option. Refer to the official documentation for more details at `https://github.com/angular/angular-cli/wiki`. To compile the application into an output directory, run the following command:

ng build

The build artifacts will be stored in the `dist` directory.

> The `--prod` option in `ng build` or `ng serve` will minify the files and remove unused (dead) code. The `--aot` option will use AOT compilation and produce even more smaller and optimized artifacts.

To run unit and e2e tests, execute `ng test` and `ng e2e` commands, respectively.

Generating scaffolding

Angular CLI allows us to generate components, services, directives, routes, pipes, and many more with `ng generate`. Here is how you would generate a component:

```
ng generate component path/name
```

For example, if we run the following command:

ng generate component shared/message

Four files will be generated and one updated. The produced output will be:

```
installing component
  create src/app/shared/message/message.component.scss
  create src/app/shared/message/message.component.html
  create src/app/shared/message/message.component.spec.ts
  create src/app/shared/message/message.component.ts
  update src/app/app.module.ts
```

The new component is registered in `app.module.ts` automatically. The generation of other scaffoldings is identical. For example, to generate a service, run this command:

```
ng generate service path/name
```

There are plenty of useful options. You can set, for example, `--spec=false` to skip test file generation.

Adding PrimeNG dependencies

Integrating PrimeNG with Angular CLI is straightforward. First, install and save the dependencies:

```
npm install primeng --save
npm install font-awesome --save
```

Second, edit the `.angular-cli.json` file and add three more CSS files to the `styles` section. These are the same files as in the SystemJS- and Webpack-based setups:

```
"styles": [
  "styles.css",
  "../node_modules/primeng/resources/themes/bootstrap/theme.css",
  "../node_modules/primeng/resources/primeng.min.css",
  "../node_modules/font-awesome/css/font-awesome.min.css"
]
```

Now, you can import desired PrimeNG modules. Refer to the *Running PrimeNG with SystemJS* section to see how to import PrimeNG modules. In the seed project on GitHub, we have imported the `MessagesModule` and put some demo code into `message.component.html` and `message.component.ts`.

Summary

After reading this chapter, you got an overview of TypeScript and Angular concepts you need to understand for the upcoming chapters. TypeScript introduces types which help to recognize errors at development time. There are primitive types, types known from object-oriented programming languages, custom types, and so on. By default, TypeScript compiler always emits an JavaScript code, even in the presence of type errors. In this way, you can quickly migrate any existing JavaScript code to TypeScript just by renaming `.js` file to `.ts` without having to fix all compilation errors at once.

A typically Angular application is written in TypeScript. Angular provides a component-based approach which decouples your UI logic from the application (business) logic. It implements a powerful dependency injection system that makes reusing services a breeze. Dependency injection also increases the code testability because you can easily mock your business logic. An Angular application consists of hierarchical components, which communicate with each other in various ways such as `@Input`, `@Output` properties, shared services, local variables, and so on.

Angular is a modular framework. Module classes annotated with `@NgModule` provide a great way to keep the code clean and organized. Angular is flexible--lifecycle hooks allow us to perform custom logic at several stages in the in the component's life. Last but not least, it is fast due to smart change detection algorithm. Angular doesn't offer any rich UI components. It is just a platform for developing single page applications. You need a third-party library to create rich UI interfaces.

PrimeNG is a collection of such rich UI components for Angular 2+. In comparison with competitors, PrimeNG was created for enterprise applications and provides 80+ components. Adding PrimeNG dependencies is easy done. You only need to add PrimeNG and FontAwesome dependencies to the `package.json` file, and three CSS files: `primeng.min.css`, `font-awesome.min.css`, and `theme.css` for any theme you like. The next chapter will cover the theming concept in detail.

An Angular and PrimeNG application consists of ES6 (ECMAScript 2015) modules. Modules can be exported and imported. All modules in an application build a dependency graph. Therefore, you need a specific tool to resolve such modules starting at some entry point(s) and to output a bundle. There are some tools doing this and other tasks such as loading modules on demand, and similar.

In this chapter, SystemJS and Webpack loaders were discussed. SystemJS is only recommended for demo applications for the purpose of learning. Webpack-based builds are more sophisticated. Webpack has a combination of loaders for every file type and plugins. Plugins include useful behaviors into the Webpack build process, for example, creating common chunks, minification of web resources, copying files and directories, creating SVG sprites, and more. To quickly start the development in TypeScript and Angular, generate your projects with Angular CLI. This is a scaffolding tool, which makes it easy to create an application that works out of the box.

2
Theming Concepts and Layouts

The main goal of this chapter is to provide an introduction to PrimeNG themes, layouts, and the concepts involved. The **theming** concept used in PrimeNG is similar to the jQuery ThemeRoller CSS Framework (`http://jqueryui.com/themeroller`). PrimeNG components are designed to allow a developer to integrate them seamlessly into the look and feel of an entire web application. At the time of writing, there are 17 free themes and 5 premium themes and layouts. Free themes include ThemeRoller themes, a Twitter Bootstrap theme, and some custom themes powered by PrimeFaces and PrimeNG. Such themes are distributed along with PrimeNG itself under Apache License.

In Chapter 1, *Getting Started with Angular and PrimeNG*, we showed three possible setups and theme installations. You can also play with the free themes in the PrimeNG showcase (`https://www.primefaces.org/primeng`) by switching them dynamically--a theme switcher is available at the top-right corner. Premium themes can be purchased as standalone themes. You can preview premium themes and layouts in the PrimeNG Theme Gallery (`http://primefaces.org/themes`).

 Elite or pro users can use some premium themes (currently Omega) without extra costs. More information about license models can be found on the license page (`https://www.primefaces.org/licenses`).

In this chapter, we will cover the following topics:

- Understanding structural and skinning CSS
- Organizing your project structure with SASS
- Simple ways to create a new theme
- Responsive grid system in PrimeNG
- Bootstrap's responsive layout meets PrimeNG

Understanding structural and skinning CSS

Each component is styled with CSS and contains two layers of style information: structural or component-specific and skinning or component-independent styles. In this section, you will understand the difference between these two types of CSS, learn some useful selectors, and see an exemplary styling of the **Paginator** component in the generated HTML. Let's start. Go to the **Paginator** showcase (`https://www.primefaces.org/primeng/#/paginator`) and explore the HTML code of the **Paginator** component. The next screenshot shows the HTML and styles in the Google Chrome DevTools.

Shortcuts for opening DevTools: *F12* (Windows), *command + option + I* (Mac).

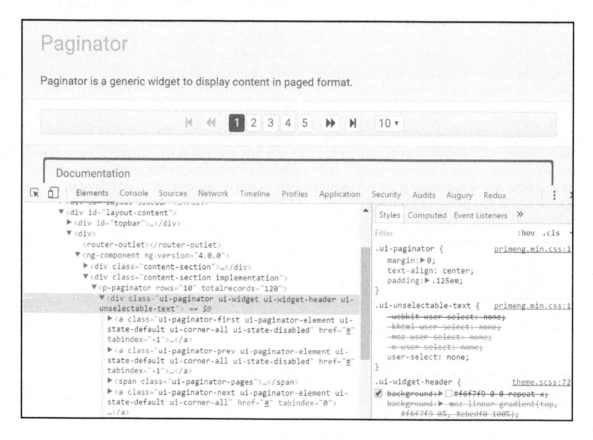

The highlighted line in the preceding screenshot represents the container element of the **Paginator** component with the following style classes:

- `ui-paginator`
- `ui-unselectable-text`
- `ui-widget`
- `ui-widget-header`

The first two style classes `ui-paginator` and `ui-unselectable-text` are generated by PrimeNG. These are structural style classes. The first one provides a semantic presentation to indicate the role of an element. Other examples for such style classes are `ui-datatable` for a table and `ui-button` for a button.

The second one is applied in situations where you want to avoid accidentally copy-pasting useless things, such as icons or images. In general, structural style classes define the skeleton of the components and include CSS properties such as margin, padding, display type, overflow behavior, dimensions, and positioning.

> Almost every component documentation in the PrimeNG showcase contains a **Styling** section with the component's structural style classes.

As already said, PrimeNG leverages the jQuery ThemeRoller CSS Framework. The `ui-widget` and `ui-widget-header` classes mentioned earlier are defined by ThemeRoller and affect the look and feel of the underlying HTML element and associated component. These are skinning style classes, which define CSS properties such as text colors, border colors, and background images.

Selector	Applies
`.ui-widget`	This is the class applied to all PrimeNG components. It applies, for example, font family and font size.
`.ui-widget-header`	This is the class applied to the header section(s) of a component.
`.ui-widget-content`	This is the class applied to the content section(s) of a component.
`.ui-state-default`	This is the default class applied to clickable, button-like components, or their elements.
`.ui-state-hover`	This is the class applied on a `mouseover` event to clickable, button-like components, or their elements.

`.ui-state-active`	This is the class applied on a `mousedown` event to clickable, button-like components, or their elements.
`.ui-state-disabled`	This is the class applied to components or their elements when they are disabled.
`.ui-state-highlight`	This is the class applied to components or their elements when they are highlighted or selected.
`.ui-corner-all`	This is the class that applies corner radius to all four corners of a component.
`.ui-corner-top`	This is the class that applies corner radius to both top corners of a component.
`.ui-corner-bottom`	This is the class that applies corner radius to both bottom corners of a component.
`.fa`	This is the class applied to elements representing an icon.

These styles are applied consistently across all PrimeNG components, so a clickable button and accordion tab have the same `ui-state-default` class applied to indicate that they are clickable. When a user moves the mouse over one of these elements, this class gets changed to `ui-state-hover`, and then to `ui-state-active` when these elements are selected.

This approach makes it easy to ensure that all elements with a similar interaction state will look identical across all components. The main advantage of the presented PrimeNG selectors is a great flexibility in theming because you don't need to know each and every skinning selector to change the styles of all available components in your web application consistently.

 In rare cases, some style classes are not generated by PrimeNG explicitly and not defined by the ThemeRoller. The **Schedule** component (`https://www.primefaces.org/primeng/#/schedule`) is one of such cases. It has structural classes `fc-head`, `fc-toolbar`, `fc-view-container`, and so on, which are controlled by the third-party plugin `FullCalendar` (`https://fullcalendar.io`).

Free themes use the relative `em` unit to define the font size of the widgets having the `.ui-widget` class. This is `1em` by default. For example, the Omega theme defines the following:

```
.ui-widget {
  font-family: "Roboto", "Trebuchet MS", Arial, Helvetica, sans-serif;
  font-size: 1em;
}
```

Thanks to the em unit, the font size is easily customizable. It is suggested to apply a base font size on the body element to adjust the size of components throughout the web application:

```
body {
    font-size: 0.9em;
}
```

Organizing your project structure with Sass

Every large frontend application needs a robust, scalable CSS architecture. A CSS preprocessor is indispensable--it helps to write cleaner, modular code with reusable pieces and maintain large and complex style sheets. A CSS preprocessor is basically a scripting language that extends CSS and compiles it into regular CSS. There are three primary CSS preprocessors today: Sass, LESS, and Stylus. As per Google Trends, Sass is the most used preprocessor today. Sass mimics the HTML structure and lets you nest CSS selectors that follow the same visual HTML hierarchy. With CSS, you would need to write this:

```
.container {
    padding: 5px;
}

.container p {
    margin: 5px;
}
```

With Sass, you can simply write this:

```
.container {
    padding: 5px;
    p {
        margin: 5px;
    }
}
```

Sass is backward compatible with CSS, so you can easily convert your existing CSS files just by renaming the .css file extension to .scss.

While nesting CSS selectors, you can use the handy & symbol. The & symbol concatenates CSS rules. For example, consider the following Sass snippet:

```
.some-class {
  &.another-class {
    color: red;
  }
}
```

This will be compiled to the following:

```
.some-class.another-class {
  color: red;
}
```

The & symbol is also useful for sandboxed UI components when every component only uses class names prefixed with a unique namespace. For example, the following imaginary header module is sandboxed with the `.mod-header` namespace:

```
.mod-header {
  &-link {
    color: blue;
  }

  &-menu {
    border: 1px solid gray;
  }
}
```

The output results in two classes: `.mod-header-link` and `.mod-header-menu`. As you see, Sass helps to avoid CSS collisions. It is recommended to write separate Sass files for each UI component and then combine them together by means of `@import` directive. With this directive, one Sass file can be imported into another one. The preprocessor will take the file that you want to import and combine it with the file you are importing into. This is a little bit different to the native CSS `@import`. The CSS `@import` always creates an HTTP request to fetch the imported file. The Sass `@import` combines the files so that one single CSS file will be sent to the browser.

Another power Sass concept is **partial files**. It is possible to create partial Sass files that contain small snippets for inclusion into other Sass files. Two typical examples of partial files are **variables** and **mixins.** Variables facilitate storing information that you want to reuse throughout your style sheets. Variables begin with dollar signs. For example:

```
$brand-color-background: white;
$brand-color-content: black;
```

Usage:

```
body {
    background-color: $brand-color-background;
    color: $brand-color-content;
}
```

A mixin lets you make groups of CSS declarations that you want to reuse throughout your style sheets. They behave like parameterized functions. A mixin begins with the @mixin directive followed by a name. Let's create a mixin to center any HTML content:

```
@mixin center($axis: "both") {
    position: absolute;
    @if $axis == "y" {
        top: 50%;
        transform: translateY(-50%);
    }
    @if $axis == "x" {
        left: 50%;
        transform: translateX(-50%);
    }
    @if $axis == "both" {
        top: 50%;
        left: 50%;
        transform: translate(-50%, -50%);
    }
}
```

The mixin name is center and the parameter $axis has a default value "both" if you don't pass the parameter value explicitly. The usage is simple--the mixin has to be included with the @include directive:

```
.centered-box {
    @include center();
}
```

This leads to the following:

```
.centered-box {
    position: absolute;
    top: 50%;
    left: 50%;
    transform: translate(-50%, -50%);
}
```

A partial file is named with a leading underscore, for example, `_variables.scss`, `_mixins.scss`. The underscore lets Sass know that the file should not be compiled to a CSS file. The underscore and file extension in the `@import` directive can be omitted:

```
@import 'variables';
@import 'mixins';
```

Sass has more powerful features such as inheritance, operators, built-in functions, and handling media queries. Refer to the official Sass site for more details (`http://sass-lang.com`). You can play with Sass online on `http://www.sassmeister.com`:

Or you can use it at `http://sass.js.org`:

It is high time to provide a guideline for organizing your Sass files. What is a good CSS architecture and project structure with a lot of Sass files? When planning your CSS architecture, you should modularize directories and files into categories. There are several proposals and recommendations. At the end, it depends on conventions in your team. One of the popular proposals is **The 7-1 Pattern** (https://sass-guidelin.es/#the-7-1-patter n). This architecture provides seven folders and one main file to import all files and compile them into a single file. These are as follows:

- base/: This folder contains global styles, such as CSS resets, typography, colors, and so on. For example:
    - _reset.scss
    - _typography.scss

- helpers/: This folder contains Sass tools and helpers, such as variables, mixins, functions, and so on. This folder should not output a single line of CSS when compiled on its own:
    - _variables.scss
    - _mixins.scss

- components/: This folder holds styles for self-contained components. These are normally widgets--small building blocks other components can be composed of. For example:
    - _button.scss
    - _carousel.scss

- layout/: This folder holds macro layout styles for larger components, such as CSS grid, header, footer, sidebar, and so on:
    - _header.scss
    - _footer.scss

- pages/: This is an optional folder, which contains page-specific styles:
    - _home.scss
    - _about.scss

- themes/: This is an optional folder, which contains styling for different themes. It makes sense for large sites with multiple themes:
    - _omega.scss
    - _ultima.scss

- vendors/: This folder contains files from external libraries and frameworks, such as Bootstrap, jQueryUI, Select2, and so on:
    - bootstrap.scss
    - jquery-ui.scss

Some folders are project specific and might not exist in many projects. Folder names are arbitrary. For instance, the `components/` folder might also be called `modules/`, depending on what you prefer. In Angular projects, each Sass file for component styling resides in the same folder as the corresponding component. There is no dedicated folder for them.

For this book, a demo project was born--an imaginary graphic editor that demonstrates styling concepts. The web application is built on top of Angular 4 and Bootstrap 3 (`http ://getbootstrap.com`). It has various panels on the left and right sides as well as a toolbar. The layout is responsive--panels get stacked on small screens. All styling files are gathered in the `main.scss` file:

```
// 1. Vendor files
@import "~font-awesome/css/font-awesome.min.css";
@import "vendor/bootstrap-custom";

// 2. Helpers (variables, mixins, functions, ...)
@import "helpers/variables";
@import "helpers/mixins";

// 3. Base stuff (common settings for all components and pages)
@import "common/viewport-workaround";
@import "common/global";
@import "common/components";

// 4. Styles for components
@import "../../app/app.component";
@import "../../app/main/main.component";
@import "../../app/layout/layout.component";
@import "../../app/panel/panel.component";
@import "../../app/panel/toolbar/toolbar.component";
```

The complete graphic editor with Sass files is available on GitHub at `https://github.com/ova2/angular-development-with-primeng/tree /master/chapter2/graphic-editor-sass`.

Once `main.scss` file is imported into the file where you bootstrap the Angular application, Webpack creates a link to the `main.css` in `index.html` automatically (thanks to `HtmlWebpackPlugin`):

```
// Webpack creates a link to the main.css and put it into the
// index.html
import './assets/css/main.scss';

import {platformBrowserDynamic} from '@angular/platform-browser-dynamic';
import {AppModule} from './app/app.module';

platformBrowserDynamic().bootstrapModule(AppModule)
                    .catch(err => console.error(err));
```

More flexible and modern responsive layout with Bootstrap 4 will be illustrated in the *Bootstrap flexbox layout meets PrimeNG* section. The graphic editor serves as a basis for a new demo application.

Simple ways to create a new theme

We sometimes need to create our own themes instead of using the predefined ones. Web applications should often feature a company-specific look and feel, which is constant and preset by company-wide style guides. Creating new themes is easy with PrimeNG, because it is powered by the ThemeRoller CSS Framework (`http://jqueryui.com/themeroller`). ThemeRoller provides a powerful and easy-to-use online visual tool. In this section, we will systematically show all the required steps to create a new theme. There are two ways how to create a new theme, either by ThemeRoller or from scratch with Sass.

ThemeRoller approach

To gain first-hand experience of the ThemeRoller online visual tool, go to the ThemeRoller home page, explore the available theme's gallery, and play with the CSS properties to see changes for widgets embedded on the page. All CSS changes will be applied on the fly.

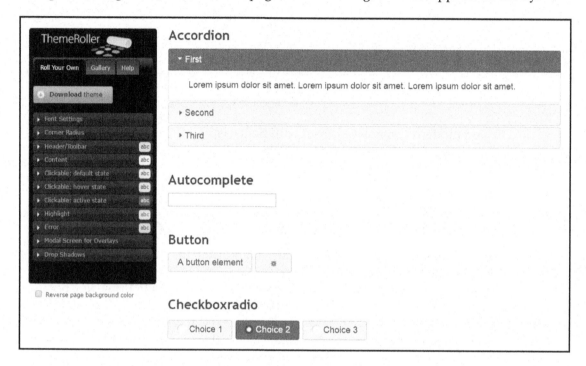

We have to select one of the existing themes (the **Gallery** tab) and edit it (the **Roll Your Own** tab). A click on the **Download theme** button accomplishes the work.

 We should deselect the **Toggle All** checkbox under the **Components** option on the **Download Builder** page so that our new theme only includes the skinning styles.

Next, we need to migrate the downloaded theme files from ThemeRoller to the PrimeNG theme infrastructure. The migration steps are straightforward:

1. The theme package that we have downloaded will have a CSS file `jquery-ui.theme.css` (as well as minified variant) and the `images` folder. Extract the package and rename the CSS file as `theme.css`.

2. In your web application, create a folder with the name of the new theme, for example, `src/assets/themes/crazy`.

3. Copy `theme.css` and the `images` folder into `src/assets/themes/crazy`.

After you are done with these steps, you can create a link to the `theme.css` in the `index.html` file:

```
<link rel="stylesheet" type="text/css"
      href="src/assets/themes/crazy/theme.css"/>
```

This was the easiest way to create your custom themes without requiring knowledge of CSS.

The Sass approach

The second way is more flexible and accurate. It is preferable to create a new theme manually by Sass because the theme is better maintainable. The main CSS settings, such as font, colors, border radius, and many more can be done configurable by Sass variables. You can create a new theme by setting custom values for those variables. This is exactly the approach followed by PrimeNG. The mostly free themes were created in such manner.

The free themes are hosted on GitHub at `https://github.com/primeface`
`s/primeng/tree/master/resources/themes`.

Every theme has a separate folder with a Sass file where variables are set. The variables themselves are used in `_theme.scss`--shared file for all free themes. This file can be found under `node_modules/primeng/resources/themes/`, if you install PrimeNG as the dependency. Sometimes, you also need to set custom fonts or special settings for particular CSS selectors. You can overwrite default style rules with your own ones--just write them after importing `_theme.scss`. The general structure of the custom theme file looks like as follows:

```
<predefined Sass variables>

@import "primeng/resources/themes/theme";

<your custom style rules>
```

Let's create the following folder structure with three Sass files for a new `crazy` theme:

```
- src
    - assets
        - themes
            - crazy
                - fonts
                    ...
                - _variables.scss
                - theme.scss
```

Sass variables can be copied from any other theme, such as Omega and placed in `_variables.scss`. Some of them get custom values as shown here:

```
$fontFamily: "Quicksand", "Trebuchet MS", Arial, Helvetica, sans-serif;
...

// Header
$headerBorderWidth: 2px;
$headerBorderColor: #f0a9df;
...

// Content
$contentBorderWidth: 2px;
$contentBorderColor: #ffafaf;
...

// Forms
$invalidInputBorderColor: #ff0000;
...
```

As you see, we would like to use a custom font `Quicksand`. You can download this font in the `.otf` format (OpenType Font) from this free resource: `https://www.fontsquirrel.com/fonts/quicksand`. For cross-browser support, we need fonts in four formats: `.ttf`, `.eot`, `.woff`, and `.svg`. There are many converter tools and one of these can be found at `http://www.font2web.com`, which allows converting any `.otf` file to the mentioned four formats. After conversion, custom fonts should be moved to the `fonts` folder and installed via the `@font-face` rule.

Furthermore, we want to have pink gradient colors for widget's header and red borders around invalid fields. All these custom rules are done in the theme file `theme.scss`. An excerpt from this file illustrates the idea:

```scss
@import 'variables';
@import "primeng/resources/themes/theme";

@font-face {
  font-family: 'Quicksand';
  src: url('fonts/Quicksand-Regular.eot');
  url('fonts/Quicksand-Regular.woff') format('woff'),
  url('fonts/Quicksand-Regular.ttf') format('truetype'),
  url('fonts/Quicksand-Regular.svg') format('svg');
  font-weight: normal;
  font-style: normal;
}

.ui-widget-header {
  background: linear-gradient(to bottom, #fffcfc 0%, #f0a9df 100%);
}

.ui-inputtext.ng-dirty.ng-invalid,
p-dropdown.ng-dirty.ng-invalid > .ui-dropdown,
... {
  border-color: $invalidInputBorderColor;
}
```

 The complete project with the `crazy` theme is available on GitHub at `https://github.com/ova2/angular-development-with-primeng/tree/master/chapter2/custom-theme`.

The proposed structure allows to create as many themes as you want. But, how to compile `theme.scss` to `theme.css`? There are two ways to compile Sass to CSS:

1. Install the Sass from the command line. The installation process is described on the Sass homepage (`http://sass-lang.com/install`). Note that you need preinstalled Ruby. Once Sass is installed, you can run `sass theme.scss theme.css` from your terminal.
2. Use `node-sass` (`https://github.com/sass/node-sass`) under Node.js.

In the project on GitHub, we used `node-sass` along with `autoprefixer` (`https://github.com/postcss/autoprefixer`) and `cssnano` (`http://cssnano.co`). All required dependencies are installed locally:

```
npm install node-sass autoprefixer cssnano postcss postcss-cli --save-dev
```

Four handy npm scripts in `package.json` help to create the theme file:

```
"premakecss": "node-sass --include-path node_modules/
src/assets/themes/crazy/theme.scss -o src/assets/themes/crazy/",
"makecss": "postcss src/assets/themes/crazy/theme.css --use
autoprefixer -d src/assets/themes/crazy/",
"prebuild:css": "npm run makecss",
"build:css": "postcss src/assets/themes/crazy/theme.css --use cssnano
            > src/assets/themes/crazy/theme.min.css"
```

 The `@import "primeng/resources/themes/theme"` path is found thanks to the `--include-path node_modules/` option, which sets the path to look for the imported files. This helps to avoid all the mess with relative paths.

The `npm run build:css` command will produce `theme.min.css`, which should be included on the page:

```
<link rel="stylesheet" type="text/css"
href="src/assets/themes/crazy/theme.min.css"/>
```

The look and feel of the new theme is amazing:

The responsive grid system in PrimeNG

PrimeNG has **Grid CSS**--a responsive and fluid layout system optimized for mobile devices, tablets, and desktops. PrimeNG components use Grid CSS internally, but this lightweight utility can be used as standalone as well. CSS Grid is based on the 12-columns layout as many other grid systems. The total width of all columns is 100%. In this section, we will explain all features of the PrimeNG grid system in details.

Basic principles

The layout container should have the ui-g style class. Children elements of the layout container become columns when they are prefixed with ui-g-* where * is any number from 1 to 12. The number expresses the taken space of 12 available units. When the number of columns exceeds 12, columns wrap to the next line:

```
<div class="ui-g">
  <div class="ui-g-2">2</div>
  <div class="ui-g-4">4</div>
  <div class="ui-g-6">6</div>
  <div class="ui-g-8">8</div>
  <div class="ui-g-4">4</div>
</div>
```

The following layout has two lines (rows):

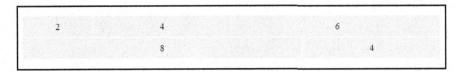

The same two-row layout is also possible with two ui-g containers:

```
<div class="ui-g">
  <div class="ui-g-2">2</div>
  <div class="ui-g-4">4</div>
  <div class="ui-g-6">6</div>
</div>
<div class="ui-g">
  <div class="ui-g-8">8</div>
  <div class="ui-g-4">4</div>
</div>
```

Generally, *n* containers with the ui-g style class creates *n* rows.

Nested columns

Columns can be nested in more complex layouts. To achieve that, just nest elements with the ui-g-* style classes:

```
<div class="ui-g">
  <div class="ui-g-8 ui-g-nopad">
    <div class="ui-g-6">6</div>
    <div class="ui-g-6">6</div>
    <div class="ui-g-12">12</div>
  </div>
  <div class="ui-g-4">4</div>
</div>
```

With this structure, columns with different content will not have equal height. There is a more robust solution to force equal height for columns with different content. Just wrap the internal div elements inside another div with the ui-g style class or even simpler, assign ui-g to the column having nested columns:

```
<div class="ui-g">
  <div class="ui-g ui-g-8 ui-g-nopad">
    <div class="ui-g-6">6<br/>6<br/>6<br/>6<br/>6<br/>6<br/></div>
    <div class="ui-g-6">6</div>
    <div class="ui-g-12">12</div>
  </div>
  <div class="ui-g-4">4</div>
</div>
```

The result looks like the following:

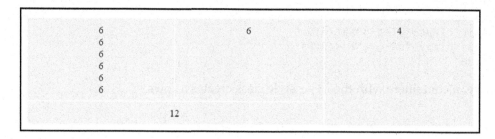

Columns have a default padding of 0.5em. To remove it, you need to apply the ui-g-nopad style class. This was demonstrated in the earlier examples.

Responsive and fluid layout

Responsive layout is achieved by applying additional classes to the columns. Four screen sizes are supported with different breakpoints.

Prefix	Device	Size
`ui-sm-*`	Small devices like phones	`max-width: 640px`
`ui-md-*`	Medium-sized devices like tablets	`min-width: 641px`
`ui-lg-*`	Large-sized devices like desktops	`min-width: 1025px`
`ui-xl-*`	Big screen monitors	`min-width: 1441px`

When an element features multiple style classes listed in the table, they get applied from the bottom to the top. Let's take an example:

```
<div class="ui-g">
  <div class="ui-g-12 ui-md-6 ui-lg-2">ui-g-12 ui-md-6 ui-lg-2</div>
  <div class="ui-g-12 ui-md-6 ui-lg-2">ui-g-12 ui-md-6 ui-lg-2</div>
  <div class="ui-g-12 ui-md-4 ui-lg-8">ui-g-12 ui-md-4 ui-lg-8</div>
</div>
```

What is happening here?

- On large screens, three columns are displayed in proportion 2:12, 2:12, and 8:12.
- On medium screens, two rows are displayed. The first row has equal columns and the second row has a column 4:12.
- On small screens (mobile devices) columns get stacked--each column is displayed in its own row.

The screenshot shows the arrangement of columns on medium-sized devices:

ui-g-12 ui-md-6 ui-lg-2   ui-g-12 ui-md-6 ui-lg-2

ui-g-12 ui-md-4 ui-lg-8

PrimeNG components have a built-in responsive mode. They understand a special `ui-fluid` style class. The Grid CSS and any other grid system can be used together with this style class, which provides a 100% width to components. This behavior helps to use the screen space efficiently. An example demonstrates various components in the fluid layout:

```
<div class="ui-fluid ui-corner-all">
  <div class="ui-g">
    <div class="ui-g ui-g-12 ui-md-6 ui-g-nopad">
      <div class="ui-g-12 ui-md-3 ui-label">
        Passenger
      </div>
      <div class="ui-g-12 ui-md-9">
        <input pInputText type="text"/>
      </div>
    </div>
    <div class="ui-g ui-g-12 ui-md-6 ui-g-nopad">
      <div class="ui-g-12 ui-md-3 ui-label">
        Flight day
      </div>
      <div class="ui-g-12 ui-md-9">
        <p-calendar [(ngModel)]="date" [showIcon]="true">
        </p-calendar>
      </div>
    </div>
  </div>
  <div class="ui-g">
    <div class="ui-g ui-g-12 ui-md-6 ui-g-nopad">
      <div class="ui-g-12 ui-md-3 ui-label">
        Notice
      </div>
      <div class="ui-g-12 ui-md-9">
        <textarea pInputTextarea type="text"></textarea>
      </div>
    </div>
    <div class="ui-g ui-g-12 ui-md-6 ui-g-nopad">
      <div class="ui-g-12 ui-md-3 ui-label">
        Destination
      </div>
      <div class="ui-g-12 ui-md-9">
        <p-listbox [options]="cities" [(ngModel)]="selectedCity">
        </p-listbox>
      </div>
    </div>
  </div>
</div>
```

The layout from medium up to big screens looks as follows:

The layout on small screens has stacked columns:

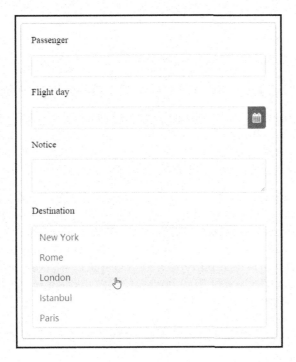

As you can see, all right-aligned labels become left aligned. You can achieve this behavior with media queries:

```
.ui-fluid .ui-g .ui-label {
  text-align: right;
  white-space: nowrap;
}

@media screen and (max-width: 640px) {
  .ui-fluid .ui-g .ui-label {
    text-align: left;
  }
}
```

The complete demo application with instructions is available on GitHub at https://github.com/ova2/angular-development-with-primeng/tree/master/chapter2/primeng-grid-css.

Bootstrap flexbox layout meets PrimeNG

In this section, we will reimplement the graphic editor introduced in the *Organizing your project structure with Sass* section with Bootstrap 4 (https://v4-alpha.getbootstrap.com) and PrimeNG components. Starting with the version v4.0.0-alpha.6, Bootstrap only has a flexbox-based layout by default, with no fallback.

Flexbox is a new layout model, which is widely supported in all modern browsers (http://caniuse.com/#search=flexbox). There are many tutorials on the Internet. You can, for example, read a comprehensive guide to the CSS flexbox layout at https://css-tricks.com/snippets/css/a-guide-to-flexbox. Flexbox tackles many layout problems. One of the main advantages of flexbox is the ability to fill extra space. All columns in the flexbox layout have the same height irrespective of their content. Let's show final screens of the graphic editor for two device resolutions.

For desktop:

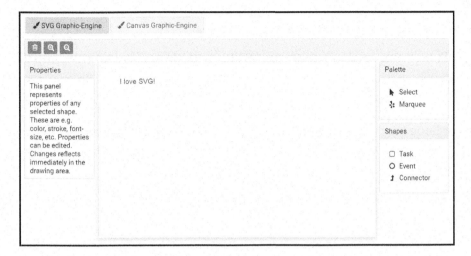

For mobile:

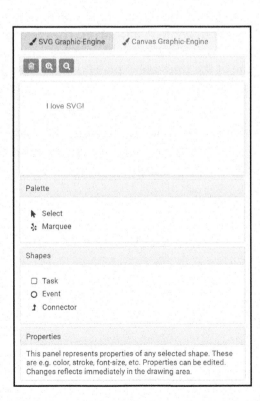

Beside PrimeNG, we need to install the latest Bootstrap 4. This is 4.0.0-alpha.6 at the time of writing:

```
npm install bootstrap@4.0.0-alpha.6 --save
```

After installation, you need to import the CSS file with flexbox layout rules into the main.scss file:

```
@import "~bootstrap/dist/css/bootstrap-grid.css";
```

In the prior Bootstrap versions, you had to enable the flexbox layout explicitly:

```
$enable-flex: true;
@import "~bootstrap/scss/bootstrap-grid.scss";
```

If you intend to use the styles for additional flex alignment options, you have to import bootstrap-grid.scss and _flex.scss:

```
@import "~bootstrap/scss/bootstrap-grid";
@import "~bootstrap/scss/utilities/flex";
```

_flex.scss is a set of utilities for vertically and horizontally alignment of columns, for controlling the visual order of your content, and so on. The file contains various CSS rules such as justify-content-start, align-items-end, align-self-auto, flex-first, flex-last, and so on. Some of the rules are explained here. Refer to the official Bootstrap documentation to learn more details (https://v4-alpha.getbootstrap.com/layout/grid).

The skeleton of the whole application resides in two files: app.component.html and layout.component.html. The first file contains a PrimeNG's tabbed menu with two menu items:

```html
<div class="container-fluid">
  <div class="row">
    <div class="col">
      <p-tabMenu [model]="items"></p-tabMenu>
    </div>
  </div>
</div>

<router-outlet></router-outlet>
```

Each item defines `routerLink`:

```
items: MenuItem[];
...
this.items = [
  {label: 'SVG Graphic-Engine', icon: 'fa-paint-brush',
    routerLink: '/svg'},
  {label: 'Canvas Graphic-Engine', icon: 'fa-paint-brush',
    routerLink: '/canvas'}
];
```

A click on a tab in the tabbed menu loads `layout.component.html` into `router-outlet`:

```html
<div class="container-fluid">
  <div class="row align-items-center ge-toolbar">
    <div class="col">
      <ge-toolbar></ge-toolbar>
    </div>
  </div>
  <div class="row no-gutters">
    <div class="col-md-8 flex-md-unordered col-drawing-area">
      <div class="drawing-area">
        <ng-content select=".ge-drawing-area"></ng-content>
      </div>
    </div>
    <div class="col-md-2 flex-md-last">
      <div class="flex-column no-gutters">
        <div class="col ge-palette">
          <ge-palette></ge-palette>
        </div>
        <div class="col ge-shapes">
          <ge-shapes></ge-shapes>
        </div>
      </div>
    </div>
    <div class="col-md-2 flex-md-first">
      <ge-properties></ge-properties>
    </div>
  </div>
</div>
```

The `ng-content` area gets replaced by SVG or Canvas surface where the user can draw shapes. The `ge-toolbar` component contains PrimeNG's `<p-toolbar>`. The other `ge-*` components contain panels, for example, `<p-panel header="Palette">`.

The most interesting part is the style classes. The short description of the style classes used in the preceding code snippet is as follows:

Style class	Description
`row`	This serves as a container for columns that go inside the row. Each column can take from 1 to 12 spaces.
`align-items-*`	This defines where flex columns inside the row are vertically positioned. The `align-items-center` class positions the column in the middle.
`no-gutters`	This removes the margin from rows and padding from columns.
`col`	This sets the `auto-layout` mode--a new feature of the Bootstrap 4 for equal width columns. The columns will automatically distribute the space in the row.
`col-<prefix>-<number>`	This indicates the number of columns you would like to use out of the possible 12 per row. The prefix defines the breakpoint. For example, the `col-md-8` class means, the column will be 8 of 12 on medium, and larger screens and 12 of 12 (default) on screens smaller than medium size.
`flex-column`	This changes `flex-direction` of items (columns). Items are laid out either in the horizontal or vertical direction. The `flex-column` class changes the direction from left-to-right to top-to-bottom.
`flex-<prefix>-first`	This reorders the column as the first column in the layout. The prefix defines the breakpoint the reordering should be applied from.
`flex-<prefix>-last`	This reorders the column as last column in the layout. The prefix described as earlier.
`flex-<prefix>-unordered`	This displays the columns between first and last. The prefix described as earlier.

Note that, on small devices, we have decreased the font size. This can be achieved with breakpoint mixins provided by Bootstrap:

```
@import "~bootstrap/scss/mixins/breakpoints";

@include media-breakpoint-down(md) {
  body {
```

```
      font-size: 0.9em;
   }
}
```

There are various breakpoint mixins, which expect one of the following parameters:

- xs: Extra small screens < 576px
- sm: Small screens >= 576px
- md: Medium screens >= 768px
- lg: Large screens >= 992px
- xl: Extra large screens >= 1200px

For example, the element with the ge-palette style class gets margin-top: 0 on screens over 768px, and margin-top: 0.5em on screens less than 768px:

```
.ge-palette {
  margin-top: 0.5em;
}

@include media-breakpoint-up(md) {
  .ge-palette {
    margin-top: 0;
  }
}
```

 The complete graphic editor with Bootstrap 4 and PrimeNG is available on GitHub at https://github.com/ova2/angular-development-with-primeng/tree /master/chapter2/graphic-editor-bootstrap4.

Summary

After reading this chapter, you can distinguish between structural and skinning style classes. In short words, structural style classes define the skeleton of the components and the skinning ones are for theming. We have seen how to set up any PrimeNG theme and create a new one. A new theme can be created either by ThemeRoller or by setting custom values for Sass variables and CSS properties of an existing theme with subsequent compilation to a CSS file. We encourage to use a CSS preprocessor for a modular CSS architecture. Sass preprocessor helps in writing better styles. A guideline for organizing the Sass files was provided as well.

After reading this chapter, you are also able to use one of the responsive grid systems, either PrimeNG own or Bootstrap's one. PrimeNG offers a lightweight responsive and fluid layout system. Furthermore, PrimeNG components having built-in responsive mode when using the `.ui-fluid` style class on the top container element. The flexbox-based layout is a new standard and a benefit for every HTML5 web application. One of the main advantages of flexbox is the ability to fill an extra space--all columns have the same height. Bootstrap 4 adds support for the flexbox model and lets you develop stunning layouts.

Starting with the next chapter, we will dive deep into each component. Our journey into the exciting PrimeNG world begins with input and select components.

3
Enhanced Inputs and Selects

chapter explains frequently used input and select components with enhanced features for any kind of application or website. Such components are the main parts of every web application. All the features of each component will cover many real-time use cases that you may encounter while developing the project. Input and select components are the first citizens while you're creating a login form or registration form or any kind of form-filling application. Due to the rapid revolution in web usage and technology improvements, there is a need for various enhanced inputs and select components that make the web more powerful. PrimeNG provides over 20 components for data input and select, which extend standard or native HTML components with skinning capabilities and useful features, such as user-friendly interface, validation, and so on.

In this chapter, we will cover the following topics:

- Formatted input with InputMask
- Autosuggestion with AutoComplete
- Entering multiple values with Chips
- Discovering checkbox - boolean, many, and TriState
- Choosing items with Single and MultiSelect components
- Basic and advanced Calendar scenarios
- Spinner and Slider – different ways to provide input
- Text editing with rich and powerful editors
- Password and star-based rating inputs
- Validation with input and select components

Formatted input with InputMask

InputMask is a special kind of input component that minimizes the chances for the user to input incorrect data. It applies flexible validation with the provided masking template. This is especially useful to enter input in a certain format, such as numeric, alphanumeric, date, currency, email, and phone. A basic example of an InputMask component for a phone number input would be as follows:

```
<p-inputMask id="basic" name="basic" mask="99-999999"
  [(ngModel)]="simple" placeholder="99-999999"/>
```

As per the preceding example, the mask value `(999) 999-9999` depicts that only a number can be input along with the parenthesis and dashed structure. Due to the usage of the placeholder with the same mask value, it suggests the kind of input format that needs to be provided. The initial display of the input looks as follows:

Once the input gets the focus, the numbers in the mask format will be replaced with an empty space and the other characters will remain in the initial phase. The default placeholder character for mask is underscore (_), so it will display underscore characters for each number digit. After each `keyPress` event, the mask character (that is, `9`) will be filled up with the actual character. If the provided input is incomplete or blurred, then the entire input will be cleared out automatically (by default, `autoClear` is `true`).

There are cases to do certain functionalities during the event occurrence in the component's DOM tree. The `inputMask` component supports the `onComplete` callback to invoke when the user completes the mask pattern. For example, the user would be notified when the mask input completes as follows:

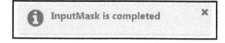

The growl message appears at the top of the page with the close icon, which allows us to remove the sticky notification at any point in time.

Mask format options

The `mask` attribute is mandatory to use for the input mask. The component not only allows the number type, but it also supports alphabetic and alphanumeric characters, so the mask format can be a combination of the following built-in definitions:

- a: Alphabetic character (A-Z, a-z)
- 9: Numeric character (0-9)
- *: Alphanumeric character (A-Z, a-z, 0-9)

Let's take an example where we can show the input mask with different mask options based on a radio button selection, as follows:

```
<div>
  <div id="phoneformat" *ngIf="format == 'Option1'">
    <span>Phone:</span>
    <p-inputMask mask="(999) 999-9999" [(ngModel)]="phone"
      placeholder="(999) 999-9999" name="phone">
    </p-inputMask>
  </div>
  <div id="dateformat" *ngIf="format == 'Option2'">
    <span>Date:</span>
    <p-inputMask mask="99/99/9999" [(ngModel)]="date"
      placeholder="99/99/9999" name="date">
    </p-inputMask>
  </div>
  <div id="serialformat" *ngIf="format == 'Option3'">
    <span>Serial Number:</span>
    <p-inputMask mask="a*-999-a999" [(ngModel)]="serial"
      placeholder="a*-999-a999" name="serial">
    </p-inputMask>
  </div>
</div>
```

As per the preceding example, only one input element will be displayed with the defined mask. The following screenshot shows a snapshot result of the mask format for a date:

 The unmask attribute can be used to control masked or unmasked output for the value bounded. For instance, it is useful if ngModel sets either a raw unmasked value or a formatted mask value to the component's bound value.

Using the slot character

As stated before, underscore (_) is the default active placeholder in a mask. But this can be customized using the slotChar attribute, as shown here:

```
<p-inputMask mask="99/99/9999" [(ngModel)]="slot" placeholder="99/99/9999"
   slotChar="mm/dd/yyyy" name="slotchar"></p-inputMask>
```

The slotChar option can be either a single character or an expression.

Making a part of the mask optional

Till now, all the examples of input masks have shown that all the characters in a mask are mandatory. It is also possible that you can make a part of the mask optional with the use of the question mark (?) character. Anything listed after the question mark within a mask definition will be treated as an optional input. A common use case is displaying the phone number with an optional extension number, as follows:

```
<span>Phone Ext</span>
<p-inputMask mask="(999) 999-9999? x99999" [(ngModel)]="optional"
   name="optionalmask" placeholder="(999) 999-9999? x99999">
</p-inputMask>
```

Once the user finishes the input by reaching the question mark character and blurs the component, the rest of the validation will be skipped. That is, the input up to that part won't be erased. For example, phone number inputs, such as (666) 234-5678 and (666) 234-5678? x1230 will be valid inputs for the mask's optional case.

 The complete demo application with instructions is available on GitHub at https://github.com/ova2/angular-development-with-primeng/tree /master/chapter3/inputmask.

Autosuggestion with AutoComplete

AutoComplete is an input component that provides real-time suggestions while the user types into the input field. This enables users to quickly find and select from a list of looked-up values as they type, which leverages the searching and filtering abilities.

A basic usage of the AutoComplete component includes the suggestions attribute to provide the list of all resulted items and completeMethod to filter items based on the typed query. For example, the following AutoComplete component displays the list of countries based on the user query:

```
<p-autoComplete [(ngModel)]="country" name="basic"
    [suggestions]="filteredCountries"
    (completeMethod)="filterCountries($event)"
    field="name" [size]="30"
    placeholder="Type your favourite Country" [minLength]="1">
</p-autoComplete>
```

In the preceding example, minLength="1" is used as minimum characters for the input to query results. This will render the output as shown in the following snapshot:

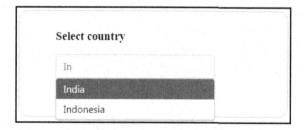

As the user types in the input field, the complete method will filter the items on demand. The method has to be defined in the component class, as shown here:

```
filterCountries(event: any) {
  let query = event.query;
  this.countryService.getCountries().
  subscribe((countries: Country[]) => {
    this.filteredCountries = this.filterCountry(query, countries);
  });
}
```

The preceding method allows filtering of the list of countries based on the user query. In this case, it will filter all the countries that start with the `query` character.

To improve the user experience, AutoComplete provides a drop-down option through the `dropdown` property. On clicking the drop-down icon, it will populate all possible items in a downwards popup immediately.

Multiple selection

With AutoComplete, it is also possible to select more than one value by setting the `multiple` property to `true`. With the help of multiple selects, the selected texts can be retrieved as an array (for example, the `countries` property). In this case, `ngModel` should refer to an array.

Working with objects

Until now, AutoComplete has shown its power on primitive types, but it can work with object types as well. The value passed to the model would be an object instance, but the `field` property defines the label to be displayed as a suggestion. That is, in this case, the `field` property is used to display any property of the object as a label. The following example shows the power of the object usage:

```
<p-autoComplete id="instance" [(ngModel)]="countryInstance" name="instance"
  [suggestions]="filteredCountryInstances"
  (completeMethod)="filterCountryInstances($event)" field="name">
</p-autoComplete>
```

In the preceding example, the `Country` object is used as a model object instance and the suggestions displayed are from the country using the `name` field property.

Advanced features - the customized content displays

In many cases, normal field population is just not enough; it would be more powerful to have customized content for a better experience. AutoComplete provides this feature using `ng-template`, which displays the custom content inside the suggestions panel. The local `template` variable passed to `ng-template` is an object from the `suggestions` array. The customized example of AutoComplete with the country's name and flag would be as follows:

```
<p-autoComplete [(ngModel)]="customCountry" name="template"
  [suggestions]="filteredCustomCountries"
  field="name" (completeMethod)="filterCustomCountries($event)"
  [size]="30" [minLength]="1" placeholder="Start your search">
  <ng-template let-country pTemplate="item">
    <div class="ui-helper-clearfix" class="template-border">
      <img src="/assets/data/images/country/
        {{country.code.toLowerCase()}}.png" class="country-image"/>
      <div class="country-text">{{country.name}}</div>
    </div>
  </ng-template>
</p-autoComplete>
```

There is no restriction on what kind of data can be shown. The following screenshot shows a snapshot result of the customized country information:

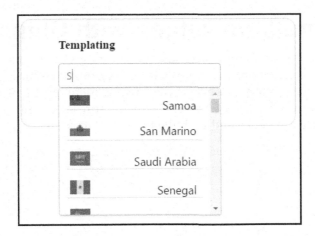

The `item` template is used to customize the content inside the suggestions panel where `selectedItem` is used to customize a selected item in the multiple selection.

The AutoComplete component supports many events as mentioned here:

Name	Parameters	Description
`completeMethod`	• `event.originalEvent`: The browser event • `event.query`: Value to search with	Callback to `invoke` to search for suggestions.
`onFocus`	`event`: Browser event	Callback to `invoke` when AutoComplete gets focus.
`onBlur`	`event`: Browser event	Callback to `invoke` when AutoComplete loses focus.
`onSelect`	`value`: The selected value	Callback to `invoke` when a suggestion is selected.
`onUnselect`	`value`: Unselected value in multiple mode	Callback to `invoke` when a selected value is removed.
`onDropdownClick`	• `event.originalEvent`: The browser event • `event.query`: The current value of the input field	Callback to `invoke` when the dropdown button is clicked.
`onClear`	`event`: The browser event	Callback to `invoke` when the `input` field is cleared.

 The complete demo application with instructions is available on GitHub at `https://github.com/ova2/angular-development-with-primeng/tree/master/chapter3/autocomplete`.

Entering multiple values with Chips

The Chip component is used to represent multiple complex entities in an input field as small blocks, such as contact information. A Chip may contain entities such as photo, title, text, rules, icons, or even a contact. This is useful to represent information in a compact way. The following basic example of the Chips component represents contact names in an order. By default, each entity can be deleted with the help of a cross icon or backspace keystroke:

```
<p-chips [(ngModel)]="contactnames" name="basic"></p-chips>
```

The following screenshot shows a snapshot result of the company contact names as a Chip example:

The Chip component supports two event callbacks named `onAdd` and `onRemove`. These event callbacks will be invoked when adding and removing Chips from the input box, respectively.

Display complex information using template

A Chip is customized using the `ng-template` element where the value is passed as the implicit variable. The content of `ng-template` consists of normal text, icons, images, and any other components. Remember that a customized Chip component doesn't have a cross icon, that is, we can remove the Chip entry with backspace only. The customized example of the Chip component with icons would be as follows:

```
<p-chips [(ngModel)]="complexcontacts" name="template">
  <ng-template let-item pTemplate="item">
    <i class="fa fa-address-card"></i>-{{item}}
  </ng-template>
</p-chips>
```

In the preceding example, customized content is displayed with the company logo and the contact name. The following screenshot shows a snapshot result of the customized Chip example:

The Chips' user entry actions will be controlled using the `max` and `disabled` properties. The maximum number of entries can be restricted using the `max` attribute. For example, if we set `max="5"`, it won't allow adding a sixth entry in the input. Whereas `disabed="true"` makes a disabled input, which restricts the Chips' entry.

The PrimeNG 4.1 release introduced `inputStyle` and `inputStyleClass` properties for customized input and the `allowDuplicate` property to control the duplicate inputs.

 The complete demo application with instructions is available on GitHub at `https://github.com/ova2/angular-development-with-primeng/tree /master/chapter3/chips`.

Discovering checkbox - boolean, many, and TriState

A checkbox is an extension to the standard checkbox element with skinning capabilities. The checkbox can either be used as a single checkbox to provide a Boolean value or in multiple selections with multiple checkboxes having the same group name.

Boolean checkbox - single selection

By default, multiple selection is enabled for the checkbox, and we can have a single selection by enabling the `binary` attribute. A basic example of a checkbox with a single selection would be as follows:

```
<p-checkbox name="single" [(ngModel)]="checked" binary="true">
</p-checkbox>
```

In the preceding example, the boolean checkbox is used to know the interest of Angular framework. The component will be displayed as shown in the following screenshot:

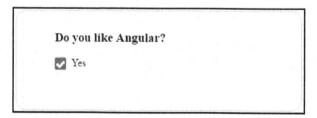

The preselection of the checkbox is also possible by enabling the Boolean property in the model.

Checkbox multiple selection

As mentioned earlier, the multiple selection is enabled by default with multiple checkbox controls having the same group name. In this case, the `model` property binds to an array to hold selected values. By assigning the individual checkbox values to the selected values, the checkbox group is displayed with preselection. The multiple checkbox selection for selecting different favorite Angular versions would be as follows:

```
<div class="ui-g" class="multicheckbox-width">
  <div class="ui-g-12"><p-checkbox name="angulargroup"
    value="AngularJS1.0" label="AngularJS V1.0"
    [(ngModel)]="selectedVersions"></p-checkbox>
  </div>
  <div class="ui-g-12"><p-checkbox name="angulargroup"
    value="AngularV2.0" label="Angular V2.0"
    [(ngModel)]="selectedVersions"></p-checkbox>
  </div>
  <div class="ui-g-12"><p-checkbox name="angulargroup"
    value="AngularV4.0" label="Angular V4.0"
    [(ngModel)]="selectedVersions"></p-checkbox>
  </div>
</div>
```

The checkbox group will be displayed with the default selection, as shown in the following screenshot:

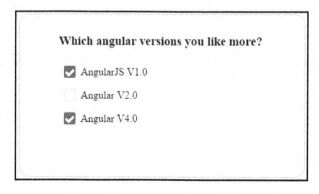

To notify the checkbox selections, there is one event callback named `onChange` that will be invoked on user actions. At the same time, the user actions are disabled through the `disabled` property.

Multistate representation - TriStateCheckbox

PrimeNG goes beyond the normal checkbox behavior of the "true/false" selection on the web. In some cases, there is a need for a "true/false/null" combination, especially to represent the status of any entity. Remember that the `model` property is assigned to any type instead of a `boolean` type. A basic example of a TriStateCheckbox used to enter the feedback for Angular 4 would be as follows:

```
<p-triStateCheckbox name="tristate" [(ngModel)]="status">
</p-triStateCheckbox>
```

TriStateCheckbox will be displayed with three different states (excellent, good, and bad) as shown in the following screenshot:

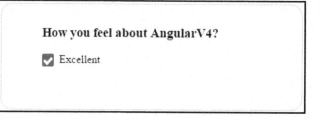

This enhanced checkbox also provides the `onChange` event callback for any user interactions. The user actions are disabled through the `disabled` property, just like the normal boolean checkbox.

 The complete demo application with instructions is available on GitHub at `https://github.com/ova2/angular-development-with-primeng/tree/master/chapter3/checkbox`.

Choosing items with single and MultiSelect components

Dropdown provides a way to select an item from a collection of available options. To list out all possible options, we should use the `SelectItem` interface that defines label-value properties, and this list will bind to the `options` attribute. The two-way binding for selected items is defined through the `model` property. Let's display a list of countries in a dropdown for user input. A basic example of a dropdown with the list of options would be as follows:

```
<p-dropdown [options]="countries" [(ngModel)]="selectedCountry"
  [styleClass]="dropdown-width" placeholder="Select a Country">
</p-dropdown>
```

The dropdown will be displayed with options as shown in the following screenshot:

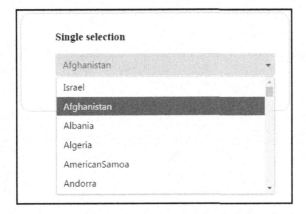

The Dropdown component provides three event callbacks, such as `onChange`, `onFocus`, and `onBlur`. When the dropdown value changes, it gets the focus and looses the focus, respectively. There is a provision to edit the input directly like any other input components using the `editable` property (that is, `editable="true"`).

> The width and height of the dropdown's viewport will be controlled through the `autoWidth` and `scrollHeight` properties. By default, the width of the dropdown is calculated based on the options width. Whereas, the scroll height is controlled through the `scrollHeight` option in pixels, the scrollbar is defined if the height of the list exceeds this value.

Customized Dropdown

The Dropdown component is more powerful with customized content over the default label text of an item. The `filter` property is used to filter all the possible options through an input in an overlay. A customized example of a Dropdown with the list of options representing a country name and a flag image would be as follows:

```
<p-dropdown [options]="countries" [(ngModel)]="selectedCountry"
  [styleClass]="dropdown-width" filter="filter">
  <ng-template let-country pTemplate="item">
    <div class="ui-helper-clearfix" class="template-border">
      <img src="/assets/data/images/country/
        {{country.code.toLowerCase()}}.png" class="country-image"/>
      <div class="country-text">{{country.name}}</div>
    </div>
  </ng-template>
</p-dropdown>
```

The dropdown will be displayed with the custom content and filtering as shown in the following screenshot:

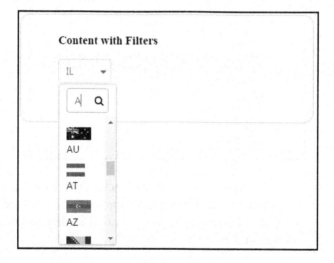

Instead of scrolling down to see a list of all the countries, there is a filter input option at the top to filter country names by their starting letters. It also supports multiproperty filtering with comma-separated values (for example, `filterBy="label, value.name".`) By default, filtering is done against the label of the `SelectItem` API.

The MultiSelect dropdown

The MultiSelect component is used to select multiple items from a collection, unlike the Dropdown component, which provides single item selection. A basic example of a MultiSelect component with the list of countries would be as follows:

```
<p-multiSelect [options]="countries" [(ngModel)]="selectedCountries">
</p-multiSelect>
```

The list of options is available through collection of the SelectItem interface, which takes a label-value pair. The list of options is bound through the options attribute of the MultiSelect component. The MultiSelect will be displayed with the countries list, as shown in the following screenshot:

In this case, the user can select multiple countries using the checkbox option, which is available for each item, and filter input to select specific options.

The complete demo application with instructions is available on GitHub at https://github.com/ova2/angular-development-with-primeng/tree /master/chapter3/select.

Basic and advanced Calendar scenarios

The Calendar is an input component that selects a date input in different customized ways, such as inline, localization, restricted to particular dates, and time-oriented. In this case, the Calendar model is backed by a date type property. The simplest component declaration for a basic date selection would be as follows:

```
<p-calendar [(ngModel)]="basicDateInput" name="basic"></p-calendar>
```

This displays an input textbox that, on being clicked opens up a pop-up date selection dialog, as shown here:

Apart from the basic date selection, there is also a provision to navigate each month for each year with the help of left and right arrow controls at the top. This will be explained in the section on advanced features.

The date selection is straightforward and can be done by clicking on a particular date in the pop-up dialog. By default, the Calendar is displayed in a popup, but this behavior can be altered with the `inline` property. The inline version of the calendar display would be as follows:

For a better user experience, there is one more option available from the component that displays the Calendar popup through the `showIcon` property. The Calendar input example, used with the icon button, would look as follows:

The visual display of the Calendar component with the `icon` attribute will change the default icon displayed next to the input.

Localization

Localization for different languages and formats is defined by binding the local settings object to the `locale` property. The default local value is `English`. To represent a different locale, we should provide the respective language text labels. For example, the German locale should provide the following labels for the German calendar:

```
this.de = {
  firstDayOfWeek: 1,
  dayNames: ['Sonntag', 'Montag', 'Dienstag', 'Mittwoch', 'Donnerstag',
             'Freitag', 'Samstag'],
  dayNamesShort: ['Son', 'Mon', 'Die', 'Mit', 'Don', 'Fre', 'Sam'],
  dayNamesMin: ['S', 'M', 'D', 'M ', 'D', 'F ', 'S'],
  monthNames: [
    'Januar', 'Februar', 'März', 'April', 'Mai', 'Juni', 'Juli',
    'August', 'September', 'Oktober', 'November', 'Dezember'
  ],
  monthNamesShort: ['Jan', 'Feb', 'Mär', 'Apr', 'Mai', 'Jun', 'Jul',
                    'Aug', 'Sep', 'Okt', 'Nov', 'Dez']
};
```

The calendar with German locale labels will be displayed as follows:

As shown before, the locale-specific labels need to be formatted as JSON in the backing component to display the locale-specific calendar.

Time picker options

Along with standard calendar dates selection, we can also display time using `showTime` and `hourFormat`. This can be further restricted to display time only using the `timeOnly` attribute, which is just a time picker. For example, the `timeOnly` option will display the time picker as follows:

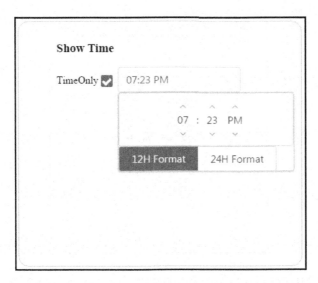

The two time formats (**12H Format** and **24H Format**) will be shown one at a time using the split button with both options. Note that the `showTime` property is enabled in this case.

Advanced features

The advanced features of the Calendar component such as the date format (using the `dateFormat` attribute), restricted dates (using the `min` and `max` dates), month and year navigators for easy access (using the `monthNavigator`, `yearNavigator`, and `yearRange` attributes), readonly input (using the `readOnlyInput` property), and useful events, such as `onSelect`, `onFocus`, `onClear`, and `onBlur`:

The preceding snapshot depicts a calendar that can be used with any possible combination of its features.

 The complete demo application with instructions is available on GitHub at `https://github.com/ova2/angular-development-with-primeng/tree /master/chapter3/calendar`.

Spinner and Slider – different ways to provide input

The input component Spinner provides a numerical input via increments and decrements using controls or buttons. But still, there is an option to use it as normal `InputText` too. A basic example of a Spinner would be as follows:

```
<p-spinner name="basic" size="30" [(ngModel)]="basicinput"></p-spinner>
```

The Spinner will be displayed with button controls, as shown in the following screenshot:

As shown in the snapshot, the value can be modified serially using the Spinner controls. Just like any other input component, Spinner supports the onChange event callback, which will be invoked upon a value change. The maximum number of characters allowed can be controlled through the maxlength property. The user interaction will be restricted through the readonly and disabled attributes.

Advanced features - going beyond basic usage

The Spinner component provides more features than just having increment and decrement controls. It can provide features such as value boundaries with min and max attributes, customized step factors (by default step factor is 1) using the step attribute, and number separators, such as decimalSeparator and thousandSeparator. The customized example of a Spinner would be as follows:

```
<p-spinner name="minmax" size="40" [(ngModel)]="customizedinput" [min]="0"
[max]="100" [step]="0.50"
    placeholder="Enter your input or use spinner controls"></p-spinner>
```

The Spinner will be displayed with button controls, as shown in the following screenshot:

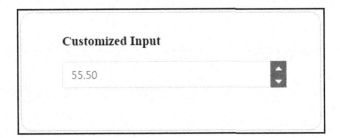

Once the user input reaches `min` and `max` limits, the value cannot be changed by either controls or input.

 The format of the input can be customized using the `formatInput` attribute.

Slider

The Slider component provides the user with the ability to input a value by using a Slider bar or using the dragging of a handle. The `model` property binds to a number type, which holds the input value. The input can be attached to Slider by providing the same model value for both. A basic example of a Slider would be as follows:

```
<p-slider [(ngModel)]="basicinput" name="basicinput"
  styleClass="slider-width">
</p-slider>
```

The Slider will be displayed with a dragging handle, as shown in the following screenshot:

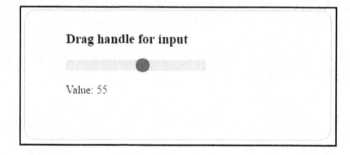

The output value will be updated every time the handle is dragged across the bar.

Advanced features - going beyond basic usage

The Slider component can be further customized in a similar way to the Spinner with input boundaries, using `min` and `max` attributes or the `range` attribute to mention both the boundaries at the same time, customized step factors (by default step factor is 1) using the `step` attribute, and the `animate` property to provide animations on the click of a Slider.

The default orientation of the Slider input is horizontal. The direction or orientation of the Slider can be changed to vertical using the `orientation` property.

Sometimes, it is good to have regular input along with the Slider handle, because it gives you the flexibility to enter input directly and is also used to display output by dragging the Slider handle. The customized example of a Slider would be as follows:

```
<input type="text" pInputText name="customizedinput"
   [(ngModel)]="customizedinput"
   styleClass="input-width"/>
<p-slider [(ngModel)]="customizedinput" name="customizedinput"
   styleClass="slider-width" [step]="20"
   [animate]="true" (onChange)="onChange()" (onSlideEnd)="onSlideEnd()">
</p-slider>
```

The Slider will be displayed with the customized features as shown in the following screenshot:

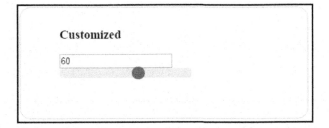

The Slider input and Slider handle bar values are mutually dependent. For example, changing one value will reflect the other one.

 The complete demo application with instructions is available on GitHub:

- https://github.com/ova2/angular-development-with-prim eng/tree/master/chapter3/spinner
- https://github.com/ova2/angular-development-with-prim eng/tree/master/chapter3/slider

Text editing with rich editors

An editor is a rich text editor (WYSIWYG) based on the Quill editor. It contains a default toolbar with common options whose controls can be customized using the header element. The latest version of Quill 1.0 is used as a dependency for this. The basic text editor with a default toolbar can be represented as follows:

```
<p-editor name="basic" [(ngModel)]="basictext"
  styleClass="editor-dimensions">
</p-editor>
```

The text editor with common options will look as follows:

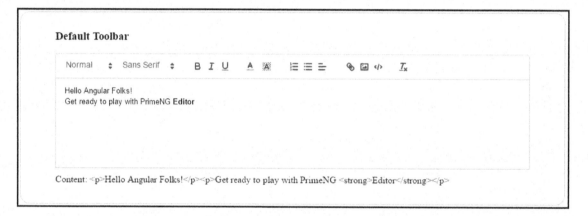

1. Add the Quill 1.0 dependency in `package.json` and install it, or use the CLI tool to install it (`npm install quill --save`).
2. Also add the Quill script and style URLs in the entry page:

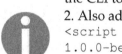

```
<script src="https://cdn.quilljs.com/
1.0.0-beta.3/quill.min.js"></script>
<link rel="stylesheet" type="text/css"
href="https://cdn.quilljs.com/1.0.0-
beta.3/quill.snow.css">
```

The editor supports `onTextChange` and `onSelectionChange` events, which will be invoked when the text of the editor changes and when the selected text of the editor changes, respectively.

The customized editor

As stated before, the editor provides a default toolbar with common options. The toolbar can be customized by defining elements inside the header element. For example, a custom toolbar created with text style controls would be as follows:

```
<p-editor name="custom" [(ngModel)]="customtext"
  styleClass="editor-dimensions">
  <p-header>
    <span class="ql-formats">
      <button class="ql-bold"></button>
      <button class="ql-italic"></button>
      <button class="ql-underline"></button>
      <button class="ql-clean"></button>
    </span>
  </p-header>
</p-editor>
```

The text editor with the customized toolbar will be displayed as follows:

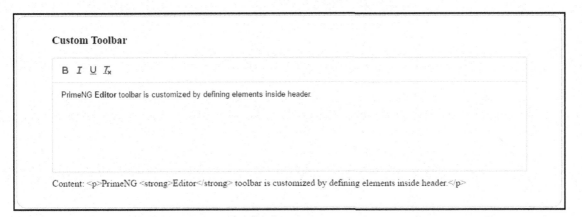

The toolbar can be customized with any number of toolbar controls in different ways. Refer to the Quill documentation for all available controls.

The complete demo application with instructions is available on GitHub at
`https://github.com/ova2/angular-development-with-primeng/tree/master/chapter3/editor`.

Password and star-based rating inputs

Password is an enhanced input with a secured entry of characters, like any other password fields on the web, but it provides strength indicators (weak, medium, and strong), which states the security strength of the user input. A basic example of a user password can be written as follows:

```
<input pPassword name="basic" type="password" />
```

The following screenshot shows a snapshot result of a basic password example:

The password is applied to the input field by attaching the pPassword directive. The ngModel property is used to bind the password value.

By default, password will display the prompt and strength indicator labels. There is an option to customize all the strength indicator labels with the help of attributes such as promptLabel, weakLabel, mediumLabel, and strongLabel. This will be helpful in localizing the password input according to the need. By default, the feedback attribute is true. The indicator labels appear once it gets the focus or key strokes in the input. But this behavior is altered by setting the feedback as false, which suppress the indicators for the input.

Rating input

The Rating component provides a star-based rating with the ability to select and cancel. The basic declaration of the component would be as follows:

```
<p-rating name="basic" [(ngModel)]="angular" ></p-rating>
```

Here, the rating-bounded value should be a number type. The default visual of an Angular rating will look as shown in the following screenshot:

Rate your faviourite Single page applications

Enter rating

Angular
⊘ ★ ★ ★ ★ ★
Rating: 5

The star attribute helps to provide the number of stars in the rating. The default value of star is 5.

The behavior of selecting and canceling the rating can be more interactive, and you can get notified with the help of onRate and onCancel callbacks. In the preceding snapshot, the rating value can be cleared with the cancel icon on the left-hand side. This is because, by default, the cancel attribute will be enabled. If the attribute is disabled then there is no chance of canceling the rating once it is selected. By disabling the cancel attribute, the rating snapshot will display without the icon, as follows:

Rate your faviourite Single page applications

Cancel Control

Ember
★ ★ ★ ★ ★ ★ ☆ ☆ ☆ ☆
Rating: 6

Due to this feature, the cancel button won't appear to cancel the given rating. Only one star can be deselected at a time.

 Currently, the Rating component doesn't support half or quarter values.

By enabling the `readonly` and `disabled` attributes on the Rating component, there is no way to select or cancel it. This can be useful for display purposes only.

The complete demo application with instructions is available on GitHub:

- https://github.com/ova2/angular-development-with-prim eng/tree/master/chapter3/password
- https://github.com/ova2/angular-development-with-prim eng/tree/master/chapter3/rating

Validation with the input and select components

Angular provides three different ways of building forms in our applications:

- **Template-driven approach**: This approach allows us to build forms with very little to no application code required
- **Model-driven (or reactive) approach using low-level APIs**: In this approach, we create our forms as testable without a DOM being required
- **Model-driven with a higher level API**: This approach uses a higher level API called `FormBuilder`.

PrimeNG created most of the input and select components with model-driven form support. Because of this, all input and select components are eligible for validation.

Let's take an example of a registration form with `firstname`, `lastname`, `password`, `address`, `phone`, and `gender` fields with validation support. PrimeNG components are backed by a model-driven API with `FormBuilder`, which groups all of the form controls to create a registration form, as shown here:

```
this.registrationform = this.formBuilder.group({
    'firstname': new FormControl('', Validators.required),
    'lastname': new FormControl('', Validators.required),
    'password': new FormControl('',
      Validators.compose([Validators.required,
      Validators.minLength(8)])),
    'address': new FormControl(''),
    'phone': new FormControl(''),
    'gender': new FormControl('', Validators.required)
});
```

HTML, however, contains the `form` element with a `formGroup` binding with the registration form. The form will wrap with the list of controls and validation conditions to display messages:

```
<form [formGroup]="registrationform"
(ngSubmit)="onSubmit(registrationform.value)">
    ...
</form>
```

A registration form with invalid input would result in an error messages, as shown in the following snapshot:

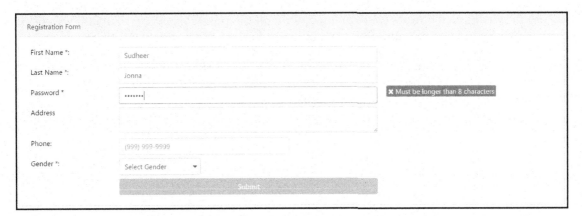

PrimeNG components provide validations through template-driven forms, as well as model-driven forms. The flexibility is given to the user on what kind of validation needs to be provided.

 The complete demo application with instructions is available on GitHub at `https://github.com/ova2/angular-development-with-primeng/tree /master/chapter3/validation`.

Summary

At the end of this chapter, you will be able to seamlessly use all available input and select components for any given use case. Initially, we covered all kinds of input components. At first, we started with formatting input with InputMask, autosuggestion with AutoComplete, and entering multiple values using Chips components.

After that, we discussed the various checkbox components, such as the boolean checkbox, many checkbox, and TriState checkbox variations. Later, we discussed the frequently used select components, such as the single and MultiSelect components. The special use case-specific input components, such as Calendar date entry, Slider, Spinner, password, star, and text editing using rich editors we explained, with all the possible features. Finally, we ended this chapter by looking at validation with input and select components. All these components and all possible features were explained in a step-by-step approach.

In the next chapter, you are going to see how the various kinds of Button and Panel components are going to make your life easier.

4

Button and Panel Components

In this chapter, initially, we will cover various Button components such as radio, split, toggle, and select buttons, and later move to various Panel components, such as Toolbar, basic Panel, FieldSet, Accordion, and tabbed view. The user input will be taken in multiple ways, among which Button input is one of the best options; on the other hand, Panel components act as container components, which allow grouping of other native HTML or PrimeNG components. Each feature of PrimeNG--enhanced Buttons and Panel components cover many real-time use case needs. Various settings to configure Button and Panel components are detailed in this chapter.

In this chapter, we will cover the following topics:

- Enhanced Button, RadioButton, and SplitButton
- Selecting value by ToggleButton and SelectButton
- Grouping buttons with Toolbar
- Arranging your view with Panels and FieldSets
- Vertical stacked panels with Accordion
- Grouping content with tabs in TabView

Enhanced Button, RadioButton, and SplitButton

Buttons are frequently used elements for any web design. PrimeNG extended plain Button behavior with awesome features.

Button

The Button component is an extension to standard input element for user interactions with icons and theming. The `pButton` directive makes a plain HTML button a PrimeNG-enhanced button. A basic example of the Button component with defined label text would be written as follows:

```
<button name="basic" pButton type="button" label="ClickMe"></button>
```

The type of the Button should be `button` type. The following screenshot shows a snapshot result of the basic Button example:

The Button component supports one event callback named `click`, which will be invoked on click of the Button element. Remember that Button's click event is basically from Angular one not specific to PrimeNG.

Icons and severity

The Button component is more useful with icons and severity properties. The `icon` attribute is used to represent font-awesome icons on top of it. Default icon position is the left-hand position. This can be customized using the `iconPos` attribute with valid values as `left` and `right`. In order to display only one icon, leave the label as undefined. An example of the Button components with various combinations of icon and label would be written as follows:

```
<button pButton type="button" icon="fa-close"></button>
<button pButton type="button" icon="fa-check" label="Yes"></button>
<button pButton type="button" icon="fa-check" iconPos="right"
label="Yes"></button>
```

In the preceding example, Buttons are defined as without a label, with the label, and right-positioned icon with the label in a respective order. The following screenshot shows a snapshot result of the Button with icons as an example:

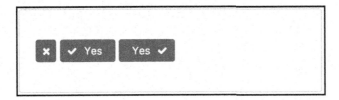

To differentiate different severity levels of user actions, PrimeNG provides five different classes, that is, these style classes are different from regular theme colors:

- ui-button-secondary
- ui-button-success
- ui-button-info
- ui-button-warning
- ui-button-danger

The following screenshot shows a snapshot result of a Button with all severity cases (compared to regular theme class) as an example:

The user interactions are prevented using the regular disabled attribute.

The complete demo application with instructions is available on GitHub at https://github.com/ova2/angular-development-with-primeng/tree/master/chapter4/button.

RadioButton

RadioButton is an extension to a standard radio button element with skinning capabilities to opt for only one value at a time. The two-way binding is provided through the ngModel directive, which enables default values as either checked or unchecked (preselection). A basic example of a RadioButton component with a defined label text is written as follows:

```
<div class="ui-g">
  <div class="ui-g-12">
    <p-radioButton name="group1" value="Angular" label="Angular"
      [(ngModel)]="basic"></p-radioButton>
  </div>
  <div class="ui-g-12">
    <p-radioButton name="group1" value="React" label="React"
      [(ngModel)]="basic"></p-radioButton>
  </div>
  <div class="ui-g-12">
    <p-radioButton name="group1" value="Polymer" label="Polymer"
      [(ngModel)]="basic"></p-radioButton>
  </div>
</div>
```

In the preceding example, all radio buttons are mapped to the same group (name="group1") in order to work as a mutual exclusive radio group. The following screenshot shows a snapshot result of the radio button example:

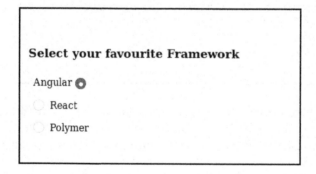

The radio button component supports one event callback named onClick, which will be invoked on the click of a radio button element. The label attribute provides a label text for the radio button. The label is also clickable and selects the value. The label components associated with the radio button need to trigger the focus of input while click on it, this can be achieved with the inputId attribute.

The complete demo application with instructions is available on GitHub at
`https://github.com/ova2/angular-development-with-primeng/tree`
`/master/chapter4/radio-button`.

SplitButton

SplitButton groups a collection of menu items in an overlay with a default command button. This button uses a common menu model API to define its items. Hence, the split button is a combination of button and menu components. A basic example of SplitButton component with defined label text would be written as follows:

```
<p-splitButton label="Create" (onClick)="create()" [model]="items">
</p-splitButton>
```

The label is applied only for the default command button. The following screenshot shows a snapshot result of the split button example:

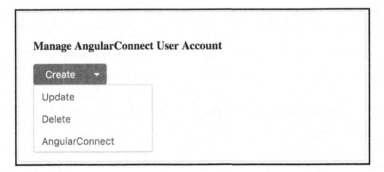

The split button component supports one event callback named `onClick`, which will be invoked on the click of the default button element.

 PrimeNG 4.1 provided `appendTo` the option which provides customization over where the overlay would be appended.

Icons and theming

There are many options to customize the plain behavior of the split button. The icons can be applied for the associated default command button and menu items separately using the `icon` property. The icons are aligned to the left side by default, but this can be applied to the right side as well, using the `iconPos` property, whereas the skinning behavior of component and overlay are modified through the `style`, `styleClass`, `menuStyle`, and `menuStyleClass` class properties. A basic example of the SplitButton component with the defined label text would be written as follows:

```
<p-splitButton label="Create" icon="fa-check" iconPos="right"
  menuStyleClass="customized-menu" [model]="itemsIcons">
</p-splitButton>
```

In the preceding example, the overlay menu default styles are changed with the help of the `menuStyleClass` property. For example, in this case, the default width of the overlay is changed by setting the `menuStyleClass` class name as shown here:

```
.customized-menu {
  width: 140%;
}
```

The following screenshot shows a snapshot result of the split button example:

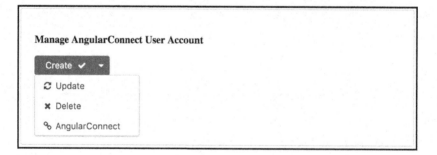

In the preceding snapshot, the split button is customized with icons, the create command button icon is aligned to the right side, and the width of the overlay increased to accommodate both icons and text.

The complete demo application with instructions is available on GitHub at https://github.com/ova2/angular-development-with-primeng/tree /master/chapter4/split-button.

Selecting a value with ToggleButton and SelectButton

ToggleButton provides a way to select a Boolean value using a button. The ngModel directive is used to define a two-way data binding to a Boolean property. That is, preselection of the toggle button is achieved by enabling the Boolean property. A basic example of ToggleButton usage would be as follows:

```
<p-toggleButton [(ngModel)]="basic" name="basic"></p-toggleButton>
```

The following screenshot shows a snapshot result of the basic example:

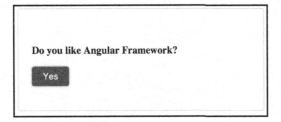

The ToggleButton also provided customized options such as onLabel, offLabel, onIcon, and offIcon over default labels and icons. The label components associated with the toggle button need to trigger the focus of button while clicking on the label, this can be achieved with the inputId attribute. The customized toggle button with labels, icons, and events would be as follows:

```
<p-toggleButton [(ngModel)]="customized" name="custom" onLabel="I
  confirm" offLabel="I reject" onIcon="fa-check-square"
  offIcon="fa-window-close">
</p-toggleButton>
```

In the preceding example, all kinds of font-awesome icons can be used for the icon attributes. The following screenshot shows a snapshot result of the customized example:

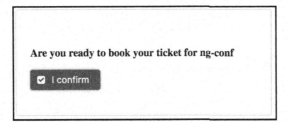

The user is notified of user actions using the onChange event. At the same time, user interactions are prevented using the disabled property.

SelectButton

The SelectButton component is used to choose single or multiple items from a list in the form of buttons. Each item in the list of options is defined as the SelectItem interface with a label-value pair properties. The options are binding through the ngModel property with a two-way binding, which results in the default selection based on the backend component data. A basic example of the select button usage would be as follows:

```
<p-selectButton [options]="types" [(ngModel)]="selectedType"
    name="basic">
</p-selectButton>
```

In the preceding example, all the Prime libraries are collected as an array for the options property. The following screenshot shows a snapshot result of the select button example:

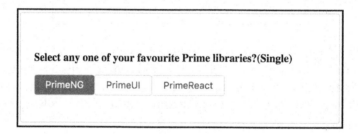

In the preceding example, only one item is selected at a time (single selection) but there is also a possibility to select multiple items using the multiple property (that is, multiple="true"). In this scenario, the selected array list should not point to a null or undefined value.

The select button components support one event callback named onChange, which will be invoked on the click of the default button element.

The complete demo application with instructions is available on GitHub:

- https://github.com/ova2/angular-development-with-prim eng/tree/master/chapter4/togglebutton
- https://github.com/ova2/angular-development-with-prim eng/tree/master/chapter4/selectbutton

Grouping buttons with Toolbar

Toolbar is a grouping or container component for buttons and other web resources. The Toolbar content is wrapped in two `div` elements, one for aligning content on the left-hand side using `.ui-toolbar-group-left` class and another one for aligning content on the right-hand side using the `.ui-toolbar-group-right` class. An example of the Toolbar component with different buttons, input controls, and text content would be as follows:

```
<p-toolbar name="toolbar">
  <div class="ui-toolbar-group-left">
    <button pButton type="button" name="open" label="Open"
      icon="fa-folder-open"></button>
    <button pButton type="button" name="new" label="New folder"
      icon="fa-plus"></button>
    <p-splitButton  name="organize" label="Organize"
      icon="fa-check" name="organize"
      [model]="items"></p-splitButton>
  </div>

  <div class="ui-toolbar-group-right">
    <input name="search" type="text" size="30" pInputText
    [(ngModel)]="search"
      placeholder="Search files here"/>
    <i class="fa fa-bars"></i>
    <button name="refresh" pButton type="button"
    icon="fa-refresh"></button>
    <button name="help" pButton type="button"
    icon="fa-question-circle"></button>
  </div>
</p-toolbar>
```

The following screenshot shows a snapshot result of the Toolbar as an example:

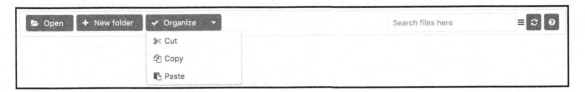

In the preceding snapshot, the commonly used Toolbar buttons are placed on left-hand side and secondary (or additional information) placed on the right-hand side. The skinning features are provided through the `style` and `styleClass` attributes.

The complete demo application with instructions is available on GitHub at `https://github.com/ova2/angular-development-with-primeng/tree/master/chapter4/toolbar`.

Arranging your view with Panels and FieldSets

Most websites and dashboards need grouping or container components to highlight title and description. PrimeNG offers many variations of container components.

Panel

As a generic grouping component for web content, Panel has features such as toggling and custom content. A basic definition of the Panel would be as follows:

```
<p-panel header="PrimeNG">
   PrimeNG is a collection of rich UI components for Angular.
   PrimeNG is a sibling of the popular JavaServer Faces Component Suite,
   PrimeFaces.
   All widgets are open source and free to use under MIT License.
   PrimeNG is developed by PrimeTek Informatics, a company with years of
   expertise in developing open source UI components.
</p-panel>
```

The preceding definition of the Panel will display PrimeNG details inside the container as shown in the following screenshot:

PrimeNG

PrimeNG is a collection of rich UI components for Angular. PrimeNG is a sibling of the popular JavaServer Faces Component Suite, PrimeFaces. All widgets are open source and free to use under MIT License. PrimeNG is developed by PrimeTek Informatics, a company with years of expertise in developing open source UI components.

The Panel is going to be more user friendly, with toggleable (`toggleable="true"`) and custom header content features. The toggleable feature defines the content as either expanded or collapsed. The initial state of the Panel content (expanded or collapsed) defined with the `collapsed` attribute; by default, the content section will be expanded, whereas the customized header and footer is defined through the `p-header` and `p-footer` tags which accepts text, images, icons, and many more. For example, the customized header with list of PrimeNG resources in the form of drop-down would be as follows:

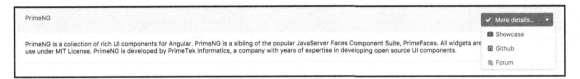

We can catch the user actions before toggling and after toggling using `onBeforeToggle` and `onAfterToggle` callbacks.

FieldSet

FieldSet is a grouping component with a content toggle feature. At the top, legend defines a caption and draws a box around the body content. The FieldSet example with `toggleable` feature would be as follows:

```
<p-fieldset legend="PrimeNG" [toggleable]="true" [collapsed]="true">
   PrimeNG is a collection of rich UI components for Angular.
   PrimeNG is a sibling of the popular JavaServer Faces Component
   Suite, PrimeFaces.
   All widgets are open source and free to use under MIT License.
   PrimeNG is developed by PrimeTek Informatics, a company with years
   of expertise in developing open source UI components.
</p-fieldset>
```

The preceding definition of the FieldSet will be displayed as shown in the following screenshot:

> — PrimeNG
>
> PrimeNG is a collection of rich UI components for Angular. PrimeNG is a sibling of the popular JavaServer Faces Component Suite, PrimeFaces. All widgets are open source and free to use under MIT License. PrimeNG is developed by PrimeTek Informatics, a company with years of expertise in developing open source UI components.

Similar to the Panel component, FieldSet provides a custom legend through the `p-header` attribute (that is, the customized header content).

The FieldSet caption text is managed by the `legend` property, whereas toggle features are controlled by `toggleable` and `collapsed` attributes. There are two event callbacks named `onBeforeToggle` and `onAfterToggle` available for any custom logic implementation.

The complete demo application with instructions is available on GitHub:

- https://github.com/ova2/angular-development-with-prim
  eng/tree/master/chapter4/panel

- https://github.com/ova2/angular-development-with-prim
  eng/tree/master/chapter4/fieldset

Vertical stacked panels with Accordion

Accordion is a container component that provides the ability to group contents in the form of multiple tabs. The content can be text, images, or any other components. All the tab contents are stacked in a vertical order. A basic definition of the Accordion component with different versions of Angular details would be as follows:

```
<p-accordion>
  <p-accordionTab header="AngularJS">
    AngularJS (commonly referred to as "Angular.js" or "AngularJS 1.X")
    is a JavaScript-based open-source front-end web application
    framework mainly maintained by Google and by a community of
    individuals and corporations to address many of the
    challenges encountered in developing single-page applications.
  </p-accordionTab>
  <p-accordionTab header="AngularV2.0">
    The successor to the older AngularJS web framework, now simply
    known as "Angular". Angular takes a web component-based
    approach to build powerful applications for the web. It is used
    along with TypeScript which provides support for both older
    and new versions of JavaScript.
  </p-accordionTab>
  <p-accordionTab header="AngularV4.0">
    Angular version 4.0.0 is a major release following announced
    adoption of Semantic Versioning, and is backwards compatible with
    2.x.x for most applications.
  </p-accordionTab>
</p-accordion>
```

The preceding Accordion will be displayed with vertical panels as shown in the following screenshot:

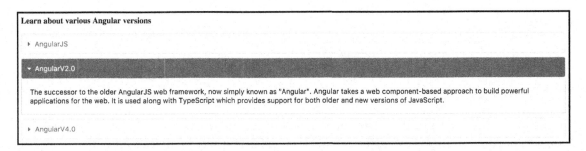

In the preceding simple example, the Accordion will display the tab contents one at a time. There is a provision in the component to display multiple tab contents by enabling the `multiple` attribute. The Accordion can be customized with powerful features such as customized headers, tab events, default selected tabs, and disabled behavior.

The customized definition of the Accordion component would be as follows:

```
<p-accordion>
  <p-accordionTab>
    <p-header>
      <img src="/assets/data/images/angularjs.png"
        alt="Smiley face" width="42" height="42">
      AngularJS
    </p-header>
    AngularJS (commonly referred to as "Angular.js" or "AngularJS 1.X")
    is a JavaScript-based open-source front-end web application
    framework mainly maintained by Google and by a community
    of individuals and corporations to address many of the challenges
    encountered in developing single-page applications.
  </p-accordionTab>
  <p-accordionTab header="AngularV2.0">
    <p-header>
      <img src="/assets/data/images/angular2.svg"
        alt="Smiley face" width="42" height="42">
      AngularV2.0
    </p-header>
    The successor to the older AngularJS web framework,
    now simply known as "Angular". Angular takes a web
    component-based approach to build powerful
    applications for the web. It is used along with TypeScript
    which provides support for both older and new versions of
    JavaScript.
  </p-accordionTab>
  <p-accordionTab header="AngularV4.0">
```

```
<p-header>
  <img src="/assets/data/images/angular4.png"
    alt="Smiley face" width="42" height="42">
  AngularV4.0
</p-header>
Angular version 4.0.0 is a major release
following announced adoption of Semantic Versioning,
and is backwards compatible with 2.x.x for most applications.
  </p-accordionTab>
</p-accordion>
```

In the preceding example, the customized header is created with the p-header tag, which consists of Angular logos and text content. The Accordion will be displayed with customized advanced features as shown in the following image:

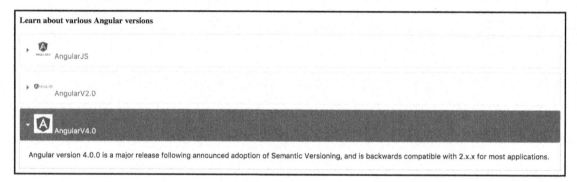

The Accordion component supports two event callbacks named onOpen and onClose, which invoked while opening and closing the tabs, respectively.

> PrimeNG 4.1 release introduced the activeIndex property, which defines the active tab or an array of indexes to change selected tab programmatically. For example, [activeIndex]="0,1".
> The complete demo application with instructions is available on GitHub at https://github.com/ova2/angular-development-with-primeng/tree/master/chapter4/accordion.

Grouping content with tabs in TabView

TabView is a tabbed Panel component to group content in the form of vertical and horizontal tabs. The default TabView will display the tabs in horizontal orientation and only one tab can be selected at a time to view the content. A basic definition of the TabView component would be as follows:

```
<p-tabView name="basic">
  <p-tabPanel header="AngularJS">
    AngularJS (commonly referred to as "Angular.js" or
    "AngularJS 1.X") is a JavaScript-based open-source front-end web
    application framework mainly maintained by Google and by a
    community of individuals and corporations to address many of
    the challenges encountered in developing single-page applications.
  </p-tabPanel>
  <p-tabPanel header="AngularV2.0">
    The successor to the older AngularJS web framework,
    now simply known as "Angular". Angular takes a
    web component-based approach to build powerful
    applications for the web. It is used along with
    TypeScript which provides support for both older
    and new versions of JavaScript.
  </p-tabPanel>
  <p-tabPanel header="AngularV4.0">
    Angular version 4.0.0 is a major release following announced
    adoption of Semantic Versioning, and is backwards compatible
    with 2.x.x for most applications.
  </p-tabPanel>
</p-tabView>
```

The preceding TabView will be displayed with horizontal panels as shown in the following screenshot:

AngularJS   **AngularV2.0**   AngularV4.0

The successor to the older AngularJS web framework, now simply known as "Angular". Angular takes a web component-based approach to build powerful applications for the web. It is used along with TypeScript which provides support for both older and new versions of JavaScript.

Each tab is represented with `p-tabPanel`. The orientation of the tabs can be altered using the `orientation` attribute. It supports four different orientations: `top`, `bottom`, `left`, and `right`. `Top` is the default orientation.

The component also supports various other advanced features such as the `closable` tabs (`closable="true"`), events (`onChange` to invoke on tab change, `onClose` to invoke on tab close), default selection using the `selection` attribute, and disable the tabs using the `disabled` attribute.

The `onChange` event object exposes two attributes which are accessible in the component class:

onChange	• `event.originalEvent`: Native click event • `event.index`: Index of the selected tab

```
onTabChange(event:any) {
  this.msgs = [];
  this.msgs.push({severity:'info', summary:'Tab Expanded',
    detail: 'Target: '+ event.originalEvent.target+'Index: '
    + event.index});
```

The `onClose` event object exposes three attributes, which are accessible in the component class:

onClose	• `event.originalEvent`: Native click event • `event.index`: Index of the closed tab • `event.close`: Callback to actually close the tab, only available if `controlClose` is enabled

```
onTabClose(event:any) {
  this.msgs = [];
  this.msgs.push({severity:'info', summary:'Tab closed',
    detail: 'Target: ' + event.originalEvent.target+'Index: '
    + event.index});
}
```

A customized definition of the TabView component would be as follows:

```
<p-tabView (onChange)="onTabChange($event)"
  (onClose)="onTabClose($event)">
  <p-tabPanel header="AngularJS" [closable]="true" [selected]="true">
    AngularJS (commonly referred to as "Angular.js" or "AngularJS 1.X")
    is a JavaScript-based open-source front-end web application
    framework mainly maintained by Google and by a community of
    individuals and corporations to address many of the challenges
    encountered in developing single-page applications.
  </p-tabPanel>
  <p-tabPanel header="AngularV2.0" [closable]="true"
   leftIcon="fa-bell-o" rightIcon="fa-bookmark-o">
    The successor to the older AngularJS web framework,
```

```
      now simply known as "Angular". Angular takes a
      web component-based approach to build powerful applications
      for the web. It is used along with TypeScript which provides
      support for both older and new versions of JavaScript.
   </p-tabPanel>
   <p-tabPanel header="AngularV4.0" [disabled]="true">
      Angular version 4.0.0 is a major release following announced
      adoption of Semantic Versioning, and is backwards compatible
      with 2.x.x for most applications.
   </p-tabPanel>
</p-tabView>
```

The preceding TabView will be displayed as shown in the following screenshot:

Remember that only the `orientation`, `activeIndex`, `style`, and `styleClass` properties applied for the TabView element whereas all other attributes need to be defined for the tab Panel element.

The complete demo application with instructions is available on GitHub at `https://github.com/ova2/angular-development-with-primeng/tree /master/chapter4/tabview`.

Summary

At the end of this chapter, you will know how to deal with various Buttons and Panel components, depending on given use case. Initially, we covered all kinds of Button components. At first, we started with click button variations such as Button, RadioButton, and SplitButton components; after that we moved on to select value button variations such as ToggleButton and SelectButton components, then followed by explaining how to group multiple buttons using the Toolbar component. Later, we moved to container components such as various Panel components available in PrimeNG suite. The Panel components tour gets started with arranging views effectively using Panels and FieldSets, then how to use vertically stacked Accordion component, followed by grouping content with multiple tabs inside the TabView component.

The next chapter will give a detailed insight on data iteration components such as DataTable, export CSV data, DataList, OrderList, PickList, Schedule, and followed by tree hierarchical components such as Tree and TreeTable components. All these components explained with all possible features in a step-by-step approach.

5
Data Iteration Components

In this chapter, we will cover the basic and advanced features to visualize data with data iteration components provided by PrimeNG, which include DataTable, DataList, PickList, OrderList, DataGrid, DataScroller, Tree, and TreeTable. We will start with the DataTable component that offers extensive features, such as filtering, sorting, pagination, selection, reordering, column resizing, toggling, and many more. We will then focus on various other components, such as DataList, that render data in a listed format and provide data selection through the listed sets such as PickList and OrderList.

After that, we will also see two more data variation components such as DataGrid that arranges large datasets in the grid-oriented layout and DataScroller that lazily loads data according to the page scroll done by the user. The Tree and TreeTable components list data in a tree format, and they are mostly based on the same data model. At the end of this chapter, we will discuss a sophisticated component called Schedule to visualize calendar data, and we will demonstrate its usage with its lazy loading feature.

In this chapter, we will cover the following topics:

- Multi feature DataTable
- Selecting rows in DataTable
- Sorting, filtering, and paginating data in DataTable
- Customizing cell content with templating
- Resizing, reordering, and toggling columns in DataTable
- In-cell editing with DataTable
- Making DataTable responsive
- Using column and row grouping

- Handling tons of data with lazy DataTable
- Row expansion by providing row template
- Exporting data in the CSV format
- DataTable events and methods
- Listing data with DataList
- Listing data with PickList
- Listing data with OrderList
- Grid-organized data with DataGrid
- On demand data loading with DataScroller
- Visualizing data with Tree
- Visualizing data with TreeTable
- Managing events with Schedule

Multi feature DataTable

DataTable displays data in a tabular format. The table is an arrangement of data in rows and columns, or possibly in a more complex structure. It requires a value as an array of objects bound through the `value` property and columns defined with the `p-column` component. A basic example of the component with browser details to display in the list format would be written as follows:

```
<p-dataTable [value]="browsers">
  <p-column field="engine" header="Engine"></p-column>
  <p-column field="browser" header="Browser"></p-column>
  <p-column field="platform" header="Platform"></p-column>
  <p-column field="grade" header="Grade"></p-column>
</p-dataTable>
```

The `browsers` array consists of objects with `engine`, `browser`, `platform`, and `grade` properties. The `field` property will map the model object property, whereas the `header` property is used to display a column's heading. In real-time applications, we use services to fetch the data from remote data sources. In this case, service is created as an injectable service and it uses the HTTP module to fetch data. The browser service would be defined with observables as shown here:

```
@Injectable()
export class BrowserService {

constructor(private http: Http) { }
```

```
getBrowsers(): Observable<Browser[]> {
    return this.http.get('/assets/data/browsers.json')
        .map(response => response.json().data as Browser[]);
    }
}
```

The component class has to define an array of `browser` objects (or items) for the `value` property. The items are retrieved from the remote service call as shown here:

```
browsers: Browser[];

constructor(private browserService: BrowserService) { }

ngOnInit() {
    this.browserService.getBrowsers().subscribe((browsers: any)
    => this.browsers = browsers);
}
```

The following screenshot shows a snapshot result presented in a tabular format:

Engine	Browser	Platform	Grade
Trident	Internet Explorer 4.0	Win 95+	B
Trident	Internet Explorer 5.0	Win 95+	C
Trident	Internet Explorer 5.5	Win 95+	A
Trident	Internet Explorer 6.0	Win 98+	A
Trident	Internet Explorer 7.0	Win XP SP2+	A
Gecko	Firefox 1.5	Win 98+ / OSX.2+	A
Gecko	Firefox 2	Win 98+ / OSX.2+	A
Gecko	Firefox 3	Win 2k+ / OSX.3+	A
Webkit	Safari 1.2	OSX.3	A
Webkit	Safari 1.3	OSX.3	A

In the preceding snapshot, we can observe alternative colors for the rows. This is a theme-specific behavior.

PrimeNG 4.1 handles the change detection feature in a more flexible manner.

Change detection

DataTable uses either setter-based checking or **ngDoCheck** to realize if the underlying data has changed to update the **user interface** (**UI**). This is configured using the immutable property. If you enabled (default) it, then the setter-based detection is utilized so your data changes such as adding or removing a record should always create a new array reference instead of manipulating an existing array. This constraint is due to Angular and does not trigger setters if the reference does not change. In this case, use slice instead of splice when removing an item or use the spread operator instead of the push method when adding an item.

On the other hand, setting the immutable property to false removes this restriction using ngDoCheck with IterableDiffers to listen to changes without the need to create a new reference of data. The setter-based method is faster; however, both methods can be used depending on your preference.

Dynamic columns

In the preceding use case, the columns are defined in a static representation using the p-column tag. There is another approach to represent columns inside a data table via dynamic columns. The table columns need to be instantiated as an array. The array will be iterated using the ngFor directive as shown here:

```
<p-dataTable [value]="basicBrowsers">
  <p-header>
    <div class="algin-left">
      <p-multiSelect [options]="columnOptions" [(ngModel)]="cols">
      </p-multiSelect>
    </div>
  </p-header>
  <p-column *ngFor="let col of cols" [field]="col.field"
[header]="col.header"></p-column>
</p-dataTable>
```

The cols property describes the given column options within the component class:

```
this.cols = [
  {field: 'engine', header: 'Engine'},
  {field: 'browser', header: 'Browser'},
  {field: 'platform', header: 'Platform'},
  {field: 'grade', header: 'Grade'}
];
```

The following screenshot shows a snapshot result of dynamic columns in a tabular format as an example:

Engine, Browser, Grade ▾		
Engine	Browser	Grade
Trident	Internet Explorer 4.0	B
Trident	Internet Explorer 5.0	C
Trident	Internet Explorer 5.5	A
Trident	Internet Explorer 6.0	A
Trident	Internet Explorer 7.0	A
Gecko	Firefox 1.5	A
Gecko	Firefox 2	A
Gecko	Firefox 3	A
Webkit	Safari 1.2	A
Webkit	Safari 1.3	A

In the preceding snapshot, the columns are dynamically added or removed using a multiselect drop-down menu. For demonstration purposes, we removed the **Version** column field from the table.

Selecting rows in DataTable

In order to perform CRUD operations on the component, there is a need for table row selection. PrimeNG supports various kinds of selections such as single, multiple, radio, and checkbox with different event callbacks.

Single selection

In single selection, the row is selected by a click event on a specific row. This selection is enabled by setting `selectionMode` as the `single` and `selection` property to hold the selected row. By default, the row is unselected with the help of the Meta key *(Ctrl* key for Windows or *Command* key for macOS). The row can be unselected without pressing the Meta key just by disabling the `metaKeySelection` property.

The component with a single selection feature to select a specific browser record would be written as follows:

```
<p-dataTable [value]="basicBrowsers" selectionMode="single"
[(selection)]="selectedBrowser">
  // Content goes here
</p-dataTable>
```

The component class has to define the `selectedBrower` object to store the selected item. The following screenshot shows a snapshot result with single selection as an example:

Single Selection			
Engine	Browser	Platform	Grade
Trident	Internet Explorer 4.0	Win 95+	B
Trident	Internet Explorer 5.0	Win 95+	C
Trident	Internet Explorer 5.5	Win 95+	A
Trident	Internet Explorer 6.0	Win 98+	A
Trident	Internet Explorer 7.0	Win XP SP2+	A
Gecko	Firefox 1.5	Win 98+ / OSX.2+	A
Gecko	Firefox 2	Win 98+ / OSX.2+	A
Gecko	Firefox 3	Win 2k+ / OSX.3+	A
Webkit	Safari 1.2	OSX.3	A
Webkit	Safari 1.3	OSX.3	A
Selected Browser: Trident - Internet Explorer 5.5 - Win 95+ - A			

To notify that single selection has worked or not, we displayed the selected record information in a footer section. The footer data should always be in sync with the selected record.

Multiple selection

In multiple selection, the row is selected by a click event on a specific row and multiple rows can be selected using the Meta key or *Shift* key. This selection is enabled by setting `selectionMode` as `multiple` and the `selection` property to hold selected rows in the form of an array. By default, the row is unselected with the help of the Meta key *(Ctrl* key for Windows or *Command* key for macOS). The row can be unselected without the help of Meta key just by disabling the `metaKeySelection` property.

The component with the multiple selection feature to select multiple browser records would be written as follows:

```
<p-dataTable [value]="basicBrowsers" selectionMode="multiple"
[(selection)]="selectedBrowsers">
  // Content goes here
</p-dataTable>
```

The component class has to define the `selectedBrowers` array object to store the selected records. The following screenshot shows a snapshot result with multiple selection as an example:

Multiple Selection			
Engine	Browser	Platform	Grade
Trident	Internet Explorer 4.0	Win 95+	B
Trident	Internet Explorer 5.0	Win 95+	C
Trident	Internet Explorer 5.5	Win 95+	A
Trident	Internet Explorer 6.0	Win 98+	A
Trident	Internet Explorer 7.0	Win XP SP2+	A
Gecko	Firefox 1.5	Win 98+ / OSX.2+	A
Gecko	Firefox 2	Win 98+ / OSX.2+	A
Gecko	Firefox 3	Win 2k+ / OSX.3+	A
Webkit	Safari 1.2	OSX.3	A
Webkit	Safari 1.3	OSX.3	A

- Trident - Internet Explorer 6.0 - Win 98+ - A
- Gecko - Firefox 1.5 - Win 98+ / OSX.2+ - A
- Webkit - Safari 1.2 - OSX.3 - A

To notify that multiple selection has worked or not, we displayed the selected records information in a footer section. The footer data should always be in sync with selected records.

Both single and multiple selection support four event callbacks, `onRowClick`, `onRowDblClick`, `onRowSelect`, and `onRowUnselect`, which carry selected data information within an event object. Refer to the events section for more details.

RadioButton selection

The single selection can be achieved through radio buttons, which exist on each row instead of using the click event on a specific row. The selection is enabled by setting `selectionMode` as `single` on a column level (remember that previously mentioned plain selection works on a table level) and the `selection` property to hold the selected row as an object.

The component with the radio selection feature to select specific browser records would be written as follows:

```
<p-dataTable [value]="basicBrowsers" [(selection)]="selectedBrowser">
  <p-header> RadioButton selection (Single Selection)</p-header>
  <p-column [style]="{'width':'38px'}" selectionMode="single">
  </p-column>
  //Content goes here
</p-dataTable>
```

The following screenshot shows a snapshot result with a radio button selection as an example:

RadioButton selection (Single Selection)			
Engine	Browser	Platform	Grade
Trident	Internet Explorer 4.0	Win 95+	B
Trident	Internet Explorer 5.0	Win 95+	C
Trident	Internet Explorer 5.5	Win 95+	A
Trident	Internet Explorer 6.0	Win 98+	A
Trident	Internet Explorer 7.0	Win XP SP2+	A
Gecko	Firefox 1.5	Win 98+ / OSX.2+	A
Gecko	Firefox 2	Win 98+ / OSX.2+	A
Gecko	Firefox 3	Win 2k+ / OSX.3+	A
Webkit	Safari 1.2	OSX.3	A
Webkit	Safari 1.3	OSX.3	A

Selected Browser: Gecko - Firefox 1.5 - Win 98+ / OSX.2+ - A

As of now, there is no unselected feature for radio button selection (that is, the row is unselected once you select another row).

Checkbox selection

The multiple selection can be achieved through checkboxes, which exist on each row instead of using a click event on a specific row. The selection is enabled by setting selectionMode as multiple on a column level (remember that plain selection provides this on a table level) and the selection property to hold the selected rows as an array of objects.

The component with the checkbox selection feature to select multiple browser records would be written as follows:

```
<p-dataTable [value]="basicBrowsers" [(selection)]="selectedBrowser">
  <p-header> Multiple Selection </p-header>
  <p-column [style]="{'width':'38px'}" selectionMode="multiple">
  </p-column>
  //Content goes here
</p-dataTable>
```

The following screenshot shows a snapshot result with a checkbox selection as an example:

	Engine	Browser	Platform	Grade
			Multiple Selection	
	Trident	Internet Explorer 4.0	Win 95+	B
✓	Trident	Internet Explorer 5.0	Win 95+	C
✓	Trident	Internet Explorer 5.5	Win 95+	A
	Trident	Internet Explorer 6.0	Win 98+	A
	Trident	Internet Explorer 7.0	Win XP SP2+	A
	Gecko	Firefox 1.5	Win 98+ / OSX.2+	A
✓	Gecko	Firefox 2	Win 98+ / OSX.2+	A
	Gecko	Firefox 3	Win 2k+ / OSX.3+	A
	Webkit	Safari 1.2	OSX.3	A
	Webkit	Safari 1.3	OSX.3	A

- Trident - Internet Explorer 5.0 - Win 95+ - C
- Trident - Internet Explorer 5.5 - Win 95+ - A
- Gecko - Firefox 2 - Win 98+ / OSX.2+ - A

In this selection, the selected records can be unselected by unselecting checkboxes. The checkbox selection supports the onHeaderCheckboxToggle event while toggling the header checkbox. Refer to the events section for more details.

When selection is enabled, use the `dataKey` attribute to avoid deep checking when comparing objects. If you cannot provide `dataKey`, use the `compareSelectionBy` property as "equals," which uses a reference for comparison instead of the default "deepEquals" comparison. The deepEquals comparison is not a good idea (especially for huge data) in terms of performance because it checks all the properties.

For example, the value of the `browserId` property could be chosen for `dataKey` as follows:

```
<p-dataTable dataKey="browserId" selection="true">
...
</p-dataTable>
```

Sorting, filtering, and paginating data in DataTable

Sorting, filtering, and pagination features are very crucial features for any kind of data iteration component. These features are going to be very helpful while working on large datasets.

Sorting

The sorting feature is provided by enabling the `sortable` property on each column. By default, the component supports single sorting (`sortMode="single"`). We can achieve multi sorting by setting `sortMode="multiple"`. The DataTable component with the sorting feature to sort browser records in either ascending or descending order would be written as follows:

```
<p-dataTable [value]="browsers" (onSort)="onSort($event)">
  <p-column field="engine" header="Engine" [sortable]="true">
  </p-column>
  <p-column field="browser" header="Browser" [sortable]="true">
  </p-column>
  <p-column field="platform" header="Platform" [sortable]="true">
  </p-column>
  <p-column field="grade" header="Grade" [sortable]="true">
  </p-column>
</p-dataTable>
```

The following screenshot shows a snapshot result with a single sorting on a limited number of records as an example:

Engine ▾	Browser ⇕	Platform ⇕	Grade ⇕
Webkit	Safari 1.2	OSX.3	A
Webkit	Safari 1.3	OSX.3	A
Trident	Internet Explorer 4.0	Win 95+	B
Trident	Internet Explorer 5.0	Win 95+	C
Trident	Internet Explorer 5.5	Win 95+	A
Trident	Internet Explorer 6.0	Win 98+	A
Trident	Internet Explorer 7.0	Win XP SP2+	A
Gecko	Firefox 1.5	Win 98+ / OSX.2+	A
Gecko	Firefox 2	Win 98+ / OSX.2+	A
Gecko	Firefox 3	Win 2k+ / OSX.3+	A

We need to use the Meta key *(Ctrl* for Windows and *Command* key for macOS) for the multi column sorting feature. The custom sorting is also supported using the `sortFunction` function instead of regular sorting on the `field` property. The sorting feature also provides the `onSort` event callback, which will be invoked on sorting a column. Refer to the event details section for more information.

Filtering

The filtering feature is provided by enabling the `filter` property on each column. The filter can be applied on a column level and whole table level as well. The table level filtering is also called **global filtering**. To enable global filter, the local template variable of input need to be referred in the `globalFilter` property. The `keyup` event of global filter input will be listened to for filtering.

The filter feature supports optional filter properties such as `filterMatchMode` to provide different types of a text search. It has five filter match modes such as `startsWith`, `contains`, `endsWith`, `equals`, and `in` and the default match mode is `startsWith`, whereas the `filterPlaceholder` property is used to display the helper place holder text. The DataTable component with the filtering feature on table columns would be written as follows:

```
<div class="ui-widget-header align-globalfilter">
  <i class="fa fa-search search-globalfilter"></i>
  <input #gb type="text" pInputText size="50"
  placeholder="Global Filter">
</div>
<p-dataTable [value]="browsers" [rows]="10" [paginator]="true"
  [globalFilter]="gb" #datatable (onFilter)="onFilter($event)">
  <p-header>List of Browsers</p-header>
  <p-column field="browser" header="Browser (contains)" [filter]="true"
    [filterMatchMode]="contains" filterPlaceholder="Search"></p-column>
  <p-column field="platform" header="Platform (startsWith)"
    [filter]="true"
    filterPlaceholder="Search"></p-column>
  <p-column field="rating" header="Rating ({{browserFilter||'No
    Filter'}}"
    [filter]="true" filterMatchMode="equals" [style]="
    {'overflow':'visible'}">
    <ng-template pTemplate="filter" let-col>
      <i class="fa fa-close"
        (click)="ratingFilter=null;
        datatable.filter(null,col.field,col.filterMatchMode)"></i>
      <p-slider [styleClass]="'slider-layout'"
        [(ngModel)]="ratingFilter" [min]="1" [max]="10"
        (onSlideEnd)="datatable.filter
        ($event.value,col.field,col.filterMatchMode)">
      </p-slider>
    </ng-template>
  </p-column>
  <p-column field="engine" header="Engine (Custom)" [filter]="true"
    filterMatchMode="equals" [style]="{'overflow':'visible'}">
    <ng-template pTemplate="filter" let-col>
      <p-dropdown [options]="engines" [style]="{'width':'100%'}"
        (onChange)="datatable.filter($event.value,col.field,
        col.filterMatchMode)" styleClass="ui-column-filter">
      </p-dropdown>
    </ng-template>
  </p-column>
  <p-column field="grade" header="Grade (Custom)" [filter]="true"
    filterMatchMode="in" [style]="{'overflow':'visible'}">
    <ng-template pTemplate="filter" let-col>
```

```
        <p-multiSelect [options]="grades" defaultLabel="All grades"
          (onChange)="datatable.filter($event.value,col.field,
            col.filterMatchMode)" styleClass="ui-column-filter">
        </p-multiSelect>
      </ng-template>
    </p-column>
  </p-dataTable>
```

The filtering feature is normally applied on a plain input component, but this behavior can also be customized by providing a filter on various other inputs such as Spinner, Slider, DropDown, and MultiSelect components. The custom input filter calls a `filter` function with three parameters. The signature of the `filter` function would be written as follows:

```
datatable.filter($event.value, col.field, col.filterMatchMode)
```

The following screenshot shows a snapshot result with a filtering feature on a limited number of records as an example:

Browser (contains)	Platform (startsWith)	Rating (No Filter ✖)	Engine (Custom)	Grade (Custom)
Search	Search	⬤	All engines ▾	B, C ▾
Internet Explorer 5.0	Win 95+	9	Trident	C
Internet Explorer 4.0	Win 95+	9	Trident	B
Internet Explorer 5.0	Win 95+	9	Trident	C

List of Browsers

Global Filter

⊲ ⊲⊲ 1 ⊳⊳ ⊳

In the preceding snapshot, we can observe that the data is filtered by a rating slider and multi select grade field. The filtering feature also provides the `onFilter` event callback, which will be invoked on filtering an input. Refer to the event details section for more information.

Pagination

If the table is backed by huge datasets, then displaying all of the data on a single page looks awkward and it is going to be a nightmare for the user when scrolling millions of records. The DataTable component supports a pagination feature just by enabling the `paginator` property and the `rows` option to display the number of records in the page.

Apart from the mentioned required features, it also supports various optional features such as:

- The `pageLinks` property shows the number of page link displayed at a time.
- The `rowsPerPageOptions` property has a provision to change the number of rows to be displayed (comma separated values as an array) in a single page.
- The `totalRecords` property displays the logical records which are useful for the lazy loading feature.
- The `paginatorPosition` property displays the paginator with possible values of `top`, `bottom`, and `both`. The default position of paginator is `bottom`.

The pagination example, which is used to display a lot of browser's information, would be written as follows:

```
<p-dataTable [value]="browsers" [rows]="10" [paginator]="true"
  [pageLinks]="3" [rowsPerPageOptions]="[10,15,20]"
  paginatorPosition="both" (onPage)="onPage($event)">
  <p-column field="engine" header="Engine"></p-column>
  <p-column field="browser" header="Browser"></p-column>
  <p-column field="platform" header="Platform"></p-column>
  <p-column field="grade" header="Grade"></p-column>
</p-dataTable>
```

The following screenshot shows a snapshot result with a pagination feature as an example:

Engine	Browser	Platform	Grade
Webkit	Safari 2.0	OSX.4+	A
Webkit	Safari 3.0	OSX.4+	A
Trident	Internet Explorer 4.0	Win 95+	B
Trident	Internet Explorer 5.0	Win 95+	C
Trident	Internet Explorer 5.5	Win 95+	A
Trident	Internet Explorer 6.0	Win 98+	A
Trident	Internet Explorer 7.0	Win XP SP2+	A
Gecko	Firefox 1.5	Win 98+ / OSX.2+	A
Gecko	Firefox 2	Win 98+ / OSX.2+	A
Gecko	Firefox 3	Win 2k+ / OSX.3+	A

We can also use an external paginator using the Paginator component apart from the one built into DataTable. The pagination feature also provides the `onPage` event callback (whereas the external paginator provides the `onPageChange` callback), which will be invoked on pagination. Refer to the event details section for more information.

Customizing the cell content with templating

By default, the value of the `field` attribute of each column is used to display the table content. The content can also be customized in every possible way with the help of the `ng-template` template tag, which can be applied on header, body, and footer levels. The `template` variable passed to the `ng-template` template is used for column definition and row data is used by the `rowData` property. There is also an optional row index available through the `rowIndex` variable.

The `ng-template` template will have the `pTemplate` directive, which holds the type of customization with the possible values of `header`, `body`, and `footer`. The customized browser content is displayed with various text colors and row data information with a button selection as follows:

```
<p-dataTable [value]="basicBrowsers">
  <p-column field="engine" header="Engine"></p-column>
  <p-column field="browser" header="Browser"></p-column>
  <p-column field="platform" header="Platform"></p-column>
  <p-column field="grade" header="Grade">
    <ng-template let-col let-browser="rowData" pTemplate="body">
      <span [style.color]="'Green'" *ngIf="browser[col.field]=='A'">
        {{browser[col.field]}}</span>
      <span [style.color]="'Blue'" *ngIf="browser[col.field]=='B'">
        {{browser[col.field]}}</span>
      <span [style.color]="'Red'" *ngIf="browser[col.field]=='C'">
        {{browser[col.field]}}</span>
    </ng-template>
  </p-column>
  <p-column styleClass="col-button">
    <ng-template pTemplate="header">
      <button type="button" pButton icon="fa-refresh"></button>
    </ng-template>
    <ng-template let-browser="rowData" pTemplate="body">
      <button type="button" pButton (click)="selectBrowser(browser)"
        icon="fa-search"></button>
    </ng-template>
  </p-column>
</p-dataTable>
```

In the preceding example, we customized the table content to display different colors based on grades, each row with button selection using body template and button at the header using a header template. The following screenshot shows a snapshot result with customized content display as an example:

Engine	Browser	Platform	Grade	⟳
Trident	Internet Explorer 4.0	Win 95+	B	🔍
Trident	Internet Explorer 5.0	Win 95+	C	🔍
Trident	Internet Explorer 5.5	Win 95+	A	🔍
Trident	Internet Explorer 6.0	Win 98+	A	🔍
Trident	Internet Explorer 7.0	Win XP SP2+	A	🔍
Gecko	Firefox 1.5	Win 98+ / OSX.2+	A	🔍
Gecko	Firefox 2	Win 98+ / OSX.2+	A	🔍
Gecko	Firefox 3	Win 2k+ / OSX.3+	A	🔍
Webkit	Safari 1.2	OSX.3	A	🔍
Webkit	Safari 1.3	OSX.3	A	🔍

As per the preceding snapshot, the `ng-template` template tag is used with different types to provide a full flexibility on customization.

Resizing, reordering, and toggling columns in DataTable

By default, all the columns of the component are in static representation without interaction. The component provides resizing, reordering, and toggling features for columns.

Resizing

Columns can be resized using drag-and-drop behavior just by setting the
`resizableColumns` property to `true`. There are two types of resize modes available. One
is the `fit` mode and the other one is the `expand` mode. The default one is the `fit` mode. In
this mode, when columns are resized, the total width of the table will not be changed;
whereas in the `expand` mode, the total width of table will be changed.

The resizing feature with the `expand` mode would be written as follows:

```
<p-dataTable [value]="basicBrowsers" resizableColumns="true"
  columnResizeMode="expand">
  <p-column field="engine" header="Engine"></p-column>
  <p-column field="browser" header="Browser"></p-column>
  <p-column field="platform" header="Platform"></p-column>
  <p-column field="grade" header="Grade"></p-column>
</p-dataTable>
```

The following screenshot shows a snapshot result with the `expand` resize mode as an
example:

Engine	Browser	Platform	Grade
Trident	Internet Explorer 4.0	Win 95+	B
Trident	Internet Explorer 5.0	Win 95+	C
Trident	Internet Explorer 5.5	Win 95+	A
Trident	Internet Explorer 6.0	Win 98+	A
Trident	Internet Explorer 7.0	Win XP SP2+	A
Gecko	Firefox 1.5	Win 98+ / OSX.2+	A
Gecko	Firefox 2	Win 98+ / OSX.2+	A
Gecko	Firefox 3	Win 2k+ / OSX.3+	A
Webkit	Safari 1.2	OSX.3	A
Webkit	Safari 1.3	OSX.3	A

In the preceding snapshot, we can observe that both **Engine** and **Grade** columns are resized considering its content size to optimize the screen area. Because of the `expand` mode, the total width of the table is also changed. It can also provides the `onColumnResize` event callback which passes the resized column header information when the column gets resized. Refer to the event details section for more information.

Reordering

Generally, the order of table columns will appear exactly as it is defined within the component. There is an option to reorder the columns using the drag-and-drop feature just by setting the `reorderableColumns` property to `true`.

The reordering feature would be written as follows:

```
<p-dataTable [value]="browsers" reorderableColumns="true">
  <p-column field="engine" header="Engine"></p-column>
  <p-column field="browser" header="Browser"></p-column>
  <p-column field="platform" header="Platform"></p-column>
  <p-column field="grade" header="Grade"></p-column>
</p-dataTable>
```

The following screenshot shows a snapshot result with a reordering feature as an example:

Engine	Platform	Browser	Grade
Trident	Win 95+	Internet Explorer 4.0	B
Trident	Win 95+	Internet Explorer 5.0	C
Trident	Win 95+	Internet Explorer 5.5	A
Trident	Win 98+	Internet Explorer 6.0	A
Trident	Win XP SP2+	Internet Explorer 7.0	A
Gecko	Win 98+ / OSX.2+	Firefox 1.5	A
Gecko	Win 98+ / OSX.2+	Firefox 2	A
Gecko	Win 2k+ / OSX.3+	Firefox 3	A
Webkit	OSX.3	Safari 1.2	A
Webkit	OSX.3	Safari 1.3	A

As per the preceding snapshot, both **Platform** and **Browser** column fields are mutually reordered (that is, the initial column order is `engine`, `browser`, `platform`, and `grade`. After reordering, the column's order will be `engine`, `platform`, `browser`, and `grade`). It also provides the `onColReorder` event callback whenever the column gets reordered. Refer to the events section for more details.

Toggling

Most of the time there will not be enough screen space (or area) to display all the columns. In this case, toggling of table columns would be really helpful to save available screen space. Because of this feature, only mandatory or primary columns can be shown. This feature can be achieved by defining MultiSelect components on a dynamic column table in order to toggle the columns. Refer to the dynamic columns example which was mentioned at the beginning of this chapter.

In-cell editing with DataTable

By default, the component's content will be in read-only mode (that is, we can't edit the content). An UI will be more interactive with the cell editing feature. The cell editing feature is enabled just by setting the `editable` property on both table and column levels. When a cell is clicked on, the edit mode will be activated. Clicking on the outside of a cell or hitting the *Enter* key switches back to the view mode after updating the value. The cell editing feature would be written as follows:

```
<p-dataTable [value]="browsers" [editable]="true">
  <p-column field="browser" header="Browser" [editable]="true">
  </p-column>
  <p-column field="platfrom" header="Platform" [editable]="false">
  </p-column>
  <p-column field="engine" header="Engine" [editable]="true">
    <ng-template let-col let-browser="rowData" pTemplate="editor">
      <p-dropdown [(ngModel)]="browser[col.field]" [options]="engines"
        [autoWidth]="false" required="true"></p-dropdown>
    </ng-template>
  </p-column>
  <p-column field="grade" header="Grade" [editable]="true">
  </p-column>
</p-dataTable>
```

The following screenshot shows a snapshot result with the cell editing feature on the engine field as an example:

Browser	Platform	Engine	Grade
Internet Explorer 4.5	Win 95+	Gecko ▼	B
Internet Explorer 5.0	Win 95+	All engines	C
Internet Explorer 5.5	Win 95+	Trident / Gecko	A
Internet Explorer 6.0	Win 98+	Webkit	A
Internet Explorer 7.0	Win XP SP2+	Trident	A
Firefox 1.5	Win 98+ / OSX.2+	Gecko	A
Firefox 2	Win 98+ / OSX.2+	Gecko	A
Firefox 3	Win 2k+ / OSX.3+	Gecko	A
Safari 1.2	OSX.3	Webkit	A
Safari 1.3	OSX.3	Webkit	A

By default, the editable mode enables the input component on the click of a particular cell. We can also use other input components such as DropDown, MultiSelect, Calendar, and so on, for a customized input editing. In the preceding example, we can edit the cells using Input and Dropdown components.

Making DataTable responsive

The responsive feature is very useful for both web and mobile apps. The component columns are displayed as stacked in a responsive mode if the screen size is smaller than a certain breakpoint value. This feature is enabled by setting the responsive property as true. This stacked behavior can also be achieved manually (irrespective of the screen size) by enabling the stacked property (that is, stacked="true").

The responsive mode feature of the Table component would be written as follows:

```
<button pButton type="button" (click)="toggle()"
  [class]="responsive-toggle"
  label="Toggle" icon="fa-list">
</button>
<p-dataTable [value]="browsers" [rows]="5" [paginator]="true"
  [pageLinks]="3" [responsive]="true" [stacked]="stacked">
  <p-header>Responsive</p-header>
  <p-column field="engine" header="Engine"></p-column>
  <p-column field="browser" header="Browser"></p-column>
```

```
    <p-column field="platform" header="Platform"></p-column>
    <p-column field="grade" header="Grade"></p-column>
</p-dataTable>
```

The component class defines the `toggle` method, which is used to toggle the responsive behavior as shown here:

```
toggle() {
    this.stacked = !this.stacked;
}
```

The following screenshot shows a snapshot result of the DataTable component with stacked columns as an example:

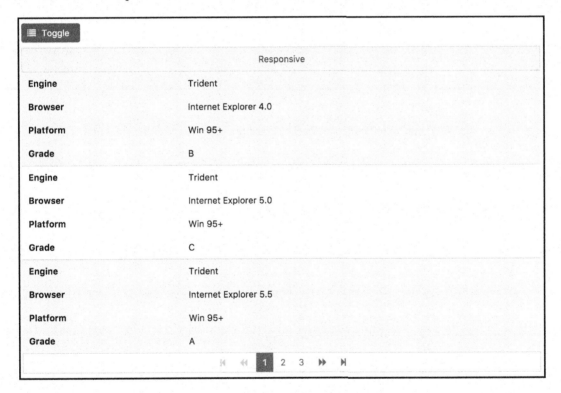

In this use case, the columns are displayed in a stacked manner by manually toggling the button, which is placed externally to the table. The responsive mode or stacked behavior can also be achieved by reducing or minimizing the screen size.

Using column and row grouping

The DataTable component provides grouping on both column and row level.

Column grouping

Columns can be grouped at the header and footer area using p-headerColumnGroup and p-footerColumnGroup tags, which define the array of columns using colspan and rowspan properties. The table rows are defined using the p-row tag, which holds the column components. The component with column grouping would be written as follows:

```
<p-dataTable [value]="basicBrowsers">
  <p-headerColumnGroup>
    <p-row>
      <p-column header="Browser" rowspan="3"></p-column>
      <p-column header="Details" colspan="4"></p-column>
    </p-row>
    <p-row>
      <p-column header="Environment" colspan="2"></p-column>
      <p-column header="Performance" colspan="2"></p-column>
    </p-row>
    <p-row>
      <p-column header="Engine"></p-column>
      <p-column header="Platform"></p-column>
      <p-column header="Rating"></p-column>
      <p-column header="Grade"></p-column>
    </p-row>
  </p-headerColumnGroup>

  <p-column field="browser"></p-column>
  <p-column field="engine"></p-column>
  <p-column field="platform"></p-column>
  <p-column field="rating"></p-column>
  <p-column field="grade"></p-column>

  <p-footerColumnGroup>
    <p-row>
      <p-column footer="*Please note that Chrome browser
        details not included"
        colspan="5"></p-column>
    </p-row>
  </p-footerColumnGroup>
</p-dataTable>
```

The following screenshot shows a snapshot result of the column grouping feature as an example:

| Browser | Details | | | | |
| | Environment | | Performance | | |
	Engine	Platform	Rating		Grade
Internet Explorer 4.0	Trident	Win 95+	7		B
Internet Explorer 5.0	Trident	Win 95+	8		C
Internet Explorer 5.5	Trident	Win 95+	5		A
Internet Explorer 6.0	Trident	Win 98+	8		A
Internet Explorer 7.0	Trident	Win XP SP2+	9		A
Firefox 1.5	Gecko	Win 98+ / OSX.2+	8		A
Firefox 2	Gecko	Win 98+ / OSX.2+	7		A
Firefox 3	Gecko	Win 2k+ / OSX.3+	6		A
Safari 1.2	Webkit	OSX.3	10		A
Safari 1.3	Webkit	OSX.3	5		A
*Please note that Chrome browser details not included					

In the preceding snapshot, we can observe that the browser-specific information is categorized with the help of column grouping.

Row grouping

By default, the table rows are individual and displayed one by one to represent unique records. In many cases, it is required to group multiple rows as one row.

Expandable row groups

The rows can be grouped on a specific field in such a way that rows can be expanded and collapsed using row expander feature. This feature is enabled by setting `rowGroupMode="subheader"`, `expandableRowGroups="true"`, and `groupField="browser"`. `groupField` is set to a specific categorized column.

The row grouping feature with expandable row group option would be written as follows:

```
<p-dataTable [value]="browsers" sortField="browser"
  rowGroupMode="subheader"  groupField="browser"
  expandableRowGroups="true" [sortableRowGroup]="false">
  <p-header>Toggleable Row Groups with Footers</p-header>
  <ng-template pTemplate="rowgroupheader" let-rowData>
    {{rowData['browser']}}
  </ng-template>
  <p-column field="engine" header="Engine"></p-column>
  <p-column field="platform" header="Platform"></p-column>
  <p-column field="rating" header="rating">
    <ng-template let-col let-browser="rowData" pTemplate="body">
      <span>{{browser[col.field]}} 'Stars'</span>
    </ng-template>
  </p-column>
  <ng-template pTemplate="rowgroupfooter" let-browser>
    <td colspan="3" style="text-align:right">Chrome browsers are not
      included</td>
  </ng-template>
</p-dataTable>
```

The following screenshot shows a snapshot result of the expandable row grouping feature as an example:

Toggleable Row Groups with Footers		
Engine	Platform	rating
❯ **Firefox 1.5**		
❯ **Firefox 2**		
❮ **Firefox 3**		
Gecko	Win 2k+ / OSX.3+	6 'Stars'
Gecko	Win 2k+ / OSX.3+	8 'Stars'
Gecko	Win 2k+ / OSX.3+	7 'Stars'
		Chrome browsers are not included
❯ **Internet Explorer 4.0**		
❯ **Internet Explorer 5.0**		
❯ **Internet Explorer 5.5**		
❯ **Internet Explorer 6.0**		
❯ **Internet Explorer 7.0**		
❯ **Safari 1.2**		
❯ **Safari 1.3**		
❯ **Safari 2.0**		
❯ **Safari 3.0**		

In this use case, we expanded Firefox version 3 group to see all the browser details over time.

Sub-headers

All related items can be grouped under one sub-group using the sub-headers feature. This use case is similar to expanded row groups but these sub-headers cannot be collapsed. This behavior is enabled by setting `rowGroupMode="subheader"` and `groupField="engine"`. The `groupField` property is set to a specific categorized column.

The row grouping feature with the sub-header option would be written as follows:

```
<p-dataTable [value]="browsers" sortField="engine"
  rowGroupMode="subheader"
  groupField="engine" [styleClass]="'rowgroup-padding'">
<p-header>Subheader</p-header>
<ng-template pTemplate="rowgroupheader" let-rowData>
  {{rowData['engine']}}
</ng-template>
<p-column field="browser" header="Browser" sortable="true">
</p-column>
<p-column field="platform" header="Platform" sortable="true">
</p-column>
<p-column field="grade" header="Grade" sortable="true">
</p-column>
</p-dataTable>
```

The following screenshot shows a snapshot result of the table with the sub-header grouping feature as an example:

	Subheader	
Browser ⇅	Platform ⇅	Grade ⇅
Gecko		
Firefox 3	Win 2k+ / OSX.3+	A
Firefox 1.5	Win 98+ / OSX.2+	A
Firefox 2	Win 98+ / OSX.2+	A
Firefox 3	Win 2k+ / OSX.3+	A
Firefox 1.5	Win 98+ / OSX.2+	A
Firefox 2	Win 98+ / OSX.2+	A
Firefox 3	Win 2k+ / OSX.3+	A
Firefox 1.5	Win 98+ / OSX.2+	A
Firefox 1.5	Win 98+ / OSX.2+	A
Firefox 2	Win 98+ / OSX.2+	A
Trident		
Internet Explorer 6.0	Win 98+	A
Internet Explorer 7.0	Win XP SP2+	A
Internet Explorer 4.0	Win 95+	B
Internet Explorer 6.0	Win 98+	A
Internet Explorer 7.0	Win XP SP2+	A
Internet Explorer 5.5	Win 95+	A
Internet Explorer 4.0	Win 95+	B
Internet Explorer 6.0	Win 95+	C
Internet Explorer 5.5	Win 95+	A
Internet Explorer 6.0	Win 98+	A
Internet Explorer 7.0	Win XP SP2+	A
Internet Explorer 4.0	Win 95+	B
Internet Explorer 4.0	Win 95+	B
Internet Explorer 5.0	Win 95+	C
Internet Explorer 5.5	Win 95+	A
Internet Explorer 6.0	Win 98+	A
Internet Explorer 7.0	Win XP SP2+	A
Internet Explorer 5.0	Win 95+	C
Internet Explorer 5.5	Win 95+	A
Internet Explorer 5.0	Win 95+	C
Webkit		
Safari 2.0	OSX.4+	A
Safari 3.0	OSX.4+	A
Safari 3.0	OSX.4+	A
Safari 1.3	OSX.3	A
Safari 1.2	OSX.3	A
Safari 1.3	OSX.3	A
Safari 2.0	OSX.4+	A
Safari 1.3	OSX.3	A
Safari 1.2	OSX.3	A
Safari 1.2	OSX.3	A

The sub-header grouping feature

In the preceding use case, all browser details are grouped based on a unique browser engine as a sub-header.

RowSpan groups

The rows can be grouped based on the sortField property. This feature is enabled by setting the rowGroupMode property value to rowspan (that is, rowGroupMode="rowspan"). An example of row grouping with row span would be written as follows:

```
<p-dataTable [value]="browsers" sortField="engine"
  rowGroupMode="rowspan"
  [styleClass]="'rowgroup-padding'">
```

```
  <p-header>RowSpan</p-header>
  <p-column field="engine" header="Engine" sortable="true"></p-column>
  <p-column field="platform" header="Platform" sortable="true">
  </p-column>
  <p-column field="browser" header="Browser" sortable="true">
  </p-column>
  <p-column field="grade" header="Grade" sortable="true"></p-column>
</p-dataTable>
```

The following screenshot shows a snapshot result of the component with the row span grouping feature as an example:

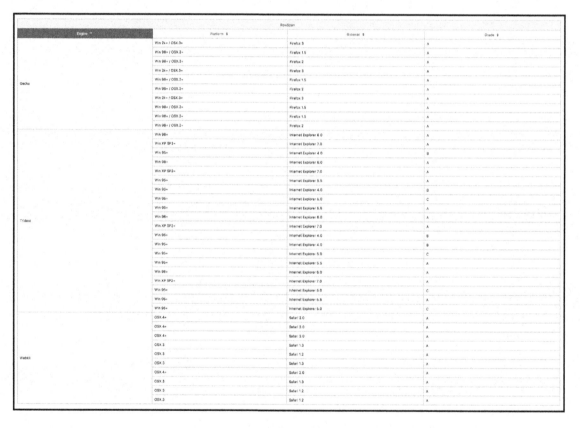

The row span grouping feature

In this version of row grouping, the browser's `engine` field is used for row grouping which spans across all of its related items.

Handling tons of data with lazy DataTable

Lazy loading is a very crucial feature to handle huge datasets. This feature provides the loading of data chunks through paging, sorting, and filtering operations instead of loading all the data at once. The lazy loading is enabled by setting the `lazy` mode (`lazy="true"`) and carrying user actions using `onLazyLoad` callback with the the event object as a parameter. The event object holds the pagination, sorting, and filter data.

It is also required to display a logical number of records to be displayed for pagination configuration using projection query. This is needed because we can retrieve only the current page data in the lazy loading. There is no information available related to the remaining records. Hence, it is required to show the paginator links based on actual records in the data source. This can be achieved through the `totalRecords` property on a Table component.

The component with lazy loading feature would be written as follows:

```
<p-dataTable [value]="browsers" [lazy]="true" [rows]="10"
  [paginator]="true" [totalRecords]="totalRecords"
  (onLazyLoad)="loadBrowsersLazy($event)">
<p-header>List of browsers</p-header>
<p-column field="engine" header="Engine" [sortable]="true"
[filter]="true">
</p-column>
<p-column field="browser" header="Browser" [sortable]="true"
[filter]="true">
</p-column>
<p-column field="platform" header="Platform" [sortable]="true"
[filter]="true">
</p-column>
<p-column field="grade" header="Grade" [sortable]="true"
[filter]="true">
</p-column>
</p-dataTable>
```

The component class defines lazy loading callback to retrieve data on demand as shown:

```
loadBrowsersLazy(event: LazyLoadEvent) {
  //event.first = First row offset
  //event.rows = Number of rows per page
  //event.sortField = Field name to sort with
  //event.sortOrder = Sort order as number, 1 for asc and -1 for dec
  //filters: FilterMetadata object having field as
  //key and filter value,
  //filter matchMode as value
```

```
this.browserService.getBrowsers().subscribe((browsers: any) =>
    this.browsers = browsers.slice(event.first,
    (event.first + event.rows)));
}
```

As a demonstration of lazy loading, we used a pagination operation for retrieving the data. We can also use sorting and filtering features. The following screenshot shows a snapshot result to illustrate as an example:

List of browsers			
Engine ⬍	Browser ⬍	Platform ⬍	Grade ⬍
Trident	Internet Explorer 4.0	Win 95+	B
Trident	Internet Explorer 5.0	Win 95+	C
Trident	Internet Explorer 5.5	Win 95+	A
Trident	Internet Explorer 6.0	Win 98+	A
Trident	Internet Explorer 7.0	Win XP SP2+	A
Gecko	Firefox 1.5	Win 98+ / OSX.2+	A
Gecko	Firefox 2	Win 98+ / OSX.2+	A
Gecko	Firefox 3	Win 2k+ / OSX.3+	A
Webkit	Safari 1.2	OSX.3	A
Webkit	Safari 1.3	OSX.3	A

|◀ ◀◀ 2 3 **4** 5 6 ▶▶ ▶|

In the preceding snapshot, we can clearly observe that the information on page 4 is retrieved dynamically from the remote data source. Refer to the events section for more details about the lazy loading event callback.

 Always prefer lazy loading for large datasets to improve the performance.

Row expansion by providing a row template

In many cases, it is not possible to accommodate all of the data in the table. The secondary or additional information of table data needs to be populated in a different representation. The row expansion features allows displaying detailed content for a particular row (that is, display data in a separate block which will appear on request). To use this feature, enable the `expandableRows` property and add an expander column using the `expander` property as a separate column along with regular columns in order to toggle the row. To declare the expanded content, provide a `pTemplate` directive with `rowexpansion` as the value. The local template reference variable from `ng-template` is used to access the table data.

The component with the row expansion feature to display full details of a browser would be written as follows:

```
<p-dataTable [value]="basicBrowsers" expandableRows="true"
  [expandedRows]="expandedRows">
<p-column expander="true" styleClass="col-icon" header="Toggle">
</p-column>
<p-column field="engine" header="Engine"></p-column>
<p-column field="browser" header="Browser"></p-column>
<p-column field="platform" header="Platform"></p-column>
<p-column field="grade" header="Grade"></p-column>
<ng-template let-browser pTemplate="rowexpansion">
  <div class="ui-grid ui-grid-responsive ui-fluid
    rowexpansion-layout">
  <div class="ui-grid-row">
    <div class="ui-grid-col-9">
      <div class="ui-grid ui-grid-responsive ui-grid-pad">
        <div class="ui-grid-row">
          <div class="ui-grid-col-2 label">Engine:</div>
          <div class="ui-grid-col-10">{{browser.engine}}</div>
        </div>
        <div class="ui-grid-row">
          <div class="ui-grid-col-2 label">Browser:</div>
          <div class="ui-grid-col-10">{{browser.browser}}</div>
        </div>
        <div class="ui-grid-row">
          <div class="ui-grid-col-2 label">Platform:</div>
          <div class="ui-grid-col-10">{{browser.platform}}</div>
        </div>
        <div class="ui-grid-row">
          <div class="ui-grid-col-2 label">Version:</div>
          <div class="ui-grid-col-10">{{browser.version}}</div>
        </div>
        <div class="ui-grid-row">
          <div class="ui-grid-col-2 label">Rating:</div>
```

```
            <div class="ui-grid-col-10">{{browser.rating}}</div>
          </div>
          <div class="ui-grid-row">
            <div class="ui-grid-col-2 label">Grade:</div>
            <div class="ui-grid-col-10">{{browser.grade}}</div>
          </div>
        </div>
      </div>
    </div>
  </div>
  </ng-template>
</p-dataTable>
```

If required, the expanded rows can be stored in an array variable inside the component class using the expandedRows property. The following screenshot shows a snapshot result of a component with the row expansion feature as an example:

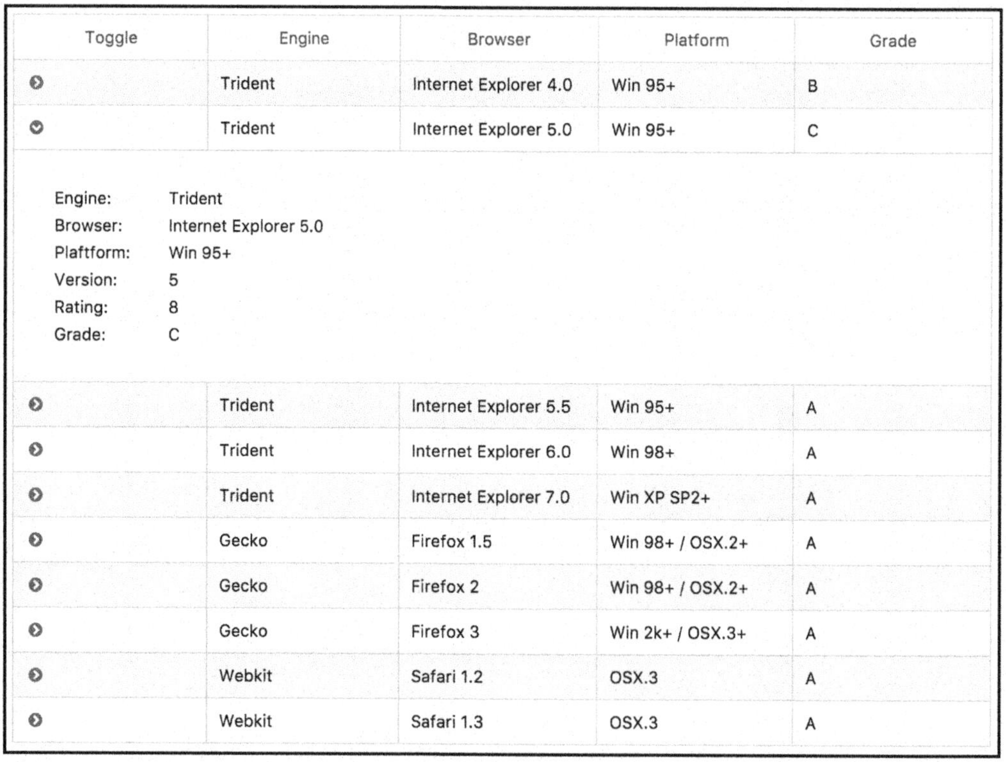

Toggle	Engine	Browser	Platform	Grade
⊙	Trident	Internet Explorer 4.0	Win 95+	B
⊙	Trident	Internet Explorer 5.0	Win 95+	C

Engine:	Trident
Browser:	Internet Explorer 5.0
Plaftform:	Win 95+
Version:	5
Rating:	8
Grade:	C

Toggle	Engine	Browser	Platform	Grade
⊙	Trident	Internet Explorer 5.5	Win 95+	A
⊙	Trident	Internet Explorer 6.0	Win 98+	A
⊙	Trident	Internet Explorer 7.0	Win XP SP2+	A
⊙	Gecko	Firefox 1.5	Win 98+ / OSX.2+	A
⊙	Gecko	Firefox 2	Win 98+ / OSX.2+	A
⊙	Gecko	Firefox 3	Win 2k+ / OSX.3+	A
⊙	Webkit	Safari 1.2	OSX.3	A
⊙	Webkit	Safari 1.3	OSX.3	A

By default, multiple rows can be expanded at once. We can make a strict single row expansion using the rowExpandMode property by setting it as single.

We can apply the row expansion behavior for grouped tables as well:

- The component provides an `expandableRowGroups` Boolean property which is used to create the icon to toggle the row groups.
- By default, all the rows will be expanded. The `expandedRowGroups` property is used to hold the row data instance to expand specific row groups by default.

 The method named `toggleRow` is provided in order to toggle table rows with the row data.

Exporting data in CSV format

The data can be viewed in table format in online mode at any time. But, there is a need of data in an offline mode. Also in many cases, we need to take huge data reports from the website. PrimeNG DataTable can be exported in CSV format using the `exportCSV()` API method. Button components placed inside or outside of the table can trigger this method for downloading the data in the CSV format. The component with export API method call would be written as follows:

```
<p-dataTable #dt [value]="basicBrowsers" exportFilename="browsers"
  csvSeparator=";">
  <p-header>
    <div class="ui-helper-clearfix">
    <button type="button" pButton icon="fa-file-o" iconPos="left"
      label="CSV" (click)="dt.exportCSV()" style="float:left"></button>
    </div>
  </p-header>
  <p-column field="engine" header="Engine"></p-column>
  <p-column field="browser" header="Browser"></p-column>
  <p-column field="platform" header="Platform"></p-column>
  <p-column field="grade" header="Grade"></p-column>
</p-dataTable>
```

By default, exported CSV uses a comma (,) operator as a separator. But, this behavior can be changed using the `csvSeparator` property on a DataTable component.

DataTable events and methods

The DataTable component provides many event callbacks and methods with respect to each feature. The following table lists out all the table event callbacks with name, parameter details, and description:

Name	Parameters	Description
onRowClick	• event.originalEvent: Browser event • event.data: Selected data	Callback to invoke when a row is clicked.
onRowSelect	• event.originalEvent: Browser event • event.data: Selected data • event.type: Type of selection, valid values are row, radiobutton, and checkbox	Callback to invoke when a row is selected.
onRowUnselect	• event.originalEvent: Browser event • event.data: Unselected data • event.type: Type of unselection, valid values are row and checkbox	Callback to invoke when a row is unselected with the Meta key.
onRowDblclick	• event.originalEvent: Browser event • event.data: Selected data	Callback to invoke when a row is selected with double-click.
onHeaderCheckboxToggle	• event.originalEvent: Browser event • event.checked: State of the header checkbox	Callback to invoke when state of header checkbox changes.
onContextMenuSelect	• event.originalEvent: Browser event • event.data: Selected data	Callback to invoke when a row is selected with right click.
onColResize	• event.element: Resized column header • event.delta: Change of width in number of pixels	Callback to invoke when a column is resized.

onColReorder	• event.dragIndex: Index of the dragged column • event.dropIndex: Index of the dropped column • event.columns: Columns array after reorder	Callback to invoke when a column is reordered.
onLazyLoad	• event.first: First row offset • event.rows: Number of rows per page • event.sortField: Field name to sort with • event.sortOrder: Sort order as number, 1 for asc and −1 for desc • filters: the FilterMetadata object having field as key and filter value, filter matchMode as value	Callback to invoke when paging, sorting, or filtering happens in lazy mode.
onEditInit	• event.column: Column object of the cell • event.data: Row data	Callback to invoke when a cell switches to the edit mode.
onEdit	• event.originalEvent: Browser event • event.column: Column object of the cell • event.data: Row data • event.index: Row index	Callback to invoke when cell data is being edited.
onEditComplete	• event.column: Column object of the cell • event.data: Row data • event.index: Row index	Callback to invoke when cell edit is completed (Supported for the *Enter* key only).
onEditCancel	• event.column: Column object of the cell • event.data: Row data • event.index: Row index	Callback to invoke when cell edit is cancelled with the *Esc* key.

onPage	• event.first: Index of first record in page • event.rows: Number of rows on the page	Callback to invoke when pagination occurs.
onSort	• event.field: Field name of the sorted column • event.order: Sort order as 1 or -1 • event.multisortmeta: Sort metadata in multi sort mode. See multiple sorting section for the structure of this object.	Callback to invoke when a column gets sorted.
onFilter	event.filters: Filters object having a field as the property key and an object with value, matchMode as the property value.	Callback to invoke when data is filtered.
onRowExpand	• event.originalEvent: Browser event • data: Row data to expand	Callback to invoke when a row is expanded.
onRowCollapse	• event.originalEvent: Browser event • data: Row data to collapse	Callback to invoke when a row is collapsed.
onRowGroupExpand	• event.originalEvent: Browser event • group: Value of the group	Callback to invoke when a row group is expanded.
onRowGroupCollapse	• event.originalEvent: Browser event • group: Value of the group	Callback to invoke when a row group is collapsed.

The following table lists out frequently used table methods with name, parameters, and description:

Name	Parameters	Description
reset	-	Resets sort, filter, and paginator state
exportCSV	-	Exports the data in CSV format
toggleRow	data	Toggles row expansion for a given row data

PrimeNG version 4.0.1 reintroduced back the `rowTrackBy` option for iteration components such as DataTable, DataGrid, and DataList to improve the DOM optimizations. That is, the DOM insertions and updates of each row are optimized by delegating the decision to the `ngForTrackBy` directive. In PrimeNG, this will be achieved through the `rowTrackBy` property. If the property is not defined, by default, the algorithm checks for an object identity. For example, the browser row is identified by ID property as

`trackById(index, browser) { return browser.id; }`.

The complete demo application with instructions is available on GitHub at `https://github.com/ova2/angular-development-with-primeng/tree /master/chapter5/datatable`.

Listing data with DataList

The DataList component is used to display the data in a list layout. It requires a collection of items as its value and `ng-template` to display content where each item can be accessed using a local template variable. This template also provides an index of each item using a variable represented by the `let-i` expression. A basic example of the DataList component with all browser details to display in a list format would be written as follows:

```
<p-dataList [value]="basicBrowsers">
  <ng-template let-browser pTemplate="item">
    <div class="ui-grid ui-grid-responsive ui-fluid"
      class="content-layout">
    <div class="ui-grid-row">
      <div class="ui-grid-col-3">
        <img src="/assets/data/images/{{browser.code}}.png"
          width="100" height="80"/>
      </div>
      <div class="ui-grid-col-9">
        <div class="ui-grid ui-grid-responsive ui-fluid">
          <div class="ui-grid-row">
            <div class="ui-grid-col-2">Engine: </div>
            <div class="ui-grid-col-10">{{browser.engine}}</div>
          </div>
          <div class="ui-grid-row">
            <div class="ui-grid-col-2">Browser: </div>
            <div class="ui-grid-col-10">{{browser.browser}}</div>
          </div>
          <div class="ui-grid-row">
            <div class="ui-grid-col-2">Platform: </div>
            <div class="ui-grid-col-10">{{browser.platform}}</div>
```

```
          </div>
          <div class="ui-grid-row">
            <div class="ui-grid-col-2">Version: </div>
            <div class="ui-grid-col-10">{{browser.version}}</div>
          </div>
          <div class="ui-grid-row">
            <div class="ui-grid-col-2">Grade: </div>
            <div class="ui-grid-col-10">{{browser.grade}}</div>
          </div>
        </div>
      </div>
     </div>
   </div>
  </ng-template>
</p-dataList>
```

The list of browser details needs to be retrieved from external services. In this case, the
BrowserService service will be injected into the component class to retrieve the browser
information. We used observables to get the data using the HTTP module. The list data will
be retrieved on page load as follows:

```
basicBrowsers: Browser[];

constructor(private browserService: BrowserService) { }

ngOnInit() {
  this.browserService.getBrowsers().subscribe(
    (browsers:any) => this.basicBrowsers = browsers.slice(0,4));
}
```

We limited the number of records to five for demonstration purposes. The following
screenshot shows a snapshot result of the DataList component in a list format as an
example:

	Engine: Browser: Platform: Version: Grade:	Trident Internet Explorer 4.0 Win 95+ 4 X
	Engine: Browser: Platform: Version: Grade:	Trident Internet Explorer 5.0 Win 95+ 5 C
	Engine: Browser: Platform: Version: Grade:	Trident Internet Explorer 5.5 Win 95+ 5.5 A
	Engine: Browser: Platform: Version: Grade:	Trident Internet Explorer 6.0 Win 98+ 6 A

The preceding snapshot just displays the data in a tabular format. In the next section, you can find many more features to make a data list a powerful component.

Facets and pagination

The DataList component supports facets such as header and footer for content using p-header and p-footer tags. In order to improve the user experience on large datasets, it supports the pagination feature. This feature is enabled by setting the paginator property as true and it sets a number of rows to be displayed using the rows property. Apart from these mandatory settings, there are some optional customized settings for pagination. Among all those optional properties, paginatorPosition is used to display the paginator either in top, bottom, or both positions; rowsPerPageOptions is used to display a drop-down with a possible number of rows to be displayed in a page, and emptyMessage is used to display a data list body when no records exist. Pagination also supports the onPage event callback, which will be invoked on page navigation. Refer to the events section for more details.

The DataList component with facets and pagination features to display browser information would be as follows:

```
<p-dataList [value]="advancedBrowsers" [paginator]="true" [rows]="5"
  (onPage)="onPagination($event)" [rowsPerPageOptions]="[5,10,15]"
  [paginatorPosition]="both" [emptyMessage]="'No records found'">
  <p-header>
    List of Browsers
  </p-header>
    .... // Content
  <p-footer>
    Note: Grades are 3 types.A,B and C.
  </p-footer>
</p-dataList>
```

The following screenshot shows a snapshot result with pagination as an example:

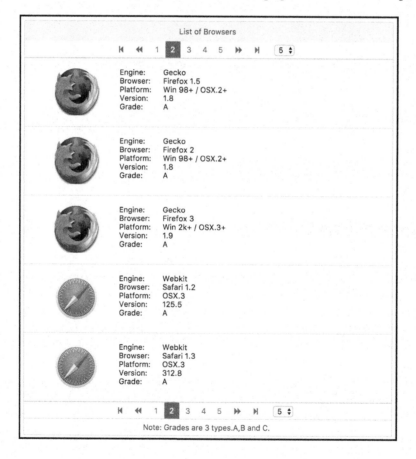

All the pagination controls are customizable with the options provided in the DataList component.

Lazy loading

Lazy loading is a very helpful feature to handle large datasets. It will not load all the data at once but as small chunks based on user demand. DataList supports lazy loading on pagination interaction. This feature is available by enabling the `lazy` attribute (that is, `lazy="true"`) and also by invoking the `onLazyLoad` callback to retrieve the data from the remote data sources. Refer to the events section for the signature and more details.

The lazy load event object provides the first record in the page and the number of rows in the current page to get the next set of data. Also you should provide the total records by projection query for pagination configuration. This is useful to display pagination links based on the total number of records available even though that many records are not available on page load (that is, only current page records exist in a lazy mode).

Let's take an example of the lazy loading feature for a DataList component with a basic prototype as shown here:

```
<p-dataList [value]="lazyloadingBrowsers" [paginator]="true" [rows]="5"
  [lazy]="true"
  (onLazyLoad)="loadData($event)" [totalRecords]="totalRecords">
  ... // Content
</p-dataList>
```

The component class has to define the lazy loading event callback to retrieve the records based on user request (in this case, it would be pagination) as shown here:

```
loadData(event:any) {
  let start = event.first;//event.first = First row offset
  let end = start + event.rows;//event.rows = Number of rows per page
  this.browserService.getBrowsers().subscribe((browsers: any) =>
    this.lazyloadingBrowsers = browsers.slice(start,end));
}
```

In the preceding code snippet, you can observe that both the `first` and `rows` properties of an event are helpful for retrieving the next bunch of records. Based on the `rows` attribute, it tries to fetch the next `rows` number of records on every instance.

Events

The component provides two event callbacks, one for pagination and the other one for lazy loading. Both events provide two arguments to get the first record and number of rows present on the page. The lazy loading event is invoked on pagination, filtering, and sorting functionalities by enabling a lazy mode.

Name	Parameters	Description
onLazyLoad	• event.first: First row offset • event.rows: Number of rows per page	Callback to invoke when paging, sorting, or filtering happens in a lazy mode.
onPage	• event.first: Index of the first record in page • event.rows: Number of rows on the page	Callback to invoke when pagination occurs.

It provides many other features such as facets for header and footer display (p-header and p-footer), pagination to navigate between multiple pages, and a lazy loading feature for retrieving the data on demand.

The complete demo application with instructions is available on GitHub at https://github.com/ova2/angular-development-with-primeng/tree/master/chapter5/datalist.

Listing data with PickList

The PickList component is used to move items between two different lists. You can also reorder the items within each list. This provides the overall status of selected items. The items can be moved/reordered using either default button controls or drag and drop behavior. PickList requires two arrays, one is used for the source list and other one is for the target list. The ng-template template tag is used to display the item's content where each item in the array can be accessed using a local ng-template variable.

A basic example of the PickList component with country information would be written as follows:

```
<p-pickList [source]="sourceCountries" [target]="targetCountries"
  [sourceStyle]="{'height':'350px'}" [targetStyle]="{'height':'350px'}">
  <ng-template let-country pTemplate="item">
    <div class="ui-helper-clearfix">
      <img src="/assets/data/images/country/
        {{country.code.toLowerCase()}}.png" />
      <span>{{country.flag}} - {{country.name}}({{country.dial_code}})
      </span>
    </div>
  </ng-template>
</p-pickList>
```

In the component class, let's define a source list for available data and the target as an empty list to indicate that there is no selection yet. The country service needs to be injected to access the country information from external resources:

```
sourceCountries: Country[];
targetCountries: Country[];

constructor(private countryService: CountryService) { }

ngOnInit() {
  this.countryService.getCountries().subscribe(
    (countries: Country[]) =>
  {
    this.sourceCountries = countries;
  });
  this.targetCountries = [];
}
```

By default, both source and target panels are available with default `width` and `height` properties. But this default behavior can be customized using `sourceStyle` and `targetStyle` properties. The following screenshot shows a snapshot result of an initial PickList as an example:

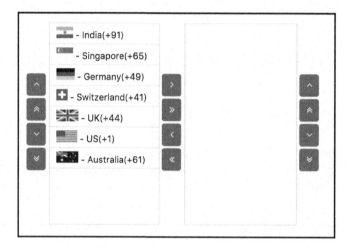

The PickList component provides six event callbacks which are used for moving items between two lists and ordering the items in both source and target areas. Among these six callbacks, four of them are used for moving items, `onMoveToTarget`, `onMoveToSource`, `onMoveAllToSource`, and `onMoveAllToSource` whereas ordering items is performed by `onSourceReorder` and `onTargetReorder`.

The component can be customized from its default behavior in different ways as mentioned here:

- Headers can be customized using headers `sourceHeader` and `targetHeader` as properties.
- The web page will become responsive using the `responsive` property (`responsive="true"`), which adjusts the button controls based on screen size.
- The default multiple selection is prevented (with the help of the Meta key) by disabling the `metaKeySelection` attribute (`metaKeySelection="false"`).
- The visibility of button controls is controlled through `showSourceControls` and `showTargetControls` properties. For example, `showSourceControls="false"` and `showTargetControls="false"`.

PrimeNG 4.1 supports the filtering feature on item fields as a new addition using the
`filterBy` property. Multiple fields can be filtered by placing the comma separated fields in
the `filterBy` property:

```
<p-pickList [source]="sourceCountries" [target]="targetCountries"
  filterBy="name, code">
  ...
</p-pickList>
```

The newer 4.1 version also supports the drag-and-drop feature (within the same list or
across lists) by enabling the `dragdrop` property. It also provides the `dragdropScope`
property, which holds the unique key to avoid conflicts with other drag-and-drop events.
The drag-and-drop feature example would be as follows:

```
<p-pickList [source]="sourceCountries" [target]="targetCountries"
  sourceHeader="Available" targetHeader="Selected" [dragdrop]="true"
  dragdropScope="name">
  ...
</p-pickList>
```

The complete demo application with instructions is available on GitHub at
`https://github.com/ova2/angular-development-with-primeng/tree`
`/master/chapter5/picklist`.

Listing data with OrderList

The OrderList component is used to sort a collection of items in different directions (up and
down). The component requires an array type variable to store its value and `ng-template`
to display content of an array of items. Each item will be accessed inside the `ng-template`
template using a local `ng-template` variable. When the position of an item changes, the
backend array is also updated to store the latest item order.

A basic example of the OrderList component with country information would be written as
follows:

```
<p-orderList [value]="countries"  header="Favourite countries" >
  <ng-template let-country pTemplate="item">
    <div class="ui-helper-clearfix">
      <img src="/assets/data/images/country/
        {{country.code.toLowerCase()}}.png" />
      <span class="content-format">
        {{country.flag}} {{country.name}}({{country.dial_code}})
      </span>
```

```
      </div>
    </ng-template>
  </p-orderList>
```

In the component class, let's define a countries list to display the collection of items. The country service needs to be injected to access the country information from the external resources or datasources as shown here:

```
countries: Country[];

constructor(private countryService: CountryService) { }

ngOnInit() {
  this.countryService.getCountries().subscribe((countries: Country[]) =>
  {
    this.countries = countries;
  });
}
```

By default, the list panel is available with default `width` and `height` properties. But this can be customized using the `listStyle` property. The following screenshot shows a snapshot result of the initial order list as an example:

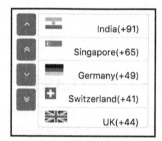

The OrderList component provides three different event callbacks as mentioned here:

Name	Parameters	Description
onReorder	event: browser event	Callback to invoke when list is reordered.
onSelectionChange	• originalEvent: browser event • value: Current selection	Callback to invoke when selection changes.
onFilterEvent	• originalEvent: browser event • value: Current filter values	Callback to invoke when filtering occurs.

The component can be customized from it's default behavior in different ways as mentioned here:

- The header can be customized using the `header` property
- The `responsive` property (`responsive="true"`) is used to apply responsive behavior, which adjusts the button controls based on the screen size
- The default multiple selection is prevented (with the help of the Meta key) by disabling the `metaKeySelection` attribute (`metaKeySelection="false"`)

The following screenshot shows a snapshot result of a countries list with the earlier mentioned customization as an example:

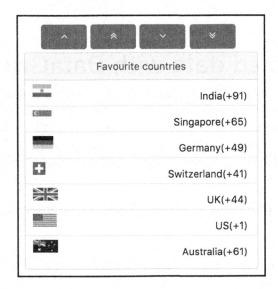

In the preceding snapshot, you can observe that controls appears at the top due to its `responsive` feature (`responsive="true"`). We can also observe that the panel width has been adjusted based on viewport size (using the `listStyle` property).

PrimeNG 4.1 version supports filtering and drag and drop features as new additions. The filter feature can be applied for single field and multiple fields using the `filterBy` property similar to the DataTable component. For example, the multi filtering feature on countries data would be as follows:

```
<p-orderList [value]="countries" filterBy="name, code">
 ...
</p-orderList>
```

The newer 4.1 version also supports a drag-and-drop feature to reorder items by enabling the `dragdrop` property. It also provides the `dragdropScope` property, which holds the unique key to avoid conflicts with other drag-and-drop events. The drag-and-drop feature example would be as follows:

```
<p-orderList [value]="countries" [dragdrop]="true" dragdropScope="name">
   ...
</p-orderList>
```

> The complete demo application with instructions is available on GitHub at https://github.com/ova2/angular-development-with-primeng/tree /master/chapter5/orderlist.

Grid-organized data with DataGrid

DataGrid displays the data in a grid-oriented layout. The data is represented in the form of a layout with multiple cells aligned in a regular pattern. It requires a collection of items as an array for the `value` attribute and the `ng-template` template tag to display its content where each item can be accessed using a local template variable. The template content needs to be wrapped within a `div` element such that the data is formatted in a grid layout using any grid CSS styles.

A basic example of a DataGrid component with browser information would be written as follows:

```
<p-dataGrid [value]="basicBrowsers">
  <ng-template let-browser pTemplate="item">
    <div style="padding:3px" class="ui-g-12 ui-md-3">
      <p-panel [header]="browser.browser" [style]="{'text-
        align':'center'}">
        <img src="/assets/data/images/{{browser.code}}.png"
          width="50"height="50">
        <div class="car-detail">{{browser.engine}} -
          {{browser.version}}
        </div>
        <hr class="ui-widget-content" style="border-top:0">
        <i class="fa fa-search" (click)="selectBrowser(browser)"
          style="cursor:pointer"></i>
      </p-panel>
    </div>
  </ng-template>
</p-dataGrid>
```

The component class has to define an array of browser objects, which are retrieved from a remote data source using the services. The service accessed on a page load would be written as follows:

```
basicBrowsers: Browser[];

constructor(private browserService: BrowserService) { }

ngOnInit() {
  this.browserService.getBrowsers().subscribe((browsers: any) =>
    this.basicBrowsers = browsers.slice(0, 12));
}
```

The following screenshot shows a snapshot result of the DataGrid component in a grid layout as an example:

In the preceding snapshot, between any one of two cells the padding will be consistent. This can be customized through skinning classes of this component.

Beyond basic usage - advanced features

In the preceding snapshot, the browser data is displayed in the grid layout. But, you can observe that there is no header or footer to summarize the context. The header and footer facets are available using `p-header` and `p-footer` tags.

To improve the usability on large sets, DataGrid provides a pagination feature to display the next chunk of data through page navigation. This feature is provided by enabling the `paginator` property and by setting the `rows` attribute. Just like any other data components, the pagination features such as `pageLinks`, `rowsPerPageOptions`, `paginatorPosition`, and `totalRecords` are available for this customization.

To handle huge amounts of data, DataGrid supports a lazy loading feature to access this huge amount of data in chunks. This feature is provided by enabling the `lazy` attribute. Also the lazy loading method should be called on the pagination operation using the `onLazyLoad` event.

The component class which defines the lazy load event callback with an `event` object as a parameter is shown here:

```
loadData(event: any) {
    let start = event.first; //event.first = First row offset
    let end = start + event.rows; //event.rows = Number of rows per page
    this.browserService.getBrowsers().subscribe((browsers: any) =>
        this.lazyloadingBrowsers = browsers.slice(start,end));
}
```

The following screenshot shows a snapshot result of the lazy loading feature as an example:

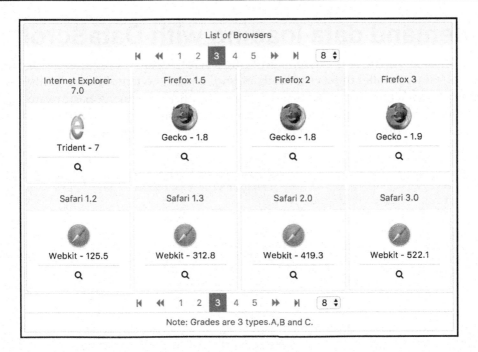

In the preceding snapshot, it displays the facets (header and footer), customized pagination options, and loading data lazily on user demand. The additional information about browsers will be displayed in a dialog popup just by clicking the search icon available in each cell. By default, the DataGrid component is responsive as a layout display across various screen sizes or devices.

The complete demo application with instructions is available on GitHub at `https://github.com/ova2/angular-development-with-primeng/tree /master/chapter5/datagrid`.

On-demand data loading with DataScroller

DataScroller displays the data on-demand using a scroll feature. It requires a collection of items as its value, number of rows to load, and `ng-template` template tag to display the content where each item can be accessed using an implicit variable. A basic example of the DataScroller component with various browser information would be written as follows (remember, here a fluid grid is used to format the content of browser records):

```
<p-dataScroller [value]="basicBrowsers" [rows]="5">
  <ng-template let-browser pTemplate="item">
    <div class="ui-grid ui-grid-responsive ui-fluid"
      class="content-layout">
    <div class="ui-grid-row">
      <div class="ui-grid-col-3">
        <img src="/assets/data/images/{{browser.code}}.png"
          width="100" height="80"/>
      </div>
      <div class="ui-grid-col-9">
        <div class="ui-grid ui-grid-responsive ui-fluid">
        <div class="ui-grid-row">
          <div class="ui-grid-col-2">Engine: </div>
          <div class="ui-grid-col-10">{{browser.engine}}</div>
        </div>
        // Other content goes here
        </div>
      </div>
    </div>
    </div>
  </ng-template>
</p-dataScroller>
```

Like any other data components, the component class of the data list should define an array of browser objects. The data is populated by making a remote call to the data source. The following screenshot shows a snapshot result as an example:

	Engine:	Trident
	Browser:	Internet Explorer 4.0
	Platform:	Win 95+
	Version:	4
	Grade:	X
	Engine:	Trident
	Browser:	Internet Explorer 5.0
	Platform:	Win 95+
	Version:	5
	Grade:	C
	Engine:	Trident
	Browser:	Internet Explorer 5.5
	Platform:	Win 95+
	Version:	5.5
	Grade:	A
	Engine:	Trident
	Browser:	Internet Explorer 6.0
	Platform:	Win 98+
	Version:	6
	Grade:	A

As shown in the preceding snapshot, the data is displayed on-demand based on a window scroll as target. To make this DataScroller element more readable, it supports facets such as header and footer using `p-header` and `p-footer` tags. By default, the DataScroller component listens to the scroll event of the window. There is also one more option to define a container of a component as an event target with the help of the inline mode. For this, we should enable the `inline` attribute as `true` (that is, `inline="true"`).

Apart from the scroll-based data loading, further data can be loaded using an explicit button action. The component should define a `loader` property which refers to the Button component. The DataScroller component with loader button would be written as follows:

```
<p-dataScroller [value]="advancedBrowsers" [rows]="5"
[loader]="loadButton">
  // Content goes here
</p-dataScroller>
<p-dataScroller [value]="advancedBrowsers" [rows]="5"
[loader]="loadButton">
```

The following screenshot shows a snapshot result with loader display as an example:

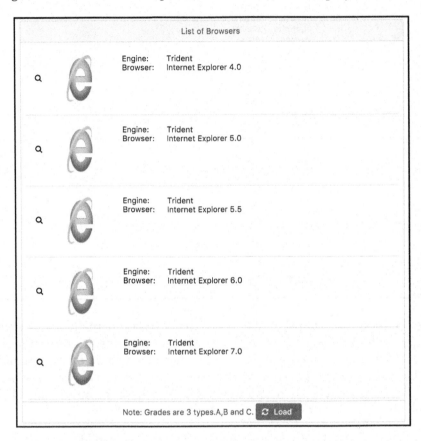

In the preceding snapshot, additional browser information is displayed in a dialog format once the user clicks the search button on the left-hand side. This gives the ability to show how to select a particular record in a DataScroller component.

Lazy loading

To deal with huge datasets, this component supports the lazy loading feature as well. Instead of loading whole data, it loads chunks of data on each scroll action. It requires both `lazy` and `onLazyLoad` properties to enable this behavior. The lazy loading example of DataScroller would be written as follows:

```
<p-dataScroller [value]="lazyloadingBrowsers" [rows]="5"
                [lazy]="true" (onLazyLoad)="loadData($event)">
```

```
    //Content goes here
</p-dataScroller>
```

The component class defines the lazy loading event callback to retrieve the data in chunks as shown here:

```
loadData(event: any) {
    let start = event.first; //event.first = First row offset
    let end = start + event.rows; //event.rows = Number of rows per page
    this.browserService.getBrowsers().subscribe((browsers: any) =>
       this.lazyloadingBrowsers = browsers.slice(start, end));
}
```

In the preceding code snippet, you can observe that the `first` and `rows` properties of an `event` object are helpful for retrieving the next bunch of records. Based on the `rows` attribute, it tries to fetch the next `rows` number of records on every fetch.

The API method `reset` is used to reset the content or data of a DataScroller component. That is, the component will reset to its default state.

The complete demo application with instructions is available on GitHub at `https://github.com/ova2/angular-development-with-primeng/tree/master/chapter5/datascroller`.

Visualizing data with Tree

The Tree component is used to display a hierarchical representation of data in a graphical format. It provides an array of the `TreeNode` objects as its value. The `TreeNode` API provides many properties to create tree node objects. The tree structure has basically three major components as listed here:

- The tree elements are called **nodes**
- The lines connecting elements are called branches
- The nodes without children are called leaf nodes or leaves

A basic example of a Tree component with nodes would be written as follows (the node will represent tourist places):

```
<p-tree [value]="basicTree"></p-tree>
```

The data for the Tree component should be provided in a nested parent-child hierarchy. Each tree node is created with a set of properties such as `label`, `data`, `expandIcon`, `collapsedIcon`, `children`, and so on. The complete list of the `TreeNode` properties is shown here:

Name	Type	Default	Description
label	string	null	Label of the node.
data	any	null	Data represented by the node.
icon	string	null	Icon of the node to display next to content.
expandedIcon	string	null	Icon to use in expanded state.
collapsedIcon	string	null	Icon to use in collapsed state.
children	TreeNode[]	null	An array of tree nodes as children.
leaf	boolean	null	Specifies if the node has children. Used in lazy loading.
style	string	null	Inline style of the node.
styleClass	string	null	Style class of the node.
expanded	boolean	null	Whether the node is in an expanded or collapsed state.
type	string	null	Type of the node to match the `ng-template` type.
parent	TreeNode	null	Parent of the node.
styleClass	string	null	Name of the style class for the node element.
draggable	boolean	null	Whether to disable dragging for a particular node even if `draggableNodes` is enabled.
droppable	boolean	null	Whether to disable dropping for a particular node even if `droppableNodes` is enabled.
selectable	boolean	null	Used to disable selection of a particular node.

 All properties of `TreeNode` are optional.

The tree node structure for the tourist places example would be as follows:

```
"data":
[
  {
    "label": "Asia",
    "data": "Documents Folder",
    "expandedIcon": "fa-folder-open",
    "collapsedIcon": "fa-folder",
    "children": [{
      "label": "India",
      "data": "Work Folder",
      "expandedIcon": "fa-folder-open",
      "collapsedIcon": "fa-folder",
      "children": [{
        "label": "Goa", "icon": "fa-file-word-o",
        "data": "Beaches& Old Goa colonial architecture"},
          {"label": "Mumbai", "icon": "fa-file-word-o", "data":
            "Shopping,Bollywood"},
          {"label": "Hyderabad", "icon": "fa-file-word-o",
            "data": "Golconda Fort"}
      ]
    },
      {
        "label": "Singapore",
        "data": "Home Folder",
        "expandedIcon": "fa-folder-open",
        "collapsedIcon": "fa-folder",
        "children": [{
          "label": "Woodlands", "icon": "fa-file-word-o",
          "data": "Parks,Sea food"}]
      },
    ]
  }
  ...
]
```

In real-time applications, the data located in a remote data source is retrieved through services. The following service is going to be injected in the component class:

```
@Injectable()
export class TreeNodeService {

  constructor(private http: Http) { }

  getTouristPlaces(): Observable<any[]> {
    return this.http.get('/assets/data/cities.json')
      .map(response => response.json().data);
```

```
    }
  }
```

The component class loads the data on page load using the service call as shown here:

```
basicTree: TreeNode[];

constructor(private nodeService: TreeNodeService) { }

ngOnInit() {
  this.nodeService.getTouristPlaces().subscribe(
    (places: any) => this.basicTree = places);
}
```

The following screenshot shows a snapshot result of the hierarchical Tree component representation as an example:

In the preceding use case, we expanded **India** and **Germany** country tree nodes to see their child nodes represented as tourist places.

Selection features - single, multiple, and checkbox

The Tree component supports three kinds of selections such as single, multiple, and checkbox. The single selection is provided by enabling both the `selectionMode` property and the `selection` attribute, which holds a selected tree node.

The Tree component with a single selection feature to select a favorite tourist place would be written as follows:

```
<p-tree [value]="singleSelectionTree" selectionMode="single"
[(selection)]="selectedPlace" (onNodeSelect)="nodeSelect($event)"
(onNodeUnselect)="nodeUnselect($event)"></p-tree>
<div>Selected Node: {{selectedPlace ? selectedPlace.label : 'none'}}</div>
```

The following screenshot shows a snapshot result of the Tree component with a single selection as an example:

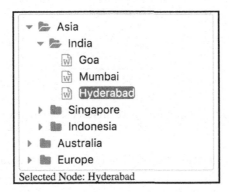

Here, multiple selection is enabled by setting `selectionMode` as `multiple` (`selectionMode="multiple"`). In this case, the `selection` property holds an array of objects as selected nodes. The multiple selection is also provided through the checkbox selection. This can be achieved just by setting `selectionMode="checkbox"`.

The Tree component with a multi checkbox selection feature to select multiple tourist places would be written as follows:

```
<p-tree [value]="checkboxSelectionTree" selectionMode="checkbox"
  [(selection)]="selectMultiplePlaces"></p-tree>
<div>Selected Nodes: <span *ngFor="let place of
selectMultiplePlaces">{{place.label}} </span></div>
```

The following screenshot shows a snapshot result of the Tree component with checkbox selection as an example:

The selection feature supports two event callbacks such as `onRowSelect` and `onRowUnselect`, which provide selected and unselected tree nodes. Refer to the events section for more details.

The propagation (upward and downward directions) of selection nodes is controlled through `propagateSelectionUp` and `propagateSelectionDown` properties, which are enabled by default.

Beyond basic usage - advanced features

The Tree component also supports many advanced features:

- The customized content can be displayed using the template tag `ng-template`.
- The lazy loading feature is available using the `onNodeExpand` event callback.
- ContextMenu for each tree node is applied using a local template reference variable.
- The horizontal layout of the Tree component is displayed using `layout="horizontal"` expression.
- The drag-and-drop feature between source and target Tree components is achieved by enabling `draggableNodes` and `droppableNodes` properties. The `dragdropScope` attribute is used to restrict drag-and-drop support to a specific area.

The row expansion or collapse behavior can be achieved in a programmatic way by externalizing the API methods. For example, a tree with external buttons, which are used to expand or collapse tree nodes in a programmatic way using event callbacks is shown here:

```
<p-tree #expandingTree [value]="programmaticTree"></p-tree>
<div>
  <button pButton type="text" label="Expand all" (click)="expandAll()">
  </button>
  <button pButton type="text" label="Collapse all"
(click)="collapseAll()"></button>
</div>
```

The component class defined with event callbacks to toggle the tree nodes in a recursive nature is shown here:

```
expandAll() {
  this.programmaticTree.forEach( (node: any) => {
    this.expandRecursive(node, true);
  } );
}

collapseAll() {
  this.programmaticTree.forEach((node: any) => {
    this.expandRecursive(node, false);
  } );
}

expandRecursive(node: TreeNode, isExpand: boolean) {
  node.expanded = isExpand;
  if (node.children) {
    node.children.forEach( childNode => {
      this.expandRecursive(childNode, isExpand);
    } );
  }
}
```

The component also supports four event callbacks such as `onNodeExpand`, `onNodeCollapse`, `onNodeDrop`, and `onNodeContextMenuSelect`. The following events table provides complete details of events, parameters, and their description:

Name	Parameters	Description
onNodeSelect	• `event.originalEvent`: Browser event • `event.node`: Selected node instance	Callback to invoke when a node is selected.
onNodeUnselect	• `event.originalEvent`: Browser event • `event.node`: Unselected node instance	Callback to invoke when a node is unselected.
onNodeExpand	• `event.originalEvent`: Browser event • `event.node`: Expanded node instance	Callback to invoke when a node is expanded.
onNodeCollapse	• `event.originalEvent`: Browser event • `event.node`: Collapsed node instance	Callback to invoke when a node is collapsed.
onNodeContextMenuSelect	• `event.originalEvent`: Browser event • `event.node`: Selected node instance	Callback to invoke when a node is selected with right-click.
onNodeDrop	• `event.originalEvent`: Browser event • `event.dragNode`: Dragged node instance • `event.dropNode`: Dropped node instance	Callback to invoke when a node is selected with right-click.

The complete demo application with instructions is available on GitHub at `https://github.com/ova2/angular-development-with-primeng/tree/master/chapter5/tree`.

Visualizing data with TreeTable

TreeTable is used to display hierarchical data in a tabular format. It requires an array of TreeNode objects as its value and provides a TreeNode API with many optional properties. TreeTable defines column components as child elements with header, footer, field, and style attributes similar to DataTable component.

A basic example of a TreeTable component with tourist place tree nodes as information would be written as follows:

```
<p-treeTable [value]="basicTreeTable">
  <p-header>Basic</p-header>
  <p-column field="name" header="Name"></p-column>
  <p-column field="days" header="Days"></p-column>
  <p-column field="type" header="Type"></p-column>
</p-treeTable>
```

The component is created by arranging TreeNode objects in a hierarchical manner. The TreeNode object consists of many properties as listed here:

Name	Type	Default	Description
label	string	null	Label of the node.
data	any	null	Data represented by the node.
icon	string	null	Icon of the node to display next to content. Not used by TreeTable.
expandedIcon	string	null	Icon to use in expanded state. Not used by TreeTable.
collapsedIcon	string	null	Icon to use in collapsed state. Not used by TreeTable.
children	TreeNode[]	null	An array of tree nodes as children.
leaf	boolean	null	Specifies if the node has children. Used in lazy loading.
style	string	null	Inline style of the node.
styleClass	string	null	Style class of the node.

The `TreeNode` structure for the tourist places example would be as follows:

```
{
  "data": [
    {
      "data": {
        "name": "Asia",
        "days": "15",
        "type": "Continent"
      },
      "children": [
        {
          "data": {
            "name": "India",
            "days": "6",
            "type": "Country"
          },
          "children": [
            {
              "data": {
                "name": "Goa",
                "days": "2",
                "type": "City"
              }...
            }]
        }]
    } }
    ...
}
```

The injected service and the same service call representation in component class is almost similar to the Tree component explained in the previous section. The following screenshot shows a snapshot result with hierarchical tourist information as an example:

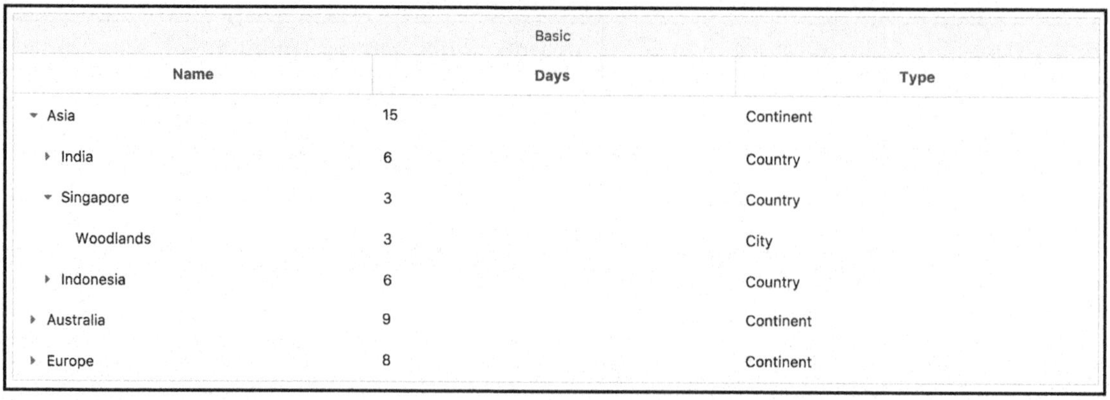

Basic		
Name	Days	Type
▾ Asia	15	Continent
▸ India	6	Country
▾ Singapore	3	Country
Woodlands	3	City
▸ Indonesia	6	Country
▸ Australia	9	Continent
▸ Europe	8	Continent

The component also supports dynamic columns where each column is created by looping through the ngFor directive.

Selection features - single, multiple, and checkbox

The TreeTable component supports three kinds of selections such as single, multiple, and checkbox. The single selection is provided by enabling the selectionMode property on tree table and the selection attribute, which holds the selected tree table node.

The TreeTable component with a single selection feature to select a favorite tourist place would be written as follows:

```
<p-treeTable [value]="singleSelectionTreeTable" selectionMode="single"
  [(selection)]="selectedTouristPlace
  (onNodeSelect)="nodeSelect($event)"
  (onNodeUnselect)="nodeUnselect($event)"
  (onRowDblclick)="onRowDblclick($event)" >
    <p-header>Singe Selection</p-header>
    <p-column field="name" header="Name"></p-column>
    <p-column field="days" header="Days"></p-column>
    <p-column field="type" header="Type"></p-column>
</p-treeTable>
```

The following screenshot shows a snapshot result with a single selection as an example:

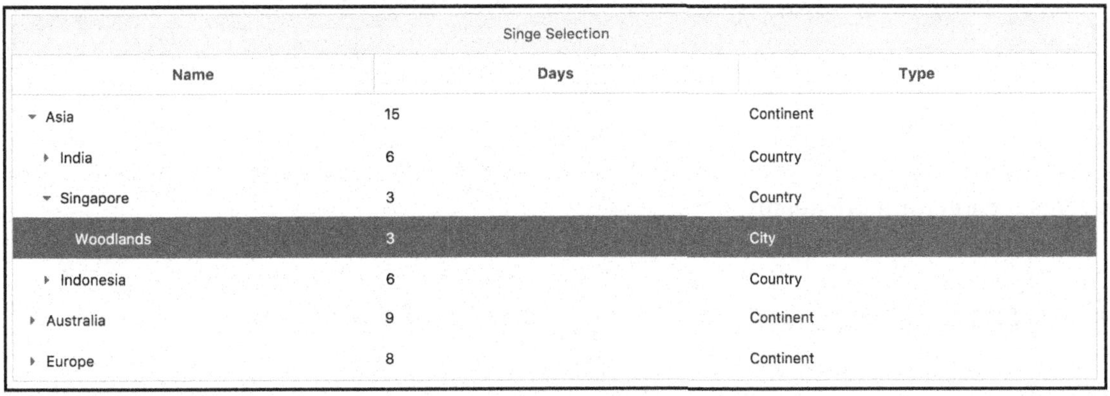

Singe Selection		
Name	**Days**	**Type**
▾ Asia	15	Continent
▸ India	6	Country
▾ Singapore	3	Country
Woodlands	3	City
▸ Indonesia	6	Country
▸ Australia	9	Continent
▸ Europe	8	Continent

Whereas, multiple selection is enabled by setting `selectionMode` as multiple (`selectionMode="multiple"`). In this case, the `selection` property holds an array of objects as selected nodes. The multiple selection is also provided through the checkbox selection. This can be achieved by setting `selectionMode="checkbox"`.

The TreeTable component with a multi checkbox selection feature to select multiple tourist places would be written as follows:

```
<p-treeTable [value]="checkboxSelectionTreeTable" selectionMode="checkbox"
    [(selection)]="selectedMultiTouristPlaces">
  <p-header>Checkbox Selection</p-header>
  <p-column field="name" header="Name"></p-column>
  <p-column field="days" header="Days"></p-column>
  <p-column field="type" header="Type"></p-column>
</p-treeTable>
```

The following screenshot shows a snapshot result with checkbox selection as an example:

Checkbox Selection		
Name	Days	Type
▶ ☐ Asia	15	Continent
▼ ▬ Australia	9	Continent
✔ Perth	3	City
☐ Brisbane	3	City
✔ Sydney	3	City
▶ ☐ Europe	8	Continent

The selection feature supports two event callbacks, such as `onNodeSelect` and `onNodeUnselect`, which provides the selected and unselected tree nodes. Refer to the events section for more details.

Beyond basic usage - advanced features

The TreeTable component also supports various advanced features such as lazy loading using the `onNodeExpand` callback, customized editable content using the `ng-template` template tag, and also context menu implementation, which is similar to the DataTable component. It also supports facets for header and footer using `p-header` and `p-footer` tags.

The content display of TreeTable is customized using `ng-template`. By default, the label of a tree node is displayed inside a tree node. To customize the content, define `ng-template` inside the column that gets the column as implicit variable (`let-col`) and `rowData` as the node instance (`let-node="rowData"`). In the same way, we can customize header and footer of this component.

Let's take an example of editable tree nodes by placing an input inside each template as shown here:

```
<p-treeTable [value]="templateTreeTable">
  <p-header>Editable Cells with Templating</p-header>
  <p-column field="name" header="Name">
    <ng-template let-node="rowData" pTemplate="body">
      <input type="text" [(ngModel)]="node.data.name"
        class="edit-input">
    </ng-template>
  </p-column>
  <p-column field="days" header="Days">
    <ng-template let-node="rowData" pTemplate="body">
      <input type="text" [(ngModel)]="node.data.days"
        class="edit-input">
    </ng-template>
  </p-column>
  <p-column field="type" header="Type">
    <ng-template let-node="rowData" pTemplate="body">
      <input type="text" [(ngModel)]="node.data.type"
        class="edit-input">
    </ng-template>
  </p-column>
</p-treeTable>
```

The following screenshot shows a snapshot result with an editable template as an example:

Editable Cells with Templating		
Name	**Days**	**Type**
▸ Asia	15	Continent
▸ Australia	20|	Continent
▸ Europe	8	Continent

In the preceding snapshot, we can edit all the tree node fields. For example, we updated tour package days from 9 to 20. TreeTable also supports event callbacks for expansion/collapsing nodes such as onNodeExpand, onNodeCollapse, and onContextmenuSelect event for context menu. Refer to the events section for more details.

 PrimeNG 4.1 introduced the toggleColumnIndex property, which is used to define the index of the column that contains the the toggler element. By default, the toggleColumnIndex value is 0 (TreeTable always shows toggler on first column if togglerColumnIndex is not defined).

The following events table provides the complete details of events, parameters, and their description:

Name	Parameters	Description
onNodeSelect	• event.originalEvent: Browser event • event.node: Selected node instance	Callback to invoke when a node is selected.
onNodeUnselect	• event.originalEvent: Browser event • event.node: Unselected node instance	Callback to invoke when a node is unselected.
onNodeExpand	• event.originalEvent: Browser event • event.node: Expanded node instance	Callback to invoke when a node is expanded.
onNodeCollapse	• event.originalEvent: Browser event • event.node: Collapsed node instance	Callback to invoke when a node is collapsed.
onContextMenuSelect	• event.originalEvent: Browser event • event.node: Selected node instance	Callback to invoke when a node is selected with right-click.
onRowDblclick	• event.originalEvent: Browser event • event.node: Selected node instance	Callback to invoke when a row is double clicked.

The complete demo application with instructions is available on GitHub at `https://github.com/ova2/angular-development-with-primeng/tree/master/chapter5/treetable`.

Managing events with Schedule

Schedule is a full-sized drag-and-drop event calendar based on a `FullCalendar` jQuery plugin. The events of Schedule should be formed as an array and defined using the `events` property. The Schedule component depends on the `FullCalendar` library, so it requires the following resources in your page as listed:

- The Schedule component is embedded in a web page using a style sheet and JavaScript files. So, we need to include the `FullCalendar` library's style sheet (`.css`) and JavaScript (`.js`) files in the HTML page's `head` section.
- Add `jQuery` and `Moment.js` libraries as mandatory libraries for a full calendar. These two libraries must be loaded before loading the `FullCalendar` library's JavaScript file.

Hence, we included `FullCalendar` and other dependent resources in a root `index.html` file as follows:

```
<!-- Schedule CSS resources-->
<link rel="stylesheet" type="text/css"
href="https://cdnjs.cloudflare.com/ajax/libs/fullcalendar/3.1.0/
fullcalendar.min.css">
<!-- Schedule Javascript resources-->
<script src="https://code.jquery.com/jquery-2.2.4.min.js"></script>
<script
src="https://cdnjs.cloudflare.com/ajax/libs/moment.js/2.13.0/moment.min.js"
></script>
<script src="https://cdnjs.cloudflare.com/ajax/libs/fullcalendar/3.1.0/
fullcalendar.min.js"></script>
```

A basic example of the Schedule component defined for the entire month would be written as follows:

```
<p-schedule [events]="events" [height]="700"
  [styleClass]="'schedule-width'">
</p-schedule>
```

Basically, all kinds of events have properties such as title, duration (start and end date), type of day (full/partial day), and so on. So, the event class would be defined as follows:

```
export class MyEvent {
  id: number;
  title: string;
  start: string;
  end: string;
  allDay: boolean = true;
}
```

The data for Schedule events should be defined exactly in the preceding format as a prototype. But in real time, data is fetched using a remote service call and updated in the Schedule UI immediately whenever there are any changes in the events. The event service, which is used to retrieve data from a data source (in this case, it retrieves data from a JSON events file) using HTTP module and observables, is defined as follows:

```
@Injectable()
export class EventService {

  constructor(private http: Http) { }

  getEvents(): Observable<any> {
    return this.http.get('/assets/data/scheduleevents.json')
      .map(response => response.json().data);
  }
}
```

The injected service gets the data during the initial load of a web page. The component class has to define the subscription for observable as shown here:

```
events: any[];

constructor(private eventService: EventService) { }

ngOnInit() {
  this.eventService.getEvents().subscribe((events: any) =>
  {this.events = events;});
}
```

The following screenshot shows a snapshot result of the embedded Schedule component display as an example:

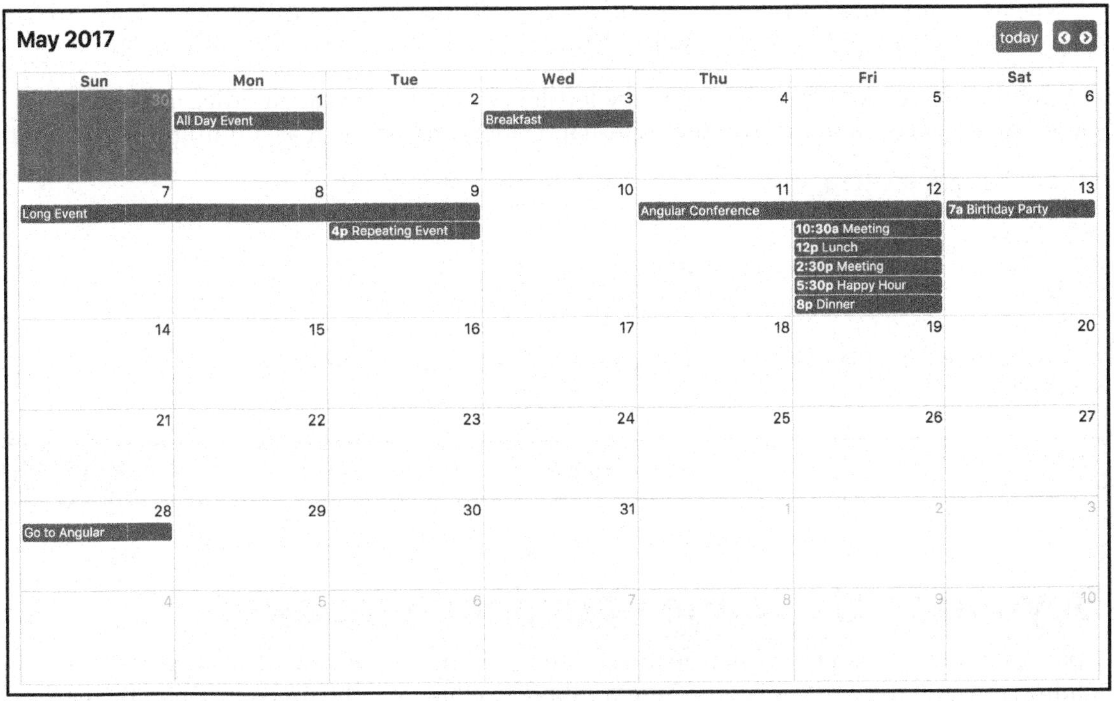

As per the preceding snapshot, the header is displayed with date (month and year), the **today** label, and month navigation controls. The main body or content area contains each day in the month and events on the specific days with a blue covered area.

Header customization

In the previous snapshot, we observed the Schedule content area along with default header text and controls. The default header configuration object for the Schedule element would be written as follows:

```
{
  left: 'title',
  center: '',
  right: 'today prev,next'
}
```

The mentioned default header display is modified through the `header` property, which holds the header configuration object as shown here:

```
<p-schedule [events]="events" [header]="headerConfig" [height]="700"
    [styleClass]="'schedule-width'"></p-schedule>
```

Let's define the navigation controls on the left-hand side, title in the middle, and type of view (month, week, and day) on the right-hand side to represent it as a configuration object:

```
this.headerConfig = {
    left: 'prev,next today',
    center: 'title',
    right: 'month,agendaWeek,agendaDay'
};
```

The following screenshot shows a snapshot result of the customized Schedule's header as an example:

 April 2017

Beyond basic usage - advanced features

Apart from the mentioned regular features, the Schedule component also supports lazy loading through the `onViewRender` event callback, which will be invoked when the new date range is rendered or when the view type changes. The Schedule component with lazy loading event callback invocation would be written as follows:

```
<p-schedule [events]="events" (onViewRender)="loadEvents($event)"
[height]="700" [styleClass]="'schedule-width'"></p-schedule>
```

The component class defines a lazy loading callback to retrieve the events data on-demand and would be written as follows:

```
loadEvents(event: any) {
    let start = event.view.start;
    let end = event.view.end;
    // In real time the service call filtered based on
    //start and end dates
    this.eventService.getEvents().subscribe((events: any) =>
    {this.events = events;});
}
```

The component also supports localization through the `locale` property. For example, German labels are represented by setting `locale="de"`. The localized labels should be defined in a component similar to calendar.

 The UI is updated automatically when there is any change in the events data. This is very helpful for CRUD operations implementation on Schedule.

Events and methods

The Schedule component provides many event callbacks on click, mouse, resize, and drag and drop user actions as listed here:

Name	Description
onDayClick	Triggered when the user clicks on a day
onEventClick	Triggered when the user clicks an event
onEventMouseover	Triggered when the user mouses over an event
onEventMouseout	Triggered when the user mouses out of an event
onEventDragStart	Triggered when event dragging begins
onEventDragStop	Triggered when event dragging stops
onEventDrop	Triggered when dragging stops and the event has moved to a *different* day/time
onEventResizeStart	Triggered when event resizing begins
onEventResizeStop	Triggered when event resizing stops
onEventResize	Triggered when resizing stops and the event has changed in duration
onViewRender	Triggered when a new date-range is rendered, or when the view type switches
onViewDestroy	Triggered when a rendered date-range needs to be torn down
onDrop	Triggered when a draggable has been dropped onto the Schedule

Also, it provides many API methods to handle different use cases as shown here:

Name	Parameters	Description
prev()	-	Moves the Schedule one step back (either by a month, week, or day)
next()	-	Moves the Schedule one step forward (either by a month, week, or day)
prevYear()	-	Moves the Schedule back one year
nextYear()	-	Moves the Schedule forward one year
today()	-	Moves the Schedule to the current date
gotoDate(date)	date: Date to navigate	Moves the Schedule to an arbitrary date
incrementDate(duration)	duration: Duration to add to current date	Moves the Schedule forward/backward an arbitrary amount of time
getDate()	-	Returns a moment for the current date of the calendar
changeView(viewName)	viewName: A valid view string to change to	Immediately switches to a different view

The preceding API methods will give full control on Schedule. There are many use cases, where these method calls are really helpful. For example, the Schedule's next view (month, week, or day) is accessed through the .next() method as shown here:

```
<p-schedule [events]="events" #schedule></p-schedule>
<button type="button" pButton (click)="next(schedule)"></p-button>
```

The component class defines the click event callback which will invoke next day, week, or month as shown here:

```
next(schedule) {
  schedule.next();
}
```

The complete demo application with instructions is available on GitHub at https://github.com/ova2/angular-development-with-primeng/tree/master/chapter5/schedule.

Summary

At this point of time, you will have an overview of all data iteration components and their most used features such as selecting rows, sorting, pagination, filtering data, and so on. Next, we were able to display (hierarchical) data in a tabular, grid, and list formats. Furthermore, you know how to achieve resizing, reordering, toggling, and grouping of columns, customizing of cell content in DataTable and visualizing the data with Tree and TreeTable components. In the next chapter, you will see amazing overlays such as dialog, confirm dialog, overlay panel, and notification components, such as growl and messages along with various features.

6
Amazing Overlays and Messages

Amazing Overlays and Messages demonstrate various variants of content displayed in modal or non-modal Overlays, such as Dialog, Lightbox, and the Overlay panel. The user does not leave the page flow when the content is displayed in the mentioned Overlays. An Overlay component overlays other components on the page. PrimeNG also offers Notification components to show any kind of messages or advisory information. These Message components will be described as well.

In this chapter, we will cover the following topics:

- Displaying content in the popup mode
- Multipurpose scenarios with OverlayPanel
- Displaying content in Lightbox
- Notifying users with Messages and Growl
- Tooltips for form components

Displaying content in the popup mode

The additional information of a website can be represented in a popup format. This will improve the user experience with optimal view port. There are two types of popup formats that exist: **Dialog** and **ConfirmDialog**.

Dialog

Dialog is a container component to display the content in an Overlay window. To save the web page's viewport, Dialog is very useful to display additional information in a popup format. The visibility of Dialog is controlled through the `visible` property.

By default, the Dialog is hidden with `visibility` as `false` and enabling the `visible` property displays the Dialog. Due to the two-way binding nature of Dialog, the `visible` property turned as `false` automatically after closing the Dialog using the close icon. The `closeOnEscape` attribute is used to close the Dialog with the *Esc* key.

A basic example of Dialog component with source button would be written as follows:

```
<p-dialog header="PrimeNG" [(visible)]="basic">
    PrimeNG content goes here.... </dialog>
```

The `visible` property is enabled on the user action. The following screenshot shows a snapshot result of the basic Dialog example:

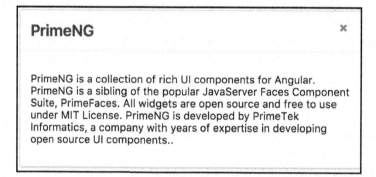

The Dialog component supports two event callbacks named `onShow` and `onHide`, which will be invoked when the Dialog is shown or hidden.

Usability features

The user experience with the Dialog component will be improved with draggable, resizable, closable, and responsive features using `draggable`, `resizable`, `closable`, and `responsive` properties. Apart from these interactive features, the `modal` property prevents user actions on the main page with a transparent background, whereas `dismissableMask` hides the Dialog if the user clicks on a transparent background.

The default values of these properties are as follows:

- `draggable = true`
- `resizable = true`
- `closable = true`
- `responsive = false`
- `modal = false`
- `dismissableMask = false`

Customized header and footer

The header of the Dialog is defined through the `header` property, and it can be controlled by the `showHeader` attribute. The header and footer sections of the Dialog component can be defined in a more flexible manner using the `p-header` and `p-footer` tags. In order to work with them, there is a need to import the header and footer components and declare it in the directives section.

A customized example of a Dialog component with customized header and footer will be written as follows:

```
<p-dialog [(visible)]="custom" modal="true">
  <p-header>
    PrimeNG License declaration
  </p-header>
  All widgets are open source and free to use under MIT License.
  If agree with the license please click 'Yes' otherwise click 'No'.
  <p-footer>
    <div class="ui-dialog-buttonpane ui-widget-content
      ui-helper-clearfix">
      <button type="button" pButton icon="fa-close"
        (click)="onComplete()" label="No"></button>
      <button type="button" pButton icon="fa-check"
        (click)="onComplete()" label="Yes"></button>
    </div>
  </p-footer>
</p-dialog>
```

The following screenshot shows a snapshot result of the custom Dialog example:

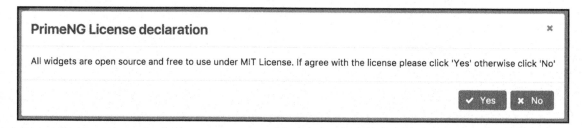

The preceding snapshot shows how the header, message, and footer icons can be customized as per the needs or requirements. By default, the Dialog component is center aligned in the viewport, but this can be customized using `positionLeft` and `positionTop` properties.

ConfirmDialog

The ConfirmDialog is a component used to display confirmation windows with multiple actions at the same time. In this case, it will be backed by the confirmation service utilizing obseravables. The service which uses a confirmed method for multiple actions needs to be imported.

A basic example of the ConfirmDialog component with a source button (or dialog generator button) would be written as follows:

```
<p-confirmDialog></p-confirmDialog>
    <button type="button" (click)="confirmAccept()" pButton
      icon="fa-check" label="Confirm"></button>
    <button type="button" (click)="confirmDelete()" pButton
      icon="fa-trash" label="Delete"></button>
```

In the preceding example, the confirm method will confirm an instance for customizing the Dialog UI along with accept and reject buttons. For example, the `accept` function invokes the confirm method of a confirmation service, which decides what action needs to be performed:

```
confirmAccept() {
  this.confirmationService.confirm({
    message: 'Do you want to subscribe for Angular news feeds?',
    header: 'Subscribe',
    icon: 'fa fa-question-circle',
    accept: () => {
      this.msgs = [];
```

```
        this.msgs.push({severity:'info', summary:'Confirmed',
                    detail: 'You have accepted'});
    }
  });
}
```

The Dialog appeared with the click of a button component. The following screenshot shows a snapshot result of the basic confirmed Dialog example:

The footer accept and reject buttons decide whether to subscribe for the Angular news feed system.

Customization

There are two ways to provide the header, message, and icons for the confirmed Dialog. One is a declarative approach in which all the features are provided through attributes (header, message, and icon), whereas the other approach is a programmatic approach in which the values can be dynamic through confirmed instance properties. Even the footer section buttons can be customized with their own UI (acceptLabel, acceptIcon, acceptVisibility, rejectLabel, rejectIcon, and rejectVisibility) along with the accept and reject methods of the local ng-template variable.

A customized example of the confirm Dialog component with header and footer would be written as follows:

```
<p-confirmDialog header="Confirmation" message="Do you like to use
  DataTable component" icon="fa fa-question-circle" width="400"
  height="200" #confirmation>
  <p-footer>
    <button type="button" pButton icon="fa-close" label="No"
    (click)="confirmation.reject()"></button>
    <button type="button" pButton icon="fa-check" label="Yes"
    (click)="confirmation.accept()"></button>
  </p-footer>
</p-confirmDialog>
```

The following screenshot shows a snapshot result of a custom confirm Dialog example:

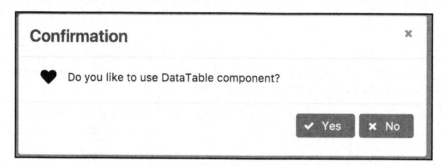

In the preceding snapshot, all headers, messages, and icons are customized in a declarative approach. The confirm Dialog provides default `closable`, `responsive`, and `closeOnEscape` properties, which is similar to the Dialog component.

The complete demo application with instructions is available on GitHub:

- https://github.com/ova2/angular-development-with-prim
  eng/tree/master/chapter6/dialog

- https://github.com/ova2/angular-development-with-primen
  g/tree/master/chapter6/confirm-dialog.

Multipurpose scenarios with OverlayPanel

The OverlayPanel is a container component that displays additional information on top of the other components in the page. This element will be displayed using the `show` or `toggle` method of a local `ng-template` variable, and it can be hidden using the `hide` or `toggle` method. Remember that the `show` method will allow a second argument as the target element, where it has to display the Overlay (instead source). A basic example of the Overlay component with the source button generator will be written as follows:

```
<p-overlayPanel #overlaybasic>
  <img src="/assets/data/images/primeng.png" alt="PrimeNG Logo" />
</p-overlayPanel>
<button type="button" pButton label="Logo"
(click)="overlaybasic.toggle($event)"></button>
```

In the preceding example, Overlay will appear by the click of the Button component. The following screenshot shows a snapshot result of the basic Overlay example:

In the preceding snapshot, the Overlay displays the PrimeNG logo as a image on the click of the logo button. By default, OverlayPanel is attached to the body of the page, but the target can be changed using the appendTo property.

Integration with other components

The OverlayPanel component can be integrated with other PrimeNG components as well. For example, the following snapshot shows how to integrate the Overlay component with the DataTable component using `ng-template`. In this case, the button needs to be placed inside DataTable `ng-template` and Overlay triggered through the `toggle` event:

Result	Name	Java	Scala	Play
🔍	Chamila	88	76	97
🔍	Alex	87	93	84
Total marks: 264 Percentage: 88% Raghu		88	83	85
🔍	Kelum	92	74	92
🔍	Darth	83	96	84
🔍	Oleg	90	80	94
🔍	Sudheer	88	87	82

In the preceding snapshot, the Overlay panel is used to display the aggregation information such as marks and percentage in the popup format by clicking on the result button in each row.

Closable properties

By default, the interaction outside the Overlay panel closes the Dialog immediately. This behavior can be prevented with the help of the `dismissable` property. At the same time, there is an option to display close at the top-right corner using the `showCloseIcon` property.

The Dialog component supports four event callbacks named `onBeforeShow`, `onAfterShow`, `onBeforeHide`, and `onAfterHide`, which will be invoked when the Dialog is shown or hidden.

> The complete demo application with instructions is available on GitHub at `https://github.com/ova2/angular-development-with-primeng/tree/master/chapter6/overlaypanel`.

Displaying content in Lightbox

LightBox component is used to display a collection of images, videos, inline HTML content, and also iframes in a modal Overlay mode. There are two types of LightBox modes that exist: one is the default `image` type and the other one is the `content` type. In the image mode, a collection of images will be displayed where each entry represents an image object which represent the source of the image, thumbnail, and title. A basic example of a LightBox with a collection (or array) of Angular conferences would be as follows:

```
<p-lightbox [images]="images" name="image"></p-lightbox>
```

The component will be rendered as shown in the following screenshot:

In the preceding snapshot, all the images are displayed as gallery of images and navigated through the next and previous icons.

Custom content mode

The content mode is enabled by setting the `type` property to `content`, which provides an anchor (or link) to open the LightBox and content to display inside of it. A customized content example of a LightBox with a collection of Angular conferences would be as follows:

```
<p-lightbox type="content" name="content">
  <a class="group" href="#">
    Watch PrimeNG Video
  </a>
  <iframe width="500" height="300"
    src="https://www.youtube.com/watch?v=Jf9nQ36e0Fw&t=754s"
    frameborder="0" allowfullscreen></iframe>
</p-lightbox>
```

The component will be rendered as iframe video inside Overlay panel as shown in the following screenshot:

As shown the preceding snapshot, the list of videos are displayed and can watch videos in a popup mode for better experience.

Transition effects

The LightBox component is more powerful with the transition effects between images. This can be achieved through the `easing` property. Here, the default value is `ease-out` (that is, the effects are customized using the `easing` property). There are many other effects available, the entire list of CSS3 effects are supported. Also, by default, the effect duration is `500ms`. This also can be customized through the `effectDuration` property.

The transition effect as an example of a LightBox with a collection of Angular conferences would be as follows:

```
<p-lightbox [images]="images" name="effects" easing="ease-out"
  effectDuration="1000ms">
</p-lightbox>
```

> The complete demo application with instructions is available on GitHub at
> https://github.com/ova2/angular-development-with-primeng/tree
> /master/chapter6/lightbox.

Notifying users with Messages and Growl

The Message component is used to display messages in an inline format to notify the users. These Messages are notified as the result of a specific action. Each Message in PrimeNG API is defined using the `Message` interface, which defines `severity`, `summary`, and `detail` properties.

A basic example of Messages to notify the user would be as follows:

```
<p-messages ([value])="messages" name="basic"></p-messages>
```

In the preceding example, Messages are displayed using the `value` property, which defines an array of the `Message` interfaces. The component will be rendered as shown in the following screenshot:

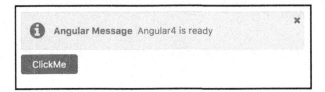

The severity of Messages are represented with the `class` property. The possible values of Messages severity would be as follows:

Severity	Class name
`success`	`.ui-button-success`
`info`	`.ui-button-info`
`warn`	`.ui-button-warn`
`error`	`.ui-button-error`

The Messages are closable by default with the help of the cross icon located at the top-right corner. This behavior can be altered through the `closable` property, that is, `[closable]="false"` disables the closable nature of Messages.

Growl - another way of notifying information

Similar to Message components, Growl is used to display Messages as a result of specific actions, but it displays in the form of the Overlay mode instead of the inline mode. Each Message is represented through the `Message` interface with `severity`, `summary`, and `details`. A basic example of Growl to notify the user would be as follows:

```
<p-growl ([value])="messages" name="basic"></p-growl>
```

The `value` property defines an array of the `Message` interfaces in the backing component model. The component will be rendered as shown in the following screenshot:

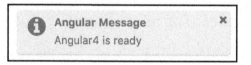

Similar to the Messages component, the same severity types can be defined in Growl as well. PrimeNG 4.1 release introduced the `onClick` event callback which will be invoked when a Message is clicked on.

Sticky behavior

By default, the Growl messages are removed after a certain span of time. The default lifespan of Growl messages is 3000ms. This can be customized using the life property (that is, life="5000"). To make the Messages as sticky, irrespective of the lifespan mentioned, you should enable the sticky behavior, that is, sticky="true".

PrimeNG Version 4.0.1 supports the two-way binding feature for Growl messages. Due to this feature, whenever the message is removed manually from UI, backend instance, or message, array will be updated immediately.

The complete demo application with instructions is available on GitHub at

- https://github.com/ova2/angular-development-with-prim eng/tree/master/chapter6/messages
- https://github.com/ova2/angular-development-with-prim eng/tree/master/chapter6/growl.

Tooltips for form components

Tooltip provides an advisory information for a component. This gives a brief insight of target component before going to use. The Tooltip is applied through the pTooltip directive with the value to define text to display. Along with that, HTML tags also displayed instead of regular text information with the help of the escape attribute. A basic example of Tooltip is to provide an advisory information for input as follows:

```
<input type="text" pInputText pTooltip="Enter your favourite component
    name" >
```

The Tooltip display on right side of input as shown in the following screenshot:

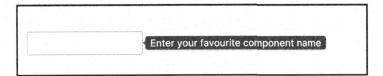

The Tooltip position is displayed on the right side of target component by default. This behavior can be changed using the `tooltipPosition` property with other values such as `top`, `right`, and `bottom`, for example, `tooltipPosition` with the `top` value will result as in the following screenshot:

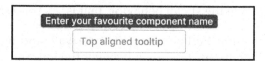

By default, the Tooltip is displayed on hover of a target element (that is, the default event to invoke Tooltip information is **hover.**) This can be customized using the `tooltipEvent` property, which provides focus event to display and blur event to hide Tooltip. Remember, Tooltips can also be disabled using the `tooltipDisabled` property.

A Tooltip event example for input would be as follows:

```
<input type="text" pInputText pTooltip="Enter your favourite component
    name" tooltipEvent="focus" placeholder="Focus inputbox"/>
```

By default, Tooltip is assigned to document body. If the target of a Tooltip placed inside scrolling containers (for example, overflown `div` element), append Tooltip to the element with the relative position. This can be achieved using the `appendTo` property (that is, `appendTo="container"`).

PrimeNG Version 4.1 provides the `showDelay` and `hideDelay` properties in order to add delay while showing and hiding Tooltips (which accept a number value in terms of milliseconds). The delay feature would be applied as follows:

```
<input type="text" pInputText pTooltip="Enter your favourite component
    name" tooltipEvent="focus" placeholder="Focus inputbox"
    showDelay="1000" hideDelay="400"/>
```

The complete demo application with instructions is available on GitHub at https://github.com/ova2/angular-development-with-primeng/tree/master/chapter6/tooltips.

Summary

By reaching this section, you will be in a position to understand how to display images, videos, iframe, and HTML content in an Overlay window without the leaving current page flow. Initially, you will see how to work with Dialog, ConfirmDialog, LightBox, and Overlay components. After that, you learned on how to display inline messages or messages in an Overlay by Messages and Growl components, respectively.

The last recipe explained about the Tooltip component for displaying advisory information. All these components are explained with all possible features in a step-by-step approach. In the next chapter, you will see how to use the Menu model API, navigation, and menu variations such as menu, mega menu, menu bar, slide menu, panel menu, tiered menu, and so on, with various features.

7
Endless Menu Variations

In this chapter, you will learn about several menu variations. PrimeNG's menus fulfill all major requirements. These days, every website contains menus. Usually, a menu is presented to a user as a list of links to be navigated or commands to be executed. Menus are sometimes organized hierarchically, allowing navigation through different levels of the menu structure.

Arranging menu items in logical groups makes it easy for users to quickly locate the related tasks. They come with various facets such as static, dynamic, tiered, hybrid, iPod-styled, and so on, and leave nothing to be desired. Readers will face a lot of recipes that discuss the menu's structure, configuration options, customizations, and integration with other components. Menu-like components helping in wizards and workflows will be explained as well.

In this chapter, we will cover the following topics:

- Creating programmatic menus with the MenuModel API
- Statically and dynamically positioned menus
- Accessing commands via MenuBar
- ContextMenu with nested items
- SlideMenu - menu in the iPod style
- TieredMenu - sub-menus in nested Overlays
- MegaMenu - the multicolumn menu
- PanelMenu - hybrid of Accordion and Tree
- TabMenu - menu items as tabs
- Breadcrumb - providing contextual information about page hierarchy

Creating programmatic menus using the MenuModel API

PrimeNG provides a `MenuModel` API, which will be shared by all menu components to specify menu items and sub-menus. The core item of the `MenuModel` API is the `MenuItem` class with options such as `label`, `icon`, `url`, child menu items with the `items` option, and so on.

Let's take an example of the Menu component to represent a common toolbar user interface. The Menu component is binding an array of the `MenuItem` classes as items through the `model` property as follows:

```
<p-menu [model]="items"></p-menu>
```

`MenuItem` is the key item in the `MenuModel` API. It has the following list of properties. Each property is described with the type, default value, and its description:

Name	Type	Default	Description
label	string	null	Text of the item.
icon	string	null	Icon of the item.
command	function	null	Callback to execute when the item is clicked.
url	string	null	External link to navigate when the item is clicked.
routerLink	array	null	RouterLink definition for internal navigation.
items	array	null	An array of children menu items.
expanded	boolean	false	Visibility of sub-menu.
disabled	boolean	false	When set as `true`, disables the menu item.
visible	boolean	true	Whether the DOM element of menu item is created or not.
target	string	null	Specifies where to open the linked document.

Table 1.0

Menu actions

The menu items with plain read-only labels and icons are not really useful. The Menu component with user actions need to perform business implementations or navigations to other resources. The major components of menu actions are command invocation and navigations. This can be achieved through the `url` and `routerLink` properties of the `MenuItem` interface.

The example usage of URL and router link options of the `MenuItem` API would be as follows:

```
{label: 'View', icon: 'fa-search', command:
  (event) => this.viewEmployee(this.selectedEmployee) }

{label: 'Help', icon: 'fa-close', url:
  'https://www.opm.gov/policy-data- oversight/worklife/employee-
  assistance-programs/' }
```

In the following sections, you will see how this `MenuModel` API is going to be used in various kinds of Menu components.

Statically and dynamically positioned menus

Menu is a navigation or command component that supports dynamic and static positioning. This is a basic Menu component among all variations of Menu components. The menus are statically positioned by default, but they are made dynamic by providing the `target` attribute. The static positioned menus are attached to the page body as target (that is, `appendTo="body"`), whereas assigning to other elements create dynamic-positioned menus.

A basic menu example, which holds project document or file types of menu items, would be as follows:

```
<p-menu [model]="items"></p-menu>
```

The list of menu items needs to be organized within a component class. For example, the root menu item titled `Edit` will have nested items as shown here:

```
this.items=[
{
    label: 'Edit',
    icon: 'fa-edit',
    items: [
        {label: 'Undo', icon: 'fa-mail-forward'},
        {label: 'Redo', icon: 'fa-mail-reply'}
    ]
},
//More items ...
}
```

The following screenshot shows a snapshot result of the basic menu (with all menu items) example:

From the preceding snapshot, you can observe that the Menu component is displayed in the inline format. But, this behavior can be changed by enabling the `popup` property in order to display as overlay.

The Menu component defines `toggle`, `show`, and `hide` methods for the Menu API. The detailed description of each method listed in tabular format is as follows:

Name	Parameters	Description
toggle	event: browser event	Toggles the visibility of the pop-up menu.
show	event: browser event	Displays the pop-up menu.
hide	-	Hides the pop-up menu.

Table 2.0

The complete demo application with instructions is available on GitHub at `https://github.com/ova2/angular-development-with-primeng/tree /master/chapter7/menu`.

Accessing commands via MenuBar

MenuBar component is a group of horizontal menu components with nested sub-menus (or a component with group of drop-down menus for page navigations). Like any other Menu component, MenuBar uses a common menu model API which holds a list of the `MenuItem` interfaces. There is no limit for nested levels of sub-menus. Let's see a basic MenuBar example for window or application-specific menus. This provides an access for common functions such as opening files, edit operations, interacting with an application, displaying help documentation, and so on, and would be as follows:

```
<p-menubar [model]="items"></p-menubar>
```

The list of menu items needs to be organized within a component class. For example, a root menu item titled `Edit` will have nested items as shown here:

```
this.items = [
  {
    label: 'Edit',
    icon: 'fa-edit',
    items: [
      {label: 'Cut', icon: 'fa-cut'},
      {label: 'Copy', icon: 'fa-copy'},
      {label: 'Paste', icon: 'fa-paste'},
      {label: 'Undo', icon: 'fa-mail-forward'},
      {label: 'Redo', icon: 'fa-mail-reply'},
      {label: 'Find', icon: 'fa-search', items: [
```

```
        {label: 'Find Next'},
        {label: 'Find Previous'}
      ]}
    ]
  },
  // more items......
];
```

The following screenshot shows a snapshot result of the basic MenuBar (with all menu items) example:

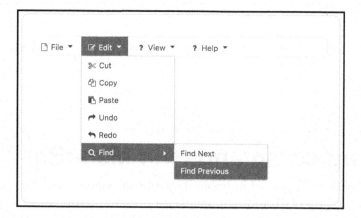

The component skinning can be achieved through the `style` and `styleClass` properties. PrimeNG 4.1 allows custom content (form controls) by placing them inside the MenuBar tags.

The complete demo application with instructions is available on GitHub at `https://github.com/ova2/angular-development-with-primeng/tree /master/chapter7/menubar`.

ContextMenu with nested items

ContextMenu is a menu with **Graphical User Interface (GUI)** representation that appears on top of your page just by right-clicking. By right-clicking, an Overlay menu is displayed on the target element. There are two types of Context menus, one for the document and the other for the specific component. Apart from these two, there is also a special integration with components such as DataTable.

By default, the ContextMenu is attached to the document with the global setting. A basic Context menu example, which displays a document or file type menu, would be as follows:

```
<p-contextMenu [global]="true" [model]="documentItems"></p-contextMenu>
```

The list of menu items needs to be organized within a component class. For example, a root menu item titled `File` will have nested items as shown here:

```
this.documentItems = [
  {
    label: 'File',
    icon: 'fa-file-o',
    items: [{
      label: 'New',
      icon: 'fa-plus',
      items: [
        {label: 'Project'},
        {label: 'Other'},
      ],
      expanded: true
    },
    {label: 'Open'},
    {label: 'Quit'}
    ],
  },
  // more items ...
];
```

The following screenshot shows a snapshot result of the basic Context menu (with all menu items) example:

The Context menu will disappear once you click on the outside of this component.

Customized target for ContextMenu

The default global settings of the Context menu can be changed using the `target` attribute (that is, the Context menu will be displayed on other elements other than the global document target). Let's take a Context menu example where the Overlay or popup appears on top of the image element on right-click as shown here:

```
<p-contextMenu [target]="image" [model]="targetItems" >
</p-contextMenu>
<img #image src="/assets/data/images/primeng.png" alt="Logo">
```

In this case, both next and previous operations can be performed from the Context menu just by defining the menu items array.

DataTable integration

In the previous section, you have seen how to integrate the context menu with other elements using the `target` property. But integration with the DataTable component is a different case which needs a special treatment. This combination is one of the frequently used use cases in web development.

The DataTable provides reference to a Context menu using the `contextMenu` property (that is, the template reference variable of the Context menu should be assigned to DataTable's `contextMenu` attribute). The Context menu integration with DataTable would be written as follows:

```
<p-contextMenu #contextmenu [model]="tableItems"></p-contextMenu>
<p-dataTable [value]="employees" selectionMode="single"
[(selection)]="selectedEmployee" [contextMenu]="contextmenu">
  <p-header>Employee Information</p-header>
  <p-column field="id" header="Employee ID"></p-column>
  <p-column field="name" header="Name"></p-column>
  <p-column field="email" header="Email"></p-column>
  <p-column field="contact" header="Telephone"></p-column>
</p-dataTable>
```

The Context menu model is bounded to an array of menu items such as `View` and `Delete` options as follows:

```
this.tableItems = [
  {label: 'View', icon: 'fa-search', command: (event) =>
    this.viewEmployee(this.selectedEmployee)},
  {label: 'Delete', icon: 'fa-close', command: (event) =>
    this.deleteEmployee(this.selectedEmployee)},
```

```
{label: 'Help', icon: 'fa-close',
  url: 'https://www.opm.gov/policy-data-oversight/worklife/
  employee-assistance-programs/'}
];
```

In the preceding example, we performed command actions which notify the user with messages. But in real time, all CRUD operations are in sync with the database. The following screenshot shows a snapshot result of the Context menu integration with DataTable component as an example:

Employee Information			
Employee ID	Name	Email	Telephone
100	Sreekanth	sreekanth@google.com	764-456-33
111	Sudheer	sudheer@geekotek.com	123-456-55
222	Darel	darel@google.com	234-432-33
333	Rishi	rishi@fb.com	678-456-333
444	Chen	chen@google.com	345-456-33
555	Raghu	raghu@amazon.com	333-456-11
666	Srini	srini@microsoft.com	555-456-88
777	Amit	amit@netflix.com	321-765-33
888	Deepak	deepak@boa.com	777-987-33
999	Anbu	anbu@dbs.com	232-545-66
1010	Kiran	kiran@google.com	345-456-22
1101	Abishek	abishek@fb.com	675-456-11
1111	Sonalee	sonalee@anz.com	222-763-99

Context menu overlay shown over row 444: Q View, ✖ Delete, ✖ Help

As per the preceding snapshot, the table row is selected on a right-click and Overlay appears on the row. The menu item selection can either do business logic or navigation to various web pages.

The complete demo application with instructions is available on GitHub at `https://github.com/ova2/angular-development-with-primeng/tree/master/chapter7/contextmenu`.

SlideMenu – menu in the iPod style

SlideMenu is a component which displays sub-menus with slide animation effects. This kind of slide menu component is the best example of iPod style menu widgets. By default, the slide menu is displayed as an inline menu component. A basic slide menu example which displays a document or file type menu would be as follows:

```
<p-slideMenu [model]="items"></p-slideMenu>
```

The list of menu items needs to be organized with in a component class. For example, a root menu item titled `File` will have nested items as shown here:

```
this.items = [
  {
    label: 'File',
    icon: 'fa-file-o',
    items: [
    {
      label: 'New',
      icon: 'fa-plus',
      items: [
        {label: 'Project'},
        {label: 'Other'},
      ]
    },
    {label: 'Open'},
    {label: 'Quit'}
    ]
  },
  // more items ...
]
```

The following screenshot shows a snapshot result of the basic slide menu, which displays file menu items on the click of the **File** menu item as an example:

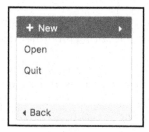

As seen in the preceding snapshot, the slide menu is displayed in an inline format. It will be displayed in pop-up mode by enabling the `popup` property. At the bottom of the slide menu popup, a back button appears with the **Back** label, but this can also be customized using the `backLabel` property.

The slide menu is accessed using API methods such as `toggle`, `show`, and `hide` methods. The slide menu provides various animation effects with the default effect `easing-out`. This default behavior can changed using the `effect` property. Similarly, the default effect duration of a slide menu is 500 milliseconds, but this can be customized using the `effectDuration` property.

The dimensions for any visual component is much needed and must be configured. Considering this standard, dimensions of Menu dimensions are configurable. The sub-menu width is controlled through the `menuWidth` property, which defaults to 180 (normally measured in pixels). Also the height of the scrollable area is controlled through the `viewportHeight` property with a default value of 175 pixels (that is, the scroll bar appears if the menu height is more than this default value).

 The complete demo application with instructions is available on GitHub at `https://github.com/ova2/angular-development-with-primeng/tree /master/chapter7/slidemenu`.

TieredMenu – sub-menus in nested overlays

The TieredMenu component displays the sub-menus in a nested Overlays mode. By default, the slide menu is displayed as an inline menu component. A basic tiered menu example, which displays the document or file type menu would be as follows:

```
<p-tieredMenu [model]="items"></p-tieredMenu>
```

The list of menu items needs to be organized with in a component class. For example, a root menu item titled `File` will have nested items as shown here:

```
this.items = [
  {
    label: 'File',
    icon: 'fa-file-o',
    items: [
  {
    label: 'New',
    icon: 'fa-plus',
```

```
    items: [
    {label: 'Project'},
    {label: 'Other'},
  ]
  },
    {label: 'Open'},
    {label: 'Quit'}
  },
  // more items
  ]
```

The following screenshot shows a snapshot result of the basic tiered menu example:

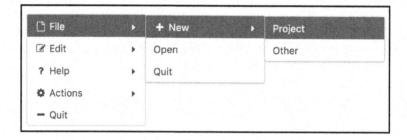

As seen in the preceding snapshot, the slide menu is displayed in an inline format. It will be displayed in pop-up mode by enabling the `popup` property. PrimeNG 4.1 introduced the `appendTo` property to attach the Overlay. The slide menu is accessed using the API methods such as `toggle`, `show`, and `hide`.

The main difference between slide menu and tiered menu components is that a slide menu displays the sub-menu by replacing the parent menu whereas a tiered menu displays the sub-menus in an Overlay mode. The API methods for both a slide menu and tiered menu with more details in a tabular format is explained in menu section *Table 2.0*.

The complete demo application with instructions is available on GitHub at
`https://github.com/ova2/angular-development-with-primeng/tree`
`/master/chapter7/tieredmenu`.

MegaMenu – the multicolumn menu

MegaMenu is like a drop-down menu that expands into a relatively large and complex interface rather than a simple list of commands. It displays the sub-menus of root items together. MegaMenu is formed with the nested menu items where each item's root item is a two-dimensional array which define columns in an Overlay menu.

A basic MegaMenu example of a retailer application to purchase clothing items would be written as follows:

```
<p-megaMenu [model]="items"></p-megaMenu>
```

The list of menu items needs to be organized with in a component class. For example, a root menu item titled **Home & Furniture** will have nested items as shown:

```
this.items = [
  {
    label: 'HOME & FURNITURE', icon: 'fa-home',
    items: [
    [
      {
        label: 'Home Furnishing',
        items: [{label: 'Cushions'}, {label: 'Throws'},
        {label: 'Rugs & Doormats'},
                {label: 'Curtains'}]
      },
      {
        label: 'Home Accessories',
        items: [{label: 'Artificial Flowers'}, {label: 'Lighting'},
                {label: 'Storage'}, {label: 'Photo Frames'}]
      }
    ],
    [
      {
        label: 'Cooking & Dinner',
        items: [{label: 'Cookware'}, {label: 'Dinnerware'},
        {label: 'Bakerware'}]
      },
      {
        label: 'Bed & Bath',
        items: [{label: 'Towels'}, {label: 'Bath Mats'}]
      }
    ]
    ]
  },
  // more items...
];
```

The following screenshot shows a snapshot result of the basic MegaMenu (with all menu items) example:

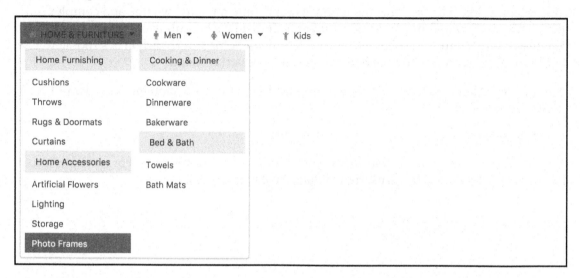

The default orientation of MegaMenu is horizontal. This can also be positioned in a vertical manner using the `orientation` attribute (that is, `orientation="vertical"`). The vertical MegaMenu looks like as the following snapshot:

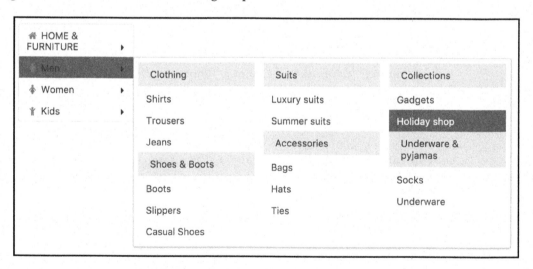

PrimeNG 4.1 allows custom content (form controls) by placing them inside MegaMenu tags.

The complete demo application with instructions is available on GitHub at
`https://github.com/ova2/angular-development-with-primeng/tree`
`/master/chapter7/megamenu`.

PanelMenu – hybrid of Accordion and Tree

PanelMenu is a hybrid of vertical stacked Accordion and hierarchical Tree components. Each parent menu item has a toggleable panel; with the panel, it shows child menu items in a hierarchical Tree format. A basic panel menu example, which displays the document or file type menu would be as follows:

```
<p-panelMenu [model]="items" ></p-panelMenu>
```

The list of menu items needs to be organized within a component class. For example, a root menu item titled **Help** will have nested items as shown here:

```
this.items = [
  {
    label: 'Help',
    icon: 'fa-question',
    items: [
        {label: 'Contents'},
        {label: 'Search', icon: 'fa-search',
          items: [{label: 'Text', items: [{label: 'Workspace'}]},
          {label: 'File'}]}
    ]
  },
  //more items ...
];
```

The following screenshot shows a snapshot result of the basic panel menu example:

```
 ▸ 🗋 File
 ▸ 🖉 Edit
 ▸ ? View
 ▾ ? Help
Contents
 ▾ 🔍 Search
    ▾ Text
       Workspace
    File
```

The initial state of each menu item is controlled through the `expanded` attribute (that is, `expanded="true"`), which is available on the `MenuItem` interface level.

 The complete demo application with instructions is available on GitHub at `https://github.com/ova2/angular-development-with-primeng/tree` `/master/chapter7/panelmenu`.

TabMenu - menu items as tabs

TabMenu is a navigation/command component that displays the items as tab headers (that is, the parent root items are represented in the form of horizontal stacked tabs). On the click of each tab, you can perform all kinds of menu actions.

A basic tabbed menu example, which displays the PrimeNG website information in the form of various tabs, would be as follows:

```
<p-tabMenu [model]="items"></p-tabMenu>
```

The list of menu items need to be organized within a component class. For example, PrimeNG's various details are explained in different horizontal tabs using menu items as follows:

```
this.items = [
  {label: 'Overview', icon: 'fa-bar-chart', routerLink:
  ['/pages/overview']},
  {label: 'Showcase', icon: 'fa-calendar', command: (event) => {
    this.msgs.length = 0;
    this.msgs.push({severity: 'info', summary: 'PrimeNG Showcase',
    detail:'Navigate all components'});}
  },
  {label: 'Documentation', icon: 'fa-book',
    url:'https://www.primefaces.org/documentation/'},
  {label: 'Downloads', icon: 'fa-download', routerLink:
    ['/pages/downloads']},
  {label: 'Support', icon: 'fa-support',
    url:'https://www.primefaces.org/support/'},
  {label: 'Social', icon: 'fa-twitter',
    url:'https://twitter.com/prime_ng'},
  {label: 'License', icon: 'fa-twitter',
    url:'https://www.primefaces.org/license/'}
];
```

The following screenshot shows a snapshot result of the tabbed panel menu example:

By default, the TabMenu displays or activates on the first tab. But the default visibility or initial display of a tab can be changed with the help of the `activeItem` property.

 The complete demo application with instructions is available on GitHub at `https://github.com/ova2/angular-development-with-primeng/tree /master/chapter7/tabmenu`.

Breadcrumb – providing contextual information about the page hierarchy

The Breadcrumb component provides contextual information about the page hierarchy. It allows you to keep track of their locations in programs, documents, and websites. This typically appears as horizontal on top of the web page separated by a greater than operator (>) as a hierarchy separator. This menu variation consists of a common menu model API to define its items. These menu items (collection of menu items) are connected to a `model` property.

A basic Breadcrumb example of an e-commerce application to purchase electrical items would be as follows:

```
<p-breadcrumb [model]="items"></p-breadcrumb>
```

The item's `model` property is an array of the `MenuItem` type. The possible options or properties for the `MenuModel` API are described in the beginning of the section. In this example, we define both label and command actions for menu items. The list of menu items need to be organized to display items as shown here:

```
this.items.push({
   label: 'Categories', command: (event) => {
     this.msgs.length = 0;
     this.msgs.push({severity: 'info', summary: event.item.label});
   }
});
this.items.push({
   label: 'Best Buy', command: (event) => {
```

```
          this.msgs.length = 0;
          this.msgs.push({severity: 'info', summary: event.item.label});
      }
  });
  this.items.push({
    label: 'TV & Video', command: (event) => {
      this.msgs.length = 0;
      this.msgs.push({severity: 'info', summary: event.item.label});
    }
  });
  this.items.push({
    label: 'TVs', command: (event) => {
      this.msgs.length = 0;
      this.msgs.push({severity: 'info', summary: event.item.label});
    }
  });
  this.items.push({
    label: 'Flat Panel TVs', command: (event) => {
      this.msgs.length = 0;
      this.msgs.push({severity: 'info', summary: event.item.label});
    }
  });
  this.items.push({label: 'LED Flat-Panel', url:
  'https://en.wikipedia.org/wiki/LED_display'});
```

The following screenshot shows a snapshot result of the basic Breadcrumb as an example:

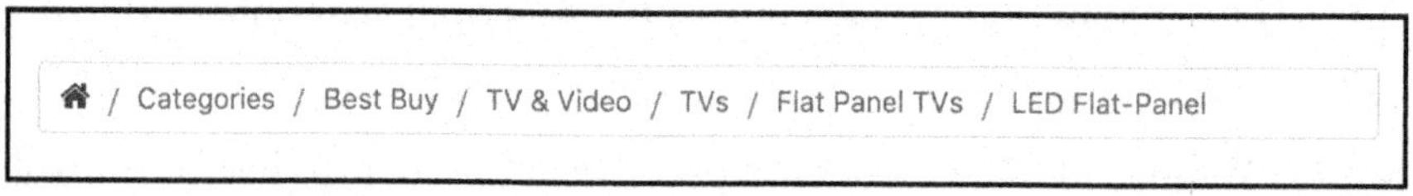

The **Home** icon is also part of the menu items and this can be customized using the home property of the MenuItem type. So, all features of the menu items apply to the **Home** menu item as well. The home property has to be defined for the Breadcrumb component as follows:

```
<p-breadcrumb [model]="items" [home]="home"></p-breadcrumb>
```

The component class holds the Home menu item as shown here:

```
home: MenuItem;

this.home = {
  label: 'Home',icon: 'fa-globe', command: (event) => {
    this.msgs.length = 0;
    this.msgs.push({severity: 'info', summary: "Home"});
  }
};
```

This is a component supported customized icon property, which can be defined from `MenuItem`.

> The complete demo application with instructions is available on GitHub at https://github.com/ova2/angular-development-with-primeng/tree /master/chapter7/breadcrumb.

Summary

At the end of this chapter, you now know how to deal with various menu components and how to put them on a page for a particular use case. At first, we started with the MenuModel API to create an array of items, after that the menu component was introduced as the basic component, then MenuBar is moved to MegaMenu components with nested complex sub-menus, and followed by other menu variations such as slide menu, tiered menu, and panel menu.

Later, we moved to the Context menu and Breadcrumb components as another kind of menu operations. In the next chapter, you will see a chart model as an API, and how to create awesome charts and maps for a visual representation of the data. All these components are explained with all possible features in a step-by-step approach.

8
Creating Charts and Maps

In this chapter, we will cover the ways to create visual charts with PrimeNG's extensive charting features and maps based on Google Maps. PrimeNG offers basic and advanced charting with its easy-to-use and user-friendly charting infrastructure. Besides standard charts, there is a special kind of chart for visualizing the hierarchical organization data. Throughout the chapter, mapping abilities such as drawing polylines, polygons, handling markers, and events will be explained as well.

In this chapter, we will cover the following topics:

- Working with the chart model
- Data representation with line and bar charts
- Data representation with pie and doughnut charts
- Data representation with radar and polar area charts
- Drawing an organization chart for relationship hierarchy
- Basic integration with the Google Map API
- Various use cases with the GMap component

Working with the chart model

The chart component provides a visual representation of data using charts on a web page. PrimeNG chart components are based on the **Charts.js 2.x** library (as a dependency), which is a HTML5 open source library. The chart model is based on the UIChart class name, and it can be represented with the element name as p-chart.

The chart components will work efficiently by attaching a chart model file (chart.js) to your project. It can be configured as either a CDN resource, local resource, or CLI configuration:

- **CDN resource configuration**:

```
<script src="https://cdnjs.cloudflare.com/ajax/libs/
    Chart.js/2.5.0/Chart.bundle.min.js"></script>
```

- **Angular CLI configuration**:

```
"scripts": [ "../node_modules/chart.js/dist/
    Chart.js", //..others ]
```

More about chart configuration and options is available in the official documentation of the Chart.js library (http://www.chartjs.org/).

Chart types

The chart type is defined through the type property. It supports seven different types of charts with an option for customizations:

- pie
- bar
- line
- doughnut
- polarArea
- radar
- horizontalBar

Each type has it's own format of data, and it can be supplied through the data property. For example, in the doughnut chart, the type should refer to doughnut and the data property should bind to the data options, as shown here:

```
<p-chart type="doughnut" [data]="doughnutdata"></p-chart>
```

The component class has to define data with the options `labels` and `datasets`, as shown here:

```
this.doughnutdata = {
  labels: ['PrimeNG', 'PrimeUI', 'PrimeReact'],
  datasets: [
    {
      data: [3000, 1000, 2000],
      backgroundColor: [
        "#6544a9",
        "#51cc00",
        "#5d4361"
      ],
      hoverBackgroundColor: [
        "#6544a9",
        "#51cc00",
        "#5d4361"
      ]
    }
  ]
};
```

Along with the labels and data options, other properties related to skinning can be applied too.

> The legends are closable by default (that is, if you want to visualize only a particular data variant, then it is possible by collapsing legends which are not required). The collapsed legend is represented with a strike line. The respective data component will disappear after the click operation on the legend.

Customization

Each series is customized on a dataset basis, but you can customize the general or common options via the `options` attribute. For example, the line chart which customizes the default options would be as follows:

```
<p-chart type="line" [data]="linedata" [options]="options">
</p-chart>
```

The component needs to define the chart options with customized `title` and `legend` properties, as shown here:

```
this.options = {
  title: {
    display: true,
    text: 'PrimeNG vs PrimeUI',
    fontSize: 16
  },
  legend: {
    position: 'bottom'
  }
};
```

As per the preceding example, the `title` option is customized with a dynamic title, font size, and conditional display of the title, whereas the `legend` attribute is used to place the legend in `top`, `left`, `bottom`, and `right` positions. The default legend position is `top`. In this example, the legend position is `bottom`.

The line chart with the preceding customized options would result as the following snapshot:

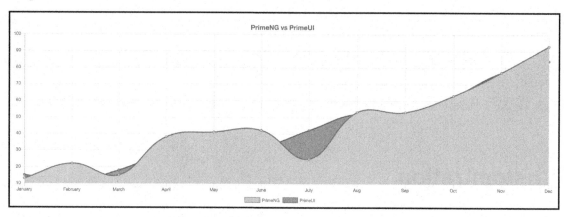

The `Chart` API also supports the utility methods shown here:

Method	Description
refresh	Redraws the graph with new data
reinit	Destroys the existing graph and then creates it again
generateLegend	Returns an HTML string of a legend for that chart

Events

The chart component provides a click event on datasets to process the selected data using the onDataSelect event callback.

Let's take a line chart example with the onDataSelect event callback by passing an event object as follows:

```
<p-chart type="line" [data]="linedata"
  (onDataSelect)="selectData($event)"></p-chart>
```

In the component class, an event callback is used to display selected data information in the following message format:

```
selectData(event: any) {
  this.msgs = [];
  this.msgs.push({
    severity: 'info',
    summary: 'Data Selected',
    'detail': this.linedata.datasets[event.element._datasetIndex]
    .data[event.element._index]
  });
}
```

In the preceding event callback (onDataSelect), we used an index of the dataset to display information. There are also many other options from an event object:

- event.element: Selected element
- event.dataset: Selected dataset
- event.element._datasetIndex: Index of the chart data series
- event.element._index: Index of the data element inside chart series

Data representation with line and bar charts

A line chart or line graph is a type of chart which displays the information as a series of data points called *markers* connected by straight line segments. A line chart is often used to visualize the real-time data in regular time intervals or time series.

A basic example of line chart usage regarding the Prime libraries downloads would be as follows:

```
<p-chart type="line" [data]="linedata" width="300" height="100">
</p-chart>
```

The component class should define a line chart data, in which one refers to the PrimeNG series and the other one refers to the PrimeUI series over the past year, as shown here:

```
this.linedata = {
  labels: ['January', 'February', 'March', 'April', 'May',
    'June', 'July', 'Aug', 'Sep', 'Oct', 'Nov', 'Dec'],
  datasets: [
    {
      label: 'PrimeNG',
      backgroundColor: '#ffb870',
      borderColor: '#cc4e0e',
      data: [13, 22, 15, 38, 41, 42, 25, 53, 53, 63, 77, 93]
    },
    {
      label: 'PrimeUI',
      backgroundColor: '#66ff00',
      borderColor: '#6544a9',
      data: [15, 11, 18, 28, 32, 32, 42, 52, 48, 62, 77, 84]
    }
  ]
};
```

As per the preceding code snippets, along with the data and labels, we can also define background and border colors to make the line chart as fancy and customizable as we like. The following screenshot shows a snapshot result of the line chart as an example:

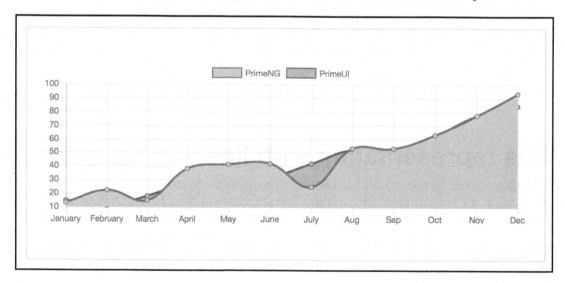

A bar chart or bar graph is a chart or graph that presents grouped data with rectangular bars, which are proportional to the values that they represent. PrimeNG also supports horizontal representation of bars in the graph.

A basic example of bar chart usage regarding the Prime libraries downloads would be as follows:

```
<p-chart type="bar" [data]="bardata" width="300" height="100">
</p-chart>
```

The component class should define the bar chart data, in which one bar refers to PrimeNG data and the other bar refers to the PrimeUI series over the past year, as shown here:

```
this.bardata = {
    labels: ['January', 'February', 'March', 'April', 'May',
      'June', 'July', 'Aug', 'Sep',
      'Oct', 'Nov', 'Dec'],
    datasets: [
      {
        label: 'PrimeNG',
        backgroundColor: '#66ff00',
        borderColor: '#6544a9',
        data: [10, 15, 13, 27, 22, 34, 44, 48, 42, 64, 77, 89]
      },
      {
        label: 'PrimeUI',
        backgroundColor: '#ffb870',
        borderColor: '#cc4e0e',
        data: [5, 14, 15, 22, 26, 24, 32, 42, 48, 62, 66, 72]
      }
    ]
};
```

The following screenshot shows a snapshot result of the bar chart with PrimeNG and PrimeUI downloads over the time period of a year as an example:

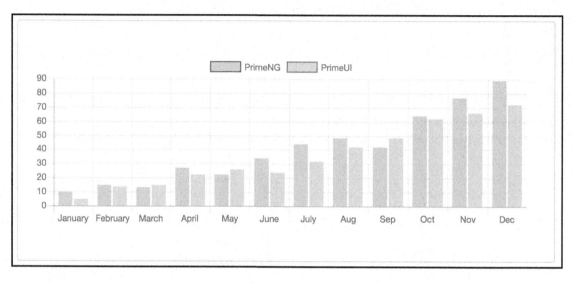

In the preceding chart, only two datasets are compared over a regular period of time. This can be applied for multi-datasets as well.

Data representation with pie and doughnut charts

A pie chart (or a circle chart) is a circular statical graphic, which is divided into slices to illustrate the numerical proportion of composite data. The arch length of each slice is equal to the quantity of data entity. A basic example of the pie chart usage regarding the Prime libraries downloads would be as follows:

```
<p-chart #pie type="pie" [data]="piedata" width="300" height="100">
</p-chart>
```

The component class should define the pie chart data with three slices for three prime libraries over the period of time, as shown here:

```
this.piedata = {
  labels: ['PrimeNG', 'PrimeUI', 'PrimeReact'],
  datasets: [
    {
      data: [3000, 1000, 2000],
```

```
      backgroundColor: [
        "#6544a9",
        "#51cc00",
        "#5d4361"
      ],
      hoverBackgroundColor: [
        "#6544a9",
        "#51cc00",
        "#5d4361"
      ]
    }
  ]
};
```

The following screenshot shows a snapshot result of the pie chart with PrimeNG, PrimeUI, and PrimeReact downloads over the time period of a year as an example:

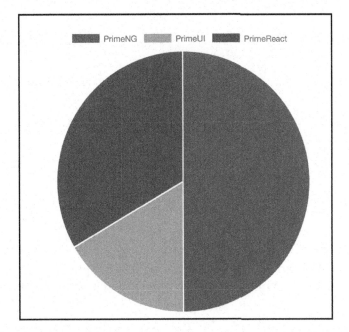

By hovering over each pie chart slice, you can observe the respective data label and it's value.

A doughnut chart is a variant of the pie chart, with a blank hollow center allowing for the additional information about the complete data (that is, each slice represents specific unique data and the general additional information applies to all slices represented by the center circle).

A basic example of doughnut chart usage for Prime libraries downloads would be as follows:

```
<p-chart type="doughnut" [data]="doughnutdata" width="300"
  height="100">
</p-chart>
```

The component class should define the pie chart data with three slices for three Prime libraries over the period of time, as shown here:

```
this.doughnutdata = {
  labels: ['PrimeNG', 'PrimeUI', 'PrimeReact'],
  datasets: [
    {
      data: [3000, 1000, 2000],
      backgroundColor: [
        "#6544a9",
        "#51cc00",
        "#5d4361"
      ],
      hoverBackgroundColor: [
        "#6544a9",
        "#51cc00",
        "#5d4361"
      ]
    }
  ]
};
```

The following screenshot shows a snapshot result of the doughnut chart with PrimeNG, PrimeUI, and PrimeReact downloads over the time period of a year as an example:

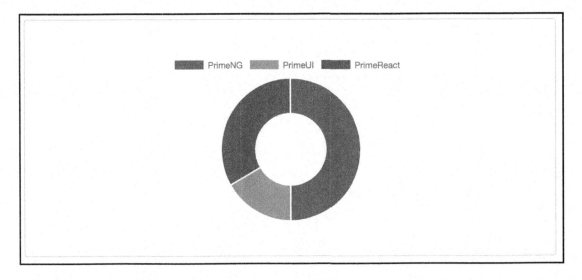

By default, the cutout percentage of the doughnut chart is 50 (where as for pie chart it is 0). This can be customized through the cutoutPercentage chart option.

Data representation with radar and polar area charts

A radar chart is a graphical representation of displaying the multivariant data in the form of a two-dimensional chart. It has at least three or more quantitative variables represented on axes starting from the same point. This chart is also called the **spider chart** or **star chart**. It is useful in measuring performance metrics of any ongoing program to control the quality of improvement.

A basic example of radar chart usage for a PrimeNG and a PrimeReact project's progress would be as follows:

```
<p-chart type="radar" [data]="radardata" width="300" height="100">
</p-chart>
```

The component class should define the radar chart data with two datasets (PrimeNG and PrimeReact) for six phases of an SDLC process as shown here:

```
this.radardata = {
  labels: ['Requirement', 'Design', 'Implementation', 'Testing',
    'Deployment', 'Maintainance'],
  datasets: [
```

```
    {
      label: 'PrimeNG',
      backgroundColor: 'rgba(162,141,158,0.4)',
      borderColor: 'rgba(145,171,188,1)',
      pointBackgroundColor: 'rgba(145,171,188,1)',
      pointBorderColor: '#fff',
      pointHoverBackgroundColor: '#fff',
      pointHoverBorderColor: 'rgba(145,171,188,1)',
      data: [76, 55, 66, 78, 93, 74]
    },
    {
      label: 'PrimeReact',
      backgroundColor: 'rgba(255,99,132,0.2)',
      borderColor: 'rgba(255,99,132,1)',
      pointBackgroundColor: 'rgba(255,99,132,1)',
      pointBorderColor: '#fff',
      pointHoverBackgroundColor: '#fff',
      pointHoverBorderColor: 'rgba(255,99,132,1)',
      data: [30, 43, 38, 17, 89, 33]
    }
  ]
};
```

In the preceding example, the datasets are not only referred to the data components but also provide skinning to the chart using background, border color, and so on. The following screenshot shows a snapshot result of the radar chart with a PrimeNG and a PrimeReact project's progress over six phases of the SDLC life cycle process as an example:

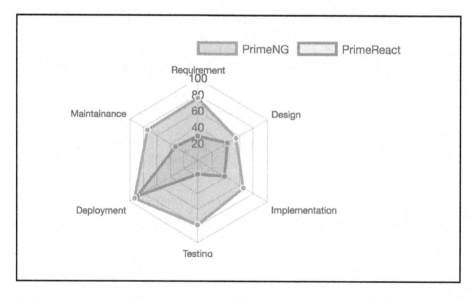

Polar area charts are similar to pie charts, but each segment has the same angle (that is, the radius of the segment differs depending on the value). This type of chart is often useful when we want to show a comparison data just similar to a pie chart. But, you can also show a scale of values for the given context.

A basic example of a polar chart usage for Prime product libraries downloads would be as follows:

```
<p-chart type="polarArea" [data]="polardata" width="300" height="100">
</p-chart>
```

The component class should define polar chart downloads data for various Prime libraries as follows:

```
this.polardata = {
  datasets: [{
    data: [45, 35, 10, 15, 5],
    backgroundColor: ["#6544a9", "#51cc00", "#5d4361", "#E7E9ED",
    "#36A2EB"],
    label: 'Prime Libraries'
  }],
  labels: ["PrimeFaces", "PrimeNG", "PrimeReact", "PrimeUI",
    "PrimeMobile"]
}
```

The component class creates the data options along with skinning properties. The following screenshot shows a snapshot result of the polar chart with PrimeFaces, PrimeNG, PrimeUI, PrimeReact, and PrimeMobile downloads for the time period of a year as an example:

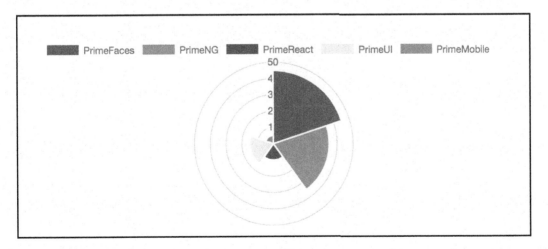

Based on the datasets, `min` and `max` values are provided, and polar chart data segment values will be adjusted (**1, 2, 3, 4, 50**).

 The complete demo application with instructions is available on GitHub at `https://github.com/ova2/angular-development-with-primeng/tree /master/chapter8/charts`.

Drawing an organization chart for the relationship hierarchy

The organization chart is a diagram that visualizes hierarchically organized data. PrimeNG provides a component called `OrganizationChart` to display such top-down relationship hierarchies. The component requires a model of the `TreeNode` instances as its value. The `TreeNode` API was explained in Chapter 5, *Data Iteration Components* in the *Visualizing data with Tree* section. In this section, we will introduce details on the `OrganizationChart` component and develop a chart which illustrates a project in an organization.

Hierarchical data with zero configuration

Drawing a simple chart is easily done--only the `value` attribute is required:

```
<p-organizationChart [value]="data"></p-organizationChart>
```

In the component class, we need to create an array of nested `TreeNode` instances. In the simple use case, providing labels is enough:

```
data: TreeNode[];

ngOnInit() {
  this.data = [
    {
      label: 'CEO',
      expanded: true,
      children: [
        {
          label: 'Finance',
          expanded: true,
          children: [
            {label: 'Chief Accountant'},
            {label: 'Junior Accountant'}
```

```
            ]
          },
          {label: 'Marketing'},
          {
            label: 'Project Manager',
            expanded: true,
            children: [
              {label: 'Architect'},
              {label: 'Frontend Developer'},
              {label: 'Backend Developer'}
            ]
          }
        ]
      }
    ];
  }
```

 By default, tree nodes having children nodes (leafs) are not expanded. To display a tree node as expanded, we can set in the model `expanded: true`. Users can expand and collapse nodes per click on the small arrow icon at the node connection point.

The simple use case is illustrated in the following diagram:

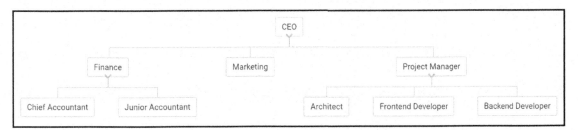

Advanced customization

Customization is enabled by templating with the `ng-template` tag. `TreeNode` has the `type` property, which is used to match the value of the `pTemplate` attribute. This matching allows you to customize the UI for every single node. Nodes without the `type` property match `pTemplate="default"`.

The next code snippet has two `ng-template` tags. The first one matches the nodes with the `type` property `department`. The second one matches the nodes without types. The current node object is exposed via the microsyntax `let-node`:

```html
<p-organizationChart [value]="data" styleClass="company">
  <ng-template let-node pTemplate="department">
    <div class="node-header ui-corner-top">
      {{node.label}}
    </div>
    <div class="node-content ui-corner-bottom">
      <img src="/assets/data/avatar/{{node.data.avatar}}" width="32">
      <div>{{node.data.name}}</div>
    </div>
  </ng-template>
  <ng-template let-node pTemplate="default">
    {{node.label}}
  </ng-template>
</p-organizationChart>
```

We will only show an excerpt of the `data` array to convey the idea.

> The complete demo application with instructions is available on GitHub at
> `https://github.com/ova2/angular-development-with-primeng/tree/master/chapter8/orgchart`.

```javascript
this.data = [
  {
    label: 'CEO',
    expanded: true,
    type: 'department',
    styleClass: 'org-dept',
    data: {id: '1', name: 'Alex Konradi', avatar: 'man.png'},
    children: [
      {
        label: 'Finance',
        expanded: true,
        type: 'department',
        styleClass: 'org-dept',
        data: {id: '2', name: 'Sara Schmidt', avatar: 'women.png'},
        children: [
          {
            label: 'Chief Accountant',
            styleClass: 'org-role'
          },
          {
            label: 'Junior Accountant',
```

```
                    styleClass: 'org-role'
                }
            ]
        },
        ...
    ]
  }
];
```

The customized organization chart looks like the following:

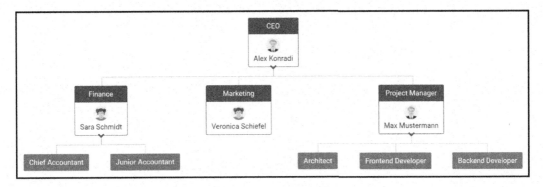

We specified custom style classes to set colors for nodes and togglers. For example:

```
.org-role {
  background-color: #00b60d;
  color: #ffffff;
}

.org-dept .ui-node-toggler {
  color: #bb0066 !important;
}
```

The complete styling settings are available on GitHub.

Selection and events

Selection is enabled by setting `selectionMode` to one of possible values: `single` or `multiple`. In the `single` mode, a single `TreeNode` is expected as the value of the `selection` property. In the `multiple` mode, an array is expected. For example:

```
<p-organizationChart [value]="data"
  selectionMode="single" [(selection)]="selectedNode">
</p-organizationChart>
```

The organization chart supports two events:

Name	Parameters	Description
`onNodeSelect`	• `event.originalEvent`: Browser event • `event.node`: Selected node instance	Callback invoked when a node is selected by a click.
`onNodeUnselect`	• `event.originalEvent`: Browser event • `event.node`: Unselected node instance	Callback invoked when a node is unselected by a click.

Let's extend the previous developed organization chart as shown here:

```
<p-organizationChart [value]="data" styleClass="company"
  selectionMode="single" [(selection)]="selectedNode"
  (onNodeSelect)="onNodeSelect($event)">
  ...
</p-organizationChart>
```

In the demo application on GitHub, we defined a `VCard` interface representing a person's VCard:

```
export interface VCard {
  id: string;
  fullName: string;
  birthday: string;
  address: string;
  email: string;
}
```

All VCard instances are lazily fetched in the `onNodeSelect` callback. After that, a VCard to the clicked person (node) is shown in the PrimeNG dialog:

```
display: boolean = false;
selectedVCard: VCard;
private availableVCards: VCard[];

onNodeSelect(event: any) {
  if (this.availableVCards == null) {
    this.vcardService.getVCards().subscribe(
      (vcards: VCard[]) => {
        this.availableVCards = vcards;
        this.showInfo(event);
      });
  } else {
    this.showInfo(event);
```

```
  }
}

private showInfo(event: any) {
  this.selectedVCard = null;

  this.availableVCards.some((element: VCard) => {
    if (event.node.data && element.id === event.node.data.id) {
      this.selectedVCard = element;
      return true;
    }
  });

  if (this.selectedVCard) {
    // show VCard in dialog
    this.display = true;
  } else {
    // show node label in growl
    this.msgs = [];
    this.msgs.push({severity: 'Label', summary: event.node.label});
  }
}
```

The dialog itself looks like the following:

```
<p-dialog header="VCard" [(visible)]="display"
 modal="modal" width="320" [responsive]="true">
  <i class="fa fa-address-card-o"></i>
  <ul style="padding: 0.2em 0.8em;">
    <li>Full name: {{selectedVCard?.fullName}}</li>
    <li>Birthday: {{selectedVCard?.birthday}}</li>
    <li>Address: {{selectedVCard?.address}}</li>
    <li>E-mail: {{selectedVCard?.email}}</li>
  </ul>
</p-dialog>
```

The result is truly amazing:

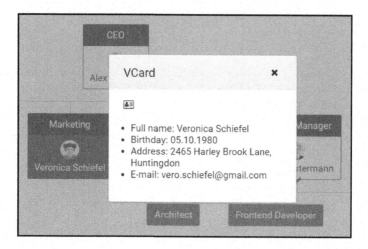

Basic integration with the Google Maps API

The GMap component provides an integration with the Google Maps API in order to use it efficiently with less configuration. It covers major features such as binding options, various overlays, events, and so on. This component requires the Google Maps API, hence it needs to be referred in the `script` section.

The JS resource file needs to be added in a script section, which has to be utilized by the GMap component, as shown here:

```
<script type="text/javascript"
  src="https://maps.google.com/maps/api/js?
  key=AIzaSyA6Ar0UymhiklJBzEPLKKn2QHwbjdz3XV0"></script>
```

A basic example of GMap usage with map options would be as follows:

```
<p-gmap [options]="options" [styleClass]="'dimensions'">
</p-gmap>
```

The option has to be defined with coordinates/positional dimensions (*latitude* and *longitude*), zoom options, and so on during the page load as follows:

```
this.options = {
  center: {lat: 14.4426, lng: 79.9865},
  zoom: 12
};
```

The following screenshot shows a snapshot result of the GMap example:

Snapshot result of the GMap example

As per the preceding snapshot, the exact area location is displayed based on the co-ordinates provided and the mode of visibility through zoom settings.

Various use cases with the GMap component

GMap can be used for various use cases apart from the basic usage of Google Maps. Maps will be more interactive using different kinds of overlays, events on maps, overlays, and so on.

Overlays

Overlays are objects on the map that are bound to latitude/longitude coordinates or dimensions. The array of overlay instances are binding through the `overlays` property. Due to the nature of one-way binding, when there are changes from an array then the map will update automatically.

GMap supports various types of overlays, as shown here:

- **Marker**: Single locations on a map. Markers can also display custom icon images.
- **Polyline**: Series of straight lines on a map.
- **Polygon**: Series of straight lines on a map but the shape is "closed."
- **Circle and rectangle**: Represents a specific region as a circle/rectangle.
- **Info windows**: Displays content within a pop-up balloon on top of a map.

The GMap example usage with overlay options would be written as follows:

```
<p-gmap [options]="options" [overlays]="overlays"
[styleClass]="'dimensions'"></p-gmap>
```

Let's define an array of overlay instances such as markers, polyline, polygon, circle, and so on, as shown here:

```
this.overlays = [
  new google.maps.Marker({position: {lat: 14.6188043,
  lng: 79.9630253}, title:"Talamanchi"}),
  new google.maps.Marker({position: {lat: 14.4290442,
  ng: 79.9456852}, title:"Nellore"}),
  new google.maps.Polygon({paths: [
    {lat: 14.1413809, lng: 79.8254154}, {lat: 11.1513809,
    lng: 78.8354154},
    {lat: 15.1313809, lng: 78.8254154},{lat: 15.1613809,
    lng: 79.8854154}
    ], strokeOpacity: 0.5, strokeWeight: 1,
    fillColor: '#1976D2', fillOpacity: 0.35
  }),
  new google.maps.Circle({center: {lat: 14.1413809, lng: 79.9513809},
  fillColor: '#197642', fillOpacity: 0.25, strokeWeight: 1,
  radius: 25000}), new google.maps.Polyline({path: [{lat: 14.1413809,
  lng: 79.9254154}, {lat: 14.6413809, lng: 79.9254154}],
  geodesic: true, strokeColor: '#F0F000', strokeOpacity: 0.5,
  strokeWeight: 2})
];
```

The following screenshot shows a snapshot result of the GMap with various overlays as an example:

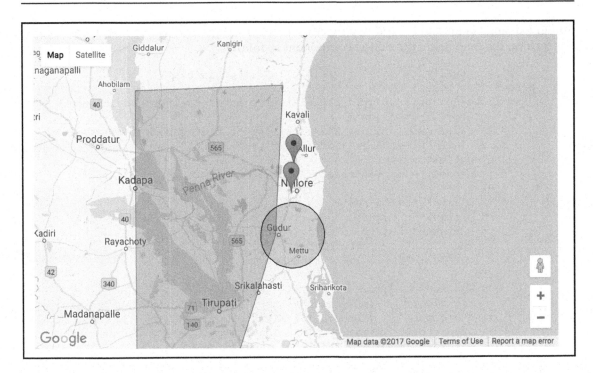

In the preceding map, you can observe that markers, a polygon, and a circle are displayed based on the co-ordinates provided and also based on other overlay-specific configurations.

Events

GMap is more powerful with interactive events on the map. There are many callbacks available to hook into events while clicking on the map, overlay clicking, and dragging the overlay.

The map component example with various types of overlay events along with event callbacks would be written as follows:

```
<p-gmap #gmap [options]="options" [overlays]="overlaysEvents"
  (onMapReady)="handleMapReady($event)"
  (onMapClick)="handleMapClick($event)"
  (onOverlayClick)="handleOverlayClick($event)"
  (onOverlayDragStart)="handleDragStart($event)"
  (onOverlayDragEnd)="handleDragEnd($event)"
  [styleClass]="'dimensions'">
</p-gmap>
```

Either existing events can be updated by clicking the overlays or new events can be created by clicking the map using the dialog component as follows:

```html
<p-dialog showEffect="fade" [(visible)]="dialogVisible"
  header="New Location">
  <div class="ui-grid ui-grid-pad ui-fluid" *ngIf="selectedPosition">
    <div class="ui-grid-row">
      <div class="ui-grid-col-2"><label for="title">Label</label></div>
      <div class="ui-grid-col-10"><input type="text"
        pInputText id="title"
        [(ngModel)]="markerTitle"></div> .
    </div>
    <div class="ui-grid-row">
      <div class="ui-grid-col-2"><label for="lat">Lat</label></div>
      <div class="ui-grid-col-10"><input id="lat"
        type="text" readonly pInputText
        [ngModel]="selectedPosition.lat()"></div>
    </div>
    <div class="ui-grid-row">
      <div class="ui-grid-col-2"><label for="lng">Lng</label></div>
      <div class="ui-grid-col-10"><input id="lng"
        type="text" readonly pInputText
        [ngModel]="selectedPosition.lng()"></div>
    </div>
    <div class="ui-grid-row">
      <div class="ui-grid-col-2"><label for="drg">Drag</label>
      </div>
      <div class="ui-grid-col-10">
        <p-checkbox [(ngModel)]="draggable" binary="true">
        </p-checkbox></div>
    </div>
  </div>
  <p-footer>
    <div class="ui-dialog-buttonpane ui-widget-content
      ui-helper-clearfix">
      <button type="button" pButton label="Add Marker"
        icon="fa-plus" (click)="addMarker()">
      </button>
    </div>
  </p-footer>
</p-dialog>
```

The component class has to define various overlay types on the initial page load, as shown here:

```
if (!this.overlaysEvents || !this.overlaysEvents.length) {
  this.overlaysEvents = [
    new google.maps.Marker({position: {lat: 14.6188043,
    lng: 79.9630253}, title:'Talamanchi'}),
    new google.maps.Marker({position: {lat: 14.4290442,
    lng: 79.9456852}, title:'Nellore'}),
    new google.maps.Polygon({paths: [
      {lat: 14.1413809, lng: 79.8254154},
      {lat: 11.1513809, lng: 78.8354154},
      {lat: 15.1313809, lng: 78.8254154},
      {lat: 15.1613809, lng: 79.8854154}],
      strokeOpacity: 0.5, strokeWeight: 1,
      fillColor: '#1976D2', fillOpacity: 0.35
    }),
    new google.maps.Circle({center: {lat: 14.1413809,
      lng: 79.9513809}, fillColor: '#197642',
      fillOpacity: 0.25, strokeWeight: 1, radius: 25000}),
    new google.maps.Polyline({path: [{lat: 14.1413809,
      lng: 79.9254154}, {lat: 14.6413809, lng: 79.9254154}],
      geodesic: true, strokeColor: '#F0F000',
      strokeOpacity: 0.5, strokeWeight: 2})];
  }
```

The following snapshot shows how the overlay events can be created or updated:

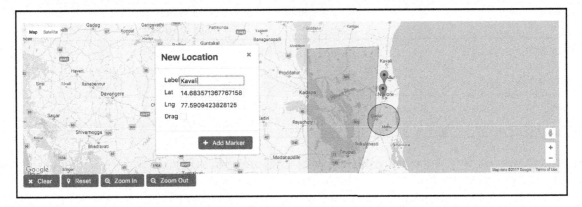

The map component supports the following listed event callbacks:

Name	Parameter	Description
onMapClick	event: Google Maps MouseEvent	When map is clicked except markers.
onOverlayClick	originalEvent: Google Maps MouseEvent overlay: Clicked overlay map: Map instance	When an overlay is clicked.
onOverlayDragStart	originalEvent: Google Maps MouseEvent overlay: Clicked overlay map: Map instance	When an overlay drag starts.
onOverlayDrag	originalEvent: Google Maps MouseEvent overlay: Clicked overlay map: Map instance	When an overlay is being dragged.
onOverlayDragEnd	originalEvent: Google Maps MouseEvent overlay: Clicked overlay map: Map instance	When an overlay drag ends.
onMapReady	event.map: Google Maps instance	When a map is ready after loading.
onMapDragEnd	originalEvent: Google Maps dragend	Callback to invoke when a map drag (that is, pan) has ended.
onZoomChanged	originalEvent: Google Maps zoom_changed	Callback to invoke when a zoom level has changed.

There are two ways of accessing the map API. One of them is the getMap() function of the GMap component (gmap.getMap()) and the other one is accessed through an event object (event.map). Once the map is ready then all map functions can be used based on our requirement. For example, the getZoom() method can be used to increase or decrease from the current state.

The complete demo application with instructions is available on GitHub at `https://github.com/ova2/angular-development-with-primeng/tree /master/chapter8/gmap`.

Summary

By reaching the end of this chapter, you will be able to visualize the data representations with PrimeNG charts and GMap components. Initially, we started with chart components. At first, we started with the chart model API and then learned how to create charts programmatically using various chart types such as pie, bar, line, doughnut, polar, and radar charts. We have seen that an organization chart fits perfectly the visualization of the relationship hierarchy.

Next, we moved to the Google Maps-based GMap component. The GMap component provides a convenient API for interactions with the Google Maps API, including drawing markers, polygons, circles, register events, and so on. In the next chapter, we will look at miscellaneous use cases and the best practices needed to be followed.

9
Miscellaneous Use Cases and Best Practices

Miscellaneous use cases and best practices introduce more interesting features of the PrimeNG library. You will learn about file uploading, drag-and-drop capabilities, displaying collection of images, practical CRUD implementation, deferred page loading, blocking page pieces, displaying confirmation dialog with guarded routes, and more. Despite a comprehensive set of components, users sometime have special requirements for existing components regarding their functionality or need new, custom components.

The purpose of this chapter is also exclusively to facilitate the start of component development on top of the PrimeNG infrastructure. We will go through the complete process of building reusable components and develop a custom wizard component. The wizard can be used for workflows, which involve multiple steps to complete a task. Furthermore, after reading this chapter, readers will be aware of the state-of-the-art state management in Angular applications.

In this chapter, we will cover the following topics:

- File uploading in all its glory
- Learning draggable and droppable directives
- Displaying collection of images with Galleria
- CRUD sample implementation with DataTable
- Deferring mechanism to optimize page loading
- Blocking page pieces during long-running AJAX calls
- Process status indicator in action
- Selecting colors with ColorPicker
- Displaying confirmation dialog with guarded routes

- Implementing custom wizard component with Steps
- Introduction to state management with @ngrx/store

File uploading in all its glory

The FileUpload component provides a file upload mechanism with enhanced features compared to the basic HTML `<input type="file">` file upload definition. The component provides an HTML5-powered UI with capabilities such as drag and drop, uploading multiple files, progress tracking, validations, and more.

File uploading component works in all modern browsers as well as IE 10 and higher.

Basic, multiple, and automatic file uploading

Two properties are required in order to be able to work with the file upload--the name of the request parameter to identify the uploaded files at backend and the remote URL to upload files. For example:

```
<p-fileUpload name="demofiles[]" url="http://demoserver.com/upload">
</p-fileUpload>
```

The component presents itself as a panel with three buttons: **Choose**, **Upload**, **Cancel**, and a content section with selected files. The **Choose** button displays a file dialog to select one or multiple files. Once selected, the files can be uploaded or canceled by the next two buttons, respectively. Filename and size are always shown by default. In addition, for images, you will see a preview as well:

The width of the previewed image can be adjusted with the `previewWidth` **attribute**.

File upload also provides a simpler UI with just one button **Choose** and without the content section. You can activate this UI by setting the `mode` attribute to `"basic"`:

```
<p-fileUpload mode="basic" name="demofiles[]"
              url="http://demoserver.com/upload">
</p-fileUpload>
```

By default, the only one file can be selected from the file dialog. Setting the `multiple` option to `true` allows selecting multiples files at once. Setting the `auto` option to `true` starts the uploading immediately without the need to press any buttons. The buttons **Upload** and **Cancel** buttons are hidden in the auto uploading mode:

```
<p-fileUpload name="demofiles[]" url="http://demoserver.com/upload"
              [multiple]="true" [auto]="true">
</p-fileUpload>
```

File selection can also be done by dragging one or more files from the filesystem and dropping them onto the content section of the FileUpload component.

At the time of writing, the backend for the FileUpload component cannot be mocked with Angular's mock API. In the demo application on GitHub, we use a simple local server `json-server` (https://github.com/typicode/json-server) to fake the backend. Otherwise, you will face exceptions. After installation, the server can be started as using the following command:

```
json-server db.json --port 3004
```

```
> json-server db.json --port 3004

\[ ^ ]/ hi!

Loading db.json
Done

Resources
http://localhost:3004/fake-backend

Home
http://localhost:3004

Type s + enter at any time to create a snapshot of the database
```

The db.json file in the project root only has a definition of endpoint:

```
{
  "fake-backend": {}
}
```

Now, you are able to use the faked remote URL without getting any exceptions:

```
<p-fileUpload name="demofiles[]" url="http://localhost:3004/
           fake-backend">
</p-fileUpload>
```

 The complete demo application with instructions is available on GitHub at https://github.com/ova2/angular-development-with-primeng/tree/master/chapter9/fileupload.

Restrictions by file types and size

By default, any file types can be uploaded. The file size is not limited either. You can restrict file types and size by setting the accept and maxFileSize options, respectively:

```
<p-fileUpload name="demofiles[]" url="http://localhost:3004/
           fake-backend" multiple="true" accept="image/*"
           maxFileSize="50000">
</p-fileUpload>
```

In the example, only images with the maximum size 50000 bytes may be uploaded. Violation of those rules causes validation messages to appear in the content section.

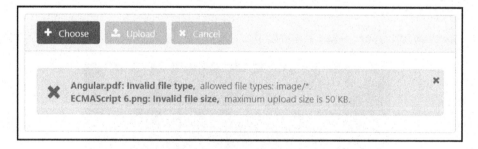

Possible values of the `accept` property:

Value	Description
`<file extension>`	A file extension starting with dot, for example, `.gif`, `.png`, `.doc` and so many.
`audio/*`	All sound files.
`video/*`	All video files.
`image/*`	All image files.
`<media type>`	A valid media type according to IANA Media Types (`http://www.ian a.org/assignments/media-types/media-types.xhtml`). For example, `application/pdf`.

To specify more than one value, separate the values with a comma, for example, `accept="audio/*,video/*,image/*"`.

Customizations

Validation messages can be customized using the following four options:

Property name	Description	Default value
`invalidFileSizeMessageSummary`	Summary message of the invalid file size. The placeholder `{0}` refers to the file name.	`{0}: Invalid file size,`
`invalidFileSizeMessageDetail`	Detail message of the invalid file size. The placeholder `{0}` refers to the file size.	`maximum upload size is {0}.`
`invalidFileTypeMessageSummary`	Summary message of the invalid file type. The placeholder `{0}` refers to the file type.	`{0}: Invalid file type,`
`invalidFileTypeMessageDetail`	Detail message of the invalid file type. The placeholder `{0}` refers to the allowed file types.	`allowed file types: {0}`

The next code snippet and screenshot demonstrate custom messages. They also show how you can set custom labels for buttons:

```
<p-fileUpload name="demofiles[]" url="http://localhost:3004/
              fake-backend"
              multiple="true" accept="image/*" maxFileSize="50000"
              invalidFileSizeMessageSummary="{0} has wrong size, "
              invalidFileSizeMessageDetail="it exceeds {0}."
              invalidFileTypeMessageSummary="{0} has wrong file type, "
              invalidFileTypeMessageDetail="it doesn't match: {0}."
              chooseLabel="Select file"
              uploadLabel="Upload it!"
              cancelLabel="Abort">
</p-fileUpload>
```

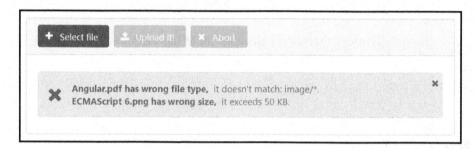

The UI is fully customizable by three named `ng-template` tags. You can customize the toolbar, the content section, and the area with selected files. The next code snippet shows a fully customizable UI:

```
<p- name="demofiles[]" url="http://localhost:3004/fake-backend"
    multiple="true" accept=".pdf" maxFileSize="1000000">
  <ng-template pTemplate="toolbar">
    <div style="font-size: 0.9em; margin-top: 0.5em;">
      Please select your PDF documents
    </div>
  </ng-template>
  <ng-template let-file pTemplate="file">
    <div style="margin: 0.5em 0 0.5em 0;">
      <i class="fa fa-file-pdf-o" aria-hidden="true"></i>
      {{file.name}}
    </div>
  </ng-template>
  <ng-template pTemplate="content">
    <i class="fa fa-cloud-upload" aria-hidden="true"></i>
    Drag and drop files onto this area
  </ng-template>
</p-fileUpload>
```

The screenshot shows the initial UI state when no file was selected:

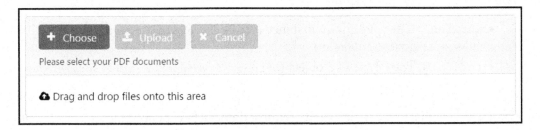

After selection from the file dialog, the UI looks like the following:

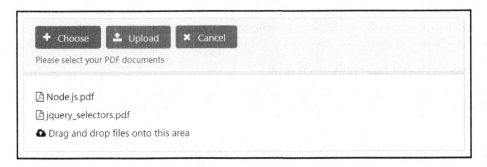

Note that only PDF files may be selected. The `ng-template` with `pTemplate="file` gets the `File` instance as an implicit variable. This instance has a property `name`, which we leverage in our custom UI.

 Refer to the official documentation to read more about `File` at `https://d eveloper.mozilla.org/en-US/docs/Web/API/File`.

The next level of customization is callback events, which are fired at a certain point of time. There are `onBeforeUpload`, `onBeforeSend`, `onUpload`, `onError`, `onClear`, `onSelect`, and `uploadHandler` events. The next code snippet demonstrates two of them:

```
<p-fileUpload name="demofiles[]" url="http://localhost:3004/
            fake-backend" accept="image/*" maxFileSize="1000000"
            (onBeforeSend)="onBeforeSend($event)"
            (onUpload)="onUpload($event)">
</p-fileUpload>
```

The `onBeforeUpload` event is fired shortly before uploading. The registered callback gets an event object with two parameters:

- `xhr`: The `XMLHttpRequest` instance (https://developer.mozilla.org/en/docs/Web/API/XMLHttpRequest).
- `formData`: The `FormData` object (https://developer.mozilla.org/en/docs/Web/API/FormData).

We can use this callback to customize the request data such as post parameters or header information. For example, we could set a token `jwt` to send it to the server. Just write the following callback method in the component class:

```
onBeforeSend(event: any) {
  (<XMLHttpRequest>event.xhr).setRequestHeader('jwt', 'xyz123');
}
```

As you see, the token has really been sent:

```
✕  Headers  Preview  Response  Timing

      Location: http://localhost:3004/fake-backend
      Pragma: no-cache
      Vary: Origin, X-HTTP-Method-Override, Accept-Encoding
      X-Content-Type-Options: nosniff
      X-Powered-By: Express
  ▼ Request Headers       view source
      Accept: */*
      Accept-Encoding: gzip, deflate, br
      Accept-Language: de-DE,de;q=0.8,en-US;q=0.6,en;q=0.4,ru;q=0.2
      Connection: keep-alive
      Content-Length: 406692
      Content-Type: multipart/form-data; boundary=----WebKitFormBoundaryvoicscK4BrXDO62o
      Host: localhost:3004
      jwt: xyz123
      Origin: http://localhost:3000
```

The onUpload event is triggered when all selected files have finished uploading. They passed event object has the mentioned XMLHttpRequest instance and an array of objects of type File. We can iterate over files and gather them together for further processing:

```
uploadMsgs: Message[] = [];
uploadedFiles: any[] = [];

onUpload(event: any) {
  for (let file of event.files) {
    this.uploadedFiles.push(file);
  }

  // produce a message for growl notification
  this.uploadMsgs = [];
  this.uploadMsgs.push({severity: 'info',
    summary: 'File Uploaded', detail: ''});
}
```

It is possible to provide a custom uploading implementation by setting customUpload="true" and defining a custom upload handler. An example:

```
<p-fileUpload name="demofiles[]" customUpload="true"
              (uploadHandler)="smartUploader($event)">
</p-fileUpload>
```

It is up to you how to implement the smartUploader callback. The callback has an access to the event.files, which is an array of objects of type File.

Learning draggable and droppable directives

Drag and drop is an action, which means grabbing an object to a different location. The components capable of being dragged and dropped enrich the web and make a solid base for modern UI patterns. The drag-and-drop utilities in PrimeNG allow us to create draggable and droppable user interfaces efficiently. They make it abstract for the developers to deal with the implementation details at the browser level.

In this section, you will learn about the `pDraggable` and `pDroppable` directives. We will introduce a DataGrid component containing some imaginary documents and make these documents draggable in order to drop them onto a recycle bin. The recycle bin is implemented as a DataTable component, which shows properties of dropped documents. For the purpose of better understanding the developed code, a picture comes first:

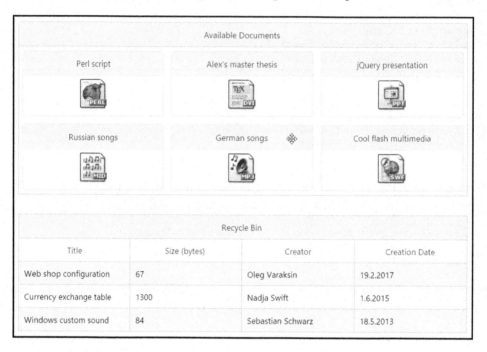

This picture shows what happens after dragging and dropping three documents.

The complete demo application with instructions is available on GitHub at `https://github.com/ova2/angular-development-with-primeng/tree /master/chapter9/dragdrop`.

Draggable

`pDraggable` is attached to an element to add a drag behavior. The value of the `pDraggable` attribute is required--it defines the scope to match draggables with droppables. By default, the whole element is draggable. We can restrict the draggable area by applying the `dragHandle` attribute. The value of `dragHandle` can be any CSS selector. In DataGrid, with available documents, we only made the panel's header draggable:

```
<p-dataGrid [value]="availableDocs">
  <p-header>
    Available Documents
  </p-header>
  <ng-template let-doc pTemplate="item">
    <div class="ui-g-12 ui-md-4" pDraggable="docs"
      dragHandle=".ui-panel-titlebar" dragEffect="move"
      (onDragStart)="dragStart($event, doc)"
        (onDragEnd)="dragEnd($event)">
      <p-panel [header]="doc.title" [style]="{'text-align':'center'}">
        <img src="/assets/data/images/docs/{{doc.extension}}.png">
      </p-panel>
    </div>
  </ng-template>
</p-dataGrid>
```

The draggable element can fire three events when the dragging process begins, proceeds, and ends. These are onDragStart, onDrag, and onDragEnd, respectively. In the component class, we buffer the dragged document at the beginning and reset it at the end of the dragging process. This task is done in two callbacks: dragStart and dragEnd:

```
class DragDropComponent {
  availableDocs: Document[];
  deletedDocs: Document[];
  draggedDoc: Document;

  constructor(private docService: DocumentService) { }

  ngOnInit() {
    this.deletedDocs = [];
    this.docService.getDocuments().subscribe((docs: Document[]) =>
      this.availableDocs = docs);
  }

  dragStart(event: any, doc: Document) {
    this.draggedDoc = doc;
  }

  dragEnd(event: any) {
    this.draggedDoc = null;
  }

  ...
}
```

In the shown code, we used the `Document` interface with the following properties:

```
interface Document {
    id: string;
    title: string;
    size: number;
    creator: string;
    creationDate: Date;
    extension: string;
}
```

In the demo application, we set the cursor to `move` when the mouse is moved over any panel's header. This trick provides a better visual feedback for the draggable area:

```
body .ui-panel .ui-panel-titlebar {
    cursor: move;
}
```

We can also set the `dragEffect` attribute to specify the effect that is allowed for a drag operation. Possible values are `none`, `copy`, `move`, `link`, `copyMove`, `copyLink`, `linkMove`, and `all`. Refer to the official documentation to read more details at `https://developer.mozilla.org/en-US/docs/Web/API/DataTransfer/effectAllowed`.

Droppable

`pDroppable` is attached to an element to add a drop behavior. The value of the `pDroppable` attribute should have the same scope as `pDraggable`.

 Droppable scope can also be an array to accept multiple droppables.

The droppable element can fire four events:

Event name	Description
onDragEnter	Invoked when a draggable element enters the drop area.
onDragOver	Invoked when a draggable element is being dragged over the drop area.
onDrop	Invoked when a draggable is dropped onto the drop area.
onDragLeave	Invoked when a draggable element leaves the drop area.

In the demo application, the whole code of the droppable area looks as follows:

```
<div pDroppable="docs" (onDrop)="drop($event)"
    [ngClass]="{'dragged-doc': draggedDoc}">
  <p-dataTable [value]="deletedDocs">
    <p-header>Recycle Bin</p-header>
    <p-column field="title" header="Title"></p-column>
    <p-column field="size" header="Size (bytes)"></p-column>
    <p-column field="creator" header="Creator"></p-column>
    <p-column field="creationDate" header="Creation Date">
      <ng-template let-col let-doc="rowData" pTemplate="body">
        {{doc[col.field].toLocaleDateString()}}
      </ng-template>
    </p-column>
  </p-dataTable>
</div>
```

Whenever a document is dragged and dropped into the recycle bin, the dropped document is removed from the list of all available documents and added to the list of deleted documents. This happens in the `onDrop` callback:

```
drop(event: any) {
  if (this.draggedDoc) {
    // add draggable element to the deleted documents list
    this.deletedDocs = [...this.deletedDocs, this.draggedDoc];
    // remove draggable element from the available documents list
    this.availableDocs = this.availableDocs.filter(
      (e: Document) => e.id !== this.draggedDoc.id);
    this.draggedDoc = null;
  }
}
```

 Both available and deleted documents are updated by creating new arrays instead of manipulating existing arrays. This is necessary in data iteration components to force Angular run change detection. Manipulating existing arrays would not run change detection and the UI would not be updated.

The **Recycle Bin** area gets a red border while dragging any panel with document. We achieved this highlighting by setting `ngClass` as `[ngClass]="{'dragged-doc':` `draggedDoc}"`. The style class `dragged-doc` is enabled when the `draggedDoc` object is set. The style class is defined as follows:

```
.dragged-doc {
  border: solid 2px red;
}
```

Displaying a collection of images with Galleria

The Galleria component can be used to display a collection of images with a transition effect.

Get it up and running

A collection of images is created programmatically--it is an array of objects with the following three attributes:

- source: The path of the image
- title: The title text in the caption section
- alt: A description in the caption section below the title

Let's create a GalleriaComponent class:

```
class GalleriaComponent {
  images: any[];

  ngOnInit() {
    this.images = [];

    this.images.push({
      source: '/assets/data/images/cars/Yeni.png',
      alt: 'This is a first car',
      title: 'Yeni Vollkswagen CC'
    });
    this.images.push({
      source: '/assets/data/images/cars/Golf.png',
      alt: 'This is a second car',
      title: 'Golf'
    });

    ... // more image definitions
  }
}
```

In the HTML code, the collection is referenced via the input property `images`:

```
<p-galleria [images]="images" panelWidth="400" panelHeight="320"
            [autoPlay]="false" [showCaption]="true">
</p-galleria>
```

The developed UI looks as follows:

The width and height of the content panel can be customized with the `panelWidth` and `panelHeight` attributes. The `showCaption` attribute enables displaying titles and descriptions in the caption section.

At the bottom, there is an area with small images called **filmstrip**. The visibility of the filmstrip is enabled by default with the `showFilmstrip` attribute. You can disable it by setting the attribute to `false`. The width and height of the frames visualized in the filmstrip can be customized with the `frameWidth` and `frameHeight` attributes, respectively. All values should be provided in pixels.

There is also the `activeIndex` attribute, which can be used to set the position of the displayed image. For example, if you want to display the second image on the initial page load, you can set `activeIndex="1"`. The default value is `0`.

Auto play mode and effects

The auto play mode turns a slideshow on. The auto play mode is enabled by default. In the example, we disabled the slideshow by setting `[autoPlay]="false"`. The transition between images in the auto play mode happens within 4000 milliseconds. This time interval can be customized with the `transitionInterval` attribute.

While iterating through the images, it is possible to apply transition effects. The `effect` attribute can have the values `blind`, `bounce`, `clip`, `drop`, `explode`, `fade` (the default), `fold`, `highlight`, `puff`, `pulsate`, `scale`, `shake`, `size`, `slide`, and `transfer`. The `effectDuration` attribute can also be used to decide on the duration of the transition. Its default value is 250 milliseconds:

```
<p-galleria [images]="images" panelWidth="400" panelHeight="320"
            effect="bounce" [effectDuration]="150">
</p-galleria>
```

Events

There is only one event `onImageClicked`, which is fired when a displayed image is clicked on:

```
<p-galleria [images]="images" panelWidth="400" panelHeight="220"
            [autoPlay]="false" [showCaption]="true"
            (onImageClicked)="onImageClicked($event)">
</p-galleria>
```

The invoked callback gets an event object. Beside index of the clicked image and the native click event, the passed in event object keeps the entire image instance from the collection. We could access the source URL in the callback and open the image in a new browser tab:

```
onImageClicked($event: any) {
  window.open($event.image.source, '_blank');
}
```

 The complete demo application with instructions is available on GitHub at https://github.com/ova2/angular-development-with-primeng/tree /master/chapter9/galleria.

CRUD sample implementation with DataTable

PrimeNG was created for enterprise applications. Implementing a **CRUD** (**create, read, update**, and **delete**) scenario is easily done. The example in this section demonstrates such a scenario with employees that are taken as domain model objects. Employees can be fetched, created, updated, and deleted. All CRUD operations happens via Angular's HTTP service, which communicates with a mock backend. We will improve our CRUD implementation later on in the section *Introduction to state management with @ngrx/store*.

The domain model object `Employee` is defined using the following interface:

```
export interface Employee {
    id: string;
    firstName: string;
    lastName: string;
    profession: string;
    department: string;
}
```

The mock backend is not shown here because it is beyond the scope of this book.

The complete demo application with instructions is available on GitHub at `https://github.com/ova2/angular-development-with-primeng/tree /master/chapter9/crud-datatable`.

The `EmployeeService` class with CRUD operations is worth to be listed here. It exposes four methods with `Observable` as return value so that the component class can invoke `subscribe()` to receive delivered data:

```
@Injectable()
export class EmployeeService {
    private static handleError(error: Response | any) {
        // error handling is done as recommended
        //in the official Angular documentation
        // https://angular.io/docs/ts/latest/guide/server-
        //communication.html#!#always-handle-errors
        ...
    }

    constructor(private http: Http) { }

    getEmployees(): Observable<Employee[]> {
        return this.http.get('/fake-backend/employees')
```

```
        .map(response => response.json() as Employee[])
        .catch(EmployeeService.handleError);
    }

    createEmployee(employee: Employee): Observable<Employee> {
      return this.http.post('/fake-backend/employees', employee)
        .map(response => response.json() as Employee)
        .catch(EmployeeService.handleError);
    }

    updateEmployee(employee: Employee): Observable<any> {
      return this.http.put('/fake-backend/employees', employee)
        .map(response => response.json())
        .catch(EmployeeService.handleError);
    }

    deleteEmployee(id: string): Observable<any> {
      return this.http.delete('/fake-backend/employees/' + id)
        .map(response => response.json())
        .catch(EmployeeService.handleError);
    }
  }
```

Employees are presented in DataTable when they are fetched from the backend:

First Name ⬍	Last Name ⬍	Profession ⬍	Department ⬍
Max	Mustermann	Junior Developer	IT
Sara	Smidth	Sofware Engineer	IT
Alexander	Konradi	Architect	IT
Jasper	Morgan	Project Manager	IT
Olga	Singen	Accountant	HR
James	Bond	Director	HR
Steve	Stevenson	Software Tester	QA
Thorsten	Koch	Business Analyst	BA

✚ Add ✎ Edit 🗑 Remove

As you can see, only the **Add** button is enabled when no employee is selected. The **Add** and **Edit** buttons trigger displaying a dialog box for employee's personal data. The **Save** button creates a new or updates an existing employee depending on what you have chosen before--the **Add** or the **Edit** button.

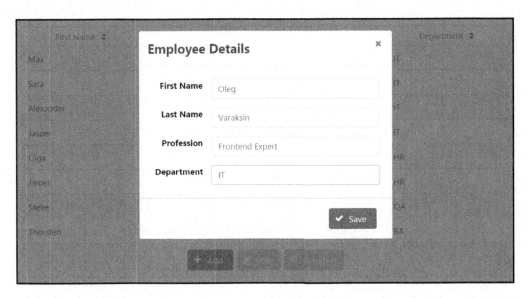

Operations triggered by buttons fade in appropriate messages:

The table is implemented with `p-dataTable` as shown here:

```
<p-dataTable [value]="employees" selectionMode="single"
             [(selection)]="selectedEmployee"
             [paginator]="true" rows="15"
             [responsive]="true"
             [alwaysShowPaginator]="false">
  <p-column field="firstName" header="First Name" [sortable]="true">
  </p-column>
  <p-column field="lastName" header="Last Name" [sortable]="true">
  </p-column>
  <p-column field="profession" header="Profession" [sortable]="true">
  </p-column>
  <p-column field="department" header="Department" [sortable]="true">
  </p-column>
  <p-footer>
    <button pButton type="button" label="Add" icon="fa-plus"
      (click)="add()"> </button>
    <button pButton type="button" label="Edit" icon="fa-pencil"
      (click)="edit()" [disabled]="!selectedEmployee"></button>
    <button pButton type="button" label="Remove" icon="fa-trash-o"
      (click)="remove()" [disabled]="!selectedEmployee"></button>
  </p-footer>
</p-dataTable>
```

The value of `p-dataTable` is bound to the array property `employees`. An employee can be selected by the click of a row and gets saved in the `selectedEmployee` property. The buttons **Edit** and **Remove** are disabled when `selectedEmployee` is not set. We will skip the code of the dialog for the sake of brevity. The most interesting part is the component class. The employees are fetched by means of `EmployeeService` in the `ngOnInit()` lifecycle callback:

```
export class DataTableCrudComponent implements OnInit,
  OnDestroy {
  employees: Employee[];
  selectedEmployee: Employee;
  employeeForDialog: Employee;
  displayDialog: boolean;
  msgs: Message[] = [];

  get$: Subscription;
  add$: Subscription;
  edit$: Subscription;
  delete$: Subscription;

  constructor(private employeeService: EmployeeService) { }
```

```
ngOnInit(): void {
  this.get$ = this.employeeService.getEmployees().subscribe(
    employees => this.employees = employees,
    error => this.showError(error)
  );
}

ngOnDestroy() {
  this.get$.unsubscribe();
  this.add$.unsubscribe();
  this.edit$.unsubscribe();
  this.delete$.unsubscribe();
}

...

private showError(errMsg: string) {
  this.msgs = [];
  this.msgs.push({severity: 'error',
                 summary: 'Sorry, an error occurred',
                 detail: errMsg});
}

private showSuccess(successMsg: string) {
  this.msgs = [];
  this.msgs.push({severity: 'success', detail: successMsg});
}
}
```

Let's explore other CRUD methods in details. The `add()` method constructs an empty employee instance and the `edit()` method clones the selected employee. Both are used in the dialog. The property `displayDialog` is set to `true` to force displaying the dialog.

This property is bound in the view to dialog's visibility as follows `[(visible)]="displayDialog"`.

```
add() {
  // create an empty employee
  this.employeeForDialog = {
    id: null, firstName: null, lastName: null, profession: null,
    department: null
  };
  this.displayDialog = true;
}
```

```
edit() {
  // create a clone of the selected employee
  this.employeeForDialog = Object.assign({}, this.selectedEmployee);
  this.displayDialog = true;
}
```

The **Save** button in the dialog invokes the `save()` method where we check if the employee exists with the help of `id`. Only employees that have been saved before contain `id` because `id` is assigned in the backend. An existing employee should be updated and the new one should be created:

```
save() {
  if (this.employeeForDialog.id) {
    // update
    this.edit$ =
      this.employeeService.updateEmployee(this.employeeForDialog)
      .finally(() => {
        this.employeeForDialog = null;
        this.displayDialog = false;
      })
      .subscribe(() => {
          this.employees.some((element: Employee, index: number) => {
            if (element.id === this.employeeForDialog.id) {
              this.employees[index] = Object.assign({},
              this.employeeForDialog);
              this.employees = [...this.employees];
              this.selectedEmployee = this.employees[index];
              return true;
            }
          });
          this.showSuccess('Employee was successfully updated');
        },
        error => this.showError(error)
      );
  } else {
    // create
    this.add$ =
      this.employeeService.createEmployee(this.employeeForDialog)
      .finally(() => {
        this.employeeForDialog = null;
        this.selectedEmployee = null;
        this.displayDialog = false;
      })
      .subscribe((employee: Employee) => {
          this.employees = [...this.employees, employee];
          this.showSuccess('Employee was successfully created');
        },
        error => this.showError(error)
```

```
        );
    }
}
```

The employee will be updated or created in the backend and the `employees` array:

As you can see, a new instance of the `employees` array is created instead of manipulating the existing one. This is necessary in data iteration components to force Angular run change detection. Manipulating elements in the existing array don't update the array's reference. As a result, the change detection would not run and the UI would not be updated.

Note that `Observable` provides a `finally` method where we can reset values of properties.

The function passed in to the `finally` method as a parameter is invoked after the source observable sequence terminates gracefully or exceptionally.

The `remove()` method gets invoked by the **Remove** button:

```
remove() {
  this.delete$ =
  this.employeeService.deleteEmployee(this.selectedEmployee.id)
    .finally(() => {
      this.employeeForDialog = null;
      this.selectedEmployee = null;
    })
    .subscribe(() => {
        this.employees = this.employees.filter(
          (element: Employee) => element.id !==
          this.selectedEmployee.id);
        this.showSuccess('Employee was successfully removed');
      },
      error => this.showError(error)
    );
}
```

The sequence logic is similar to the other CRUD operations.

Deferring mechanism to optimize page loading

Large-scale applications always need best practices to improve the page loading time. It is not advisable to wait for the landing page to display until all contents in the page have been fully loaded. PrimeNG provided a defer directive which postpones the content loading until the component appears in the view port. The content will be lazily loaded when it becomes visible by the page scroll.

The pDefer directive is applied to a container element and the content needs to be wrapped with ng-template directive as follows:

```
<div pDefer (onLoad)="loadData()">
  <ng-template>
    deferred content
  </ng-template>
</div>
```

The defer directive is very helpful to lazily load huge datasets when you use data iteration components such as p-dataTable, p-dataList, p-dataGrid, and so on. The onLoad callback is used to query data from the data source on demand when the component becomes visible through page scrolling. The query is not initiated on page load so that the page is loaded quickly. A concrete example is implemented here:

```
<div pDefer (onLoad)="loadData()">
  <ng-template>
    <p-dataTable [value]="employees">
      <p-column field="firstName" header="First Name"></p-column>
      <p-column field="lastName" header="Last Name"></p-column>
      <p-column field="profession" header="Profession"></p-column>
      <p-column field="department" header="Department"></p-column>
    </p-dataTable>
  </ng-template>
</div>
```

The loadData() method fetches the employees:

```
loadData(): void {
  this.employeeService.getEmployees().subscribe(
    employees => this.employees = employees,
    error => this.showError(error)
  );
}
```

Blocking page pieces during long-running AJAX calls

The BlockUI component allows us to block any piece of a page, for example, during AJAX calls. The BlockUI component adds a layer over the target element and gives the appearance and behavior of blocking user interaction. It is very handy if you have, for example, a large DataTable component and CRUD operations take much time. You can block almost everything--even the whole page. In this section, we will demonstrate how to deal with BlockUI.

The BlockUI component blocks a blockable *target* component. The `target` property points to a template reference variable of such target component. The visibility of BlockUI is controlled by the Boolean property `blocked`. For instance, the following BlockUI blocks the Panel component when the property `blocked` is set to `true` and unblocks it otherwise:

```
<p-blockUI [blocked]="blocked" [target]="pnl">
  // any custom content or empty
</p-blockUI>

<p-panel #pnl header="Panel Header">
  Content of Panel
</p-panel>
```

The default value of `target` is the `document` object. That means, if no `target` is provided, the whole page is blocked. As you can also see, it is possible to place any custom content within the `p-blockUI` tag. The custom content gets displayed on a semi-transparent layer.

We will leverage the CRUD example from the previous section to demonstrate the BlockUI component in action. For the sake of brevity, only two buttons will be available--a **Reload** button, which performs data fetching, and a **Remove** button.

Let's specify the blocking as--the **Reload** button should block the whole page and the **Remove** button should only block the table. Furthermore, we want to display a loading indicator and the text **Loading...** as shown in the picture:

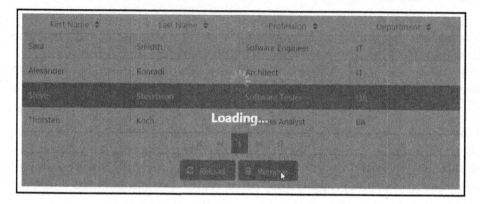

These acceptance criteria results in two BlockUI components:

```
<p-dataTable ... #dtable>
  ...
</p-dataTable>

<p-blockUI [blocked]="blockedTable" [target]="dtable">
  <div class="center">
    <div class="box">
      <div class="content">
        <img src="/assets/data/images/loader.svg"/>
        <h1>Loading...</h1>
      </div>
    </div>
  </div>
</p-blockUI>

<p-blockUI [blocked]="blockedPage">
  <div class="center">
    <div class="box">
      <div class="content">
        <img src="/assets/data/images/loader.svg"/>
        <h1>Loading...</h1>
      </div>
    </div>
  </div>
</p-blockUI>
```

The properties `blockedTable` and `blockedPage` are set to `true` immediately on button clicks. After CRUD operations are done, the properties are set to `false`. This approach is outlined in the next code block:

```
export class DataTableCrudComponent {
  ...
  selectedEmployee: Employee;
  blockedTable: boolean;
  blockedPage: boolean;

  reload() {
    this.blockedPage = true;
    this.employeeService.getEmployees()
      .finally(() => {this.blockedPage = false;})
      .subscribe(...);
  }

  remove() {
    this.blockedTable = true;
    this.employeeService.deleteEmployee(this.selectedEmployee.id)
      .finally(() => {this.blockedTable = false;
        this.selectedEmployee = null;})
      .subscribe(...);
  }
}
```

The semi-transparent layer over blocked components can be customized as follows:

`.ui-blockui.ui-widget-overlay {opacity: 0.5;}`

The complete demo application with instructions is available on GitHub at `https://github.com/ova2/angular-development-with-primeng/tree /master/chapter9/blockui`.

Process status indicator in action

The ProgressBar component indicates a status of some process, task, or whatever. It can deal with static as well as dynamic values. A dynamic value is a value changing in time. The next code snippet demonstrates two progress bars, with a static and dynamic value:

```
<p-growl [value]="msgs"></p-growl>

<h3>Static value</h3>
<p-progressBar [value]="40"></p-progressBar>

<h3>Dynamic value</h3>
<p-progressBar [value]="value"></p-progressBar>
```

The dynamic value gets produced every 800 milliseconds from 1 to 100 with the Observable methods as follows:

```
export class ProgressBarComponent implements OnInit, OnDestroy {
  msgs: Message[];
  value: number;
  interval$: Subscription;

  ngOnInit() {
    const interval = Observable.interval(800).take(100);
    this.interval$ = interval.subscribe(
      x => this.value = x + 1,
      () => {/** no error handling */ },
      () => this.msgs = [{severity: 'info', summary: 'Success',
        detail: 'Process completed'}]
    );
  }

  ngOnDestroy() {
    this.interval$.unsubscribe();
  }
}
```

At the end, a growl message with the text **Process completed** will be displayed. A snapshot picture is shown here:

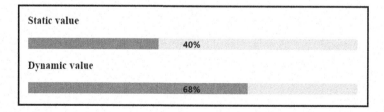

The complete demo application with instructions is available on GitHub at
`https://github.com/ova2/angular-development-with-primeng/tree`
`/master/chapter9/progressbar`.

Selecting colors with ColorPicker

ColorPicker is a graphical user interface input widget used to select colors from a two-dimensional square box. The component uses the `ngModel` directive for two-way value binding. Basically, it supports three kinds of color formats such as hex, RGB, and HSB with a hex default type. The color format is denoted with the `format` attribute, for example, as `format="rgb"`. ColorPicker is an editable component and can be used in model-driven forms as well. A basic example would be as follows:

```
<p-colorPicker [(ngModel)]="color1"></p-colorPicker>
```

The component has to define the `string` type color property for default hex values, whereas the color property should be object type for RGB and HSB formats as shown here:

```
color1: string;
color2: any = {r: 100, g: 120, b: 140};
color3: any = {h: 80, s: 50, b: 40};
```

The color picker will display the selected color as follows:

By default, the color picker is displayed in overlay format, but this default behavior can be changed using the `inline` property, which allows a inline format by enabling the inline setting. The color picker component in the inline format would be written as follows:

```
<p-colorPicker [(ngModel)]="color3" inline="true"
    (onChange)="change($event)"></p-colorPicker>
```

This component also supports the `onChange` callback with an `event` object as argument. The `event` object holds the browser event and the selected color value to notify the changes as follows:

```
change(event){
    this.msgs = [];
    this.msgs.push({severity: 'success',
        summary: 'The color is changed from ColorPicker',
        detail: 'The selected color is ' + event.value});
}
```

Like other input components, ColorPicker supports model-driven forms, disabled property to disable the user interactions, and so on.

The complete demo application with instructions is available on GitHub at `https://github.com/ova2/angular-development-with-primeng/tree /master/chapter9/colorpicker`.

Displaying confirmation dialog with guarded routes

In Angular 2+, you can protect routes with guards. The most likely used guard types are `CanActivate` and `CanDeactivate`. The first guard type decides if a route can be activated, and the second one decides if a route can be deactivated. In this section, we will discuss `CanDeactivate`. This is an interface having only one method `canDeactivate`:

```
export interface CanDeactivate<T> {
    canDeactivate(component: T, route: ActivatedRouteSnapshot,
        state: RouterStateSnapshot):
        Observable<boolean> | Promise<boolean> | boolean;
}
```

This method can return `Observable<boolean>`, `Promise<boolean>`, or `boolean`. If the value of `boolean` is `true`, the user can navigate away from the route. If the value of `boolean` is `false`, the user will stay on the same view. If you want to protect your route from navigating away under some circumstances, you have to do three steps:

1. Create a class that implements the `CanDeactivate` interface. The class acts as a guard, which will be checked by the router when navigating away from the current view. As you can see, the interface expects a generic component class. This is the current component rendered within the `<router-outlet>` tag.

2. Register this guard as provider in a module annotated with `@NgModule`.

3. Add this guard to the router configuration. A router configuration has the `canDeactivate` property where such guards can be added multiple times.

> You might want to check out an example from the official Angular documentation
> `https://angular.io/docs/ts/latest/api/router/index/CanDeactiva te-interface.html`.

In this book, we would like to implement a typical use case where we will check if there are some unsaved input changes made by user. If the current view has unsaved input values and the user tries to navigate away to another view, a confirmation dialog should be shown. We will use ConfirmDialog from PrimeNG:

Now, hitting the **Yes** button leads to navigating to another view:

> # Hello second view!

Hitting the **No** button prevents the the process of navigating from the current route. Let's create the first view with an `input` element, a `submit` button, and the `<p-confirmDialog>` component:

```
<h1>This is the first view</h1>

<form novalidate (ngSubmit)="onSubmit(f)" #f="ngForm">
  <label for="username">Username:</label>
  <input id="username" name="username" type="text"
    pInputText [(ngModel)]="username"/>
  <button type="submit" pButton label="Confirm"></button>
</form>

<p-confirmDialog header="Confirmation" icon="fa fa-question-circle"
  width="400">
</p-confirmDialog>
```

The corresponding component for this template keeps the `dirty` state of the form, which indicates that the form is being edited:

```
export class FirstViewComponent {
  dirty: boolean;
  username: string;

  constructor(private router: Router) { }

  onSubmit(f: FormGroup) {
    this.dirty = f.dirty;
    this.router.navigate(['/chapter9/second-view']);
  }
}
```

We will not implement any sophisticated algorithms in order to check if the input value was really changed. We just check the form's `dirty` state. If the form is not being edited, the navigation on submit should be fine. No need to ask the user about unsaved changes. Now, we have to inject the PrimeNG `ConfirmationService` into our guard implementation, which is required to display a confirmation dialog, and use it like this within the `canDeactivate` method:

```
this.confirmationService.confirm({
  message: 'You have unsaved changes.
  Are you sure you want to leave this page?',
  accept: () => {
    // logic to perform a confirmation
  },
  reject: () => {
    // logic to cancel a confirmation
  }
});
```

But there is a problem. The `confirm` method doesn't return required `Observable<boolean>`, `Promise<boolean>`, or `boolean`. The solution is to create and return an `Observable` object by invoking `Observable.create()`. The `create` method expects a callback with one parameter `observer: Observer<boolean>`. Now we need to do two steps:

- Put the call `this.confirmationService.confirm()` into the callback's body.
- Pass `true` or `false` to the subscriber by invoking `observer.next(true)` and `observer.next(false)` respectively. The subscriber is the PrimeNG's component `ConfirmDialog` which needs to be informed about user's choice.

The full implementation of the `UnsavedChangesGuard` is shown next:

```
@Injectable()
export class UnsavedChangesGuard implements
  CanDeactivate<FirstViewComponent> {

  constructor(private confirmationService: ConfirmationService) { }

  canDeactivate(component: FirstViewComponent) {
    // Allow navigation if the form is unchanged
    if (!component.dirty) { return true; }

    return Observable.create((observer: Observer<boolean>) => {
      this.confirmationService.confirm({
        message: 'You have unsaved changes.
        Are you sure you want to leave this page?',
        accept: () => {
          observer.next(true);
          observer.complete();
        },
        reject: () => {
          observer.next(false);
          observer.complete();
        }
```

```
          });
      });
    }
  }
```

As we already said, the guard is registered in the router configuration:

```
{path: 'chapter9/first-view', component: FirstViewComponent,
    canDeactivate: [UnsavedChangesGuard]}
```

If you prefer `Promise` instead of `Observable`, you can return `Promise` as follows:

```
return new Promise((resolve, reject) => {
  this.confirmationService.confirm({
    message: "You have unsaved changes.
    Are you sure you want to leave this page?",
    accept: () => {
      resolve(true);
    },
    reject: () => {
      resolve(false);
    }
  });
});
```

 The complete demo application with instructions is available on GitHub at
https://github.com/ova2/angular-development-with-primeng/tree
/master/chapter9/guarded-routes.

Implementing a custom wizard component with Steps

PrimeNG has a component called Steps, which indicates the steps in a workflow. The usage is simple:

```
<p-steps [model]="items" [(activeIndex)]="activeIndex"></p-steps>
```

The `model` is a collection of objects of type `MenuItem` which we met in the Chapter 7, *Endless Menu Variations*. The property `activeIndex` points to an index of the active item (step) in the collection of items. The default value is 0 what means that the first item is selected by default. We can also make the items clickable by setting `[readonly]="false"`.

Refer to the PrimeNG showcase to see Steps in action:
`https://www.primefaces.org/primeng/#/steps`

On basis of `<p-steps>`, we will implement a wizard like behavior with two custom components named `<pe-steps>` and `<pe-step>`. The prefix pe should hint at "PrimeNG extensions". The component `<pe-steps>` acts as container for multiple steps. The basic structure:

```
<pe-steps [(activeIndex)]="activeIndex" (change)="onChange($event)">
  <pe-step label="First Step">
    // content of the first step
  </pe-step>
  <pe-step label="Second Step">
    // content of the second step
  </pe-step>
  <pe-step label="Third Step">
    // content of the third step
  </pe-step>
</pe-steps>
```

We can grasp this structure as wizard. The navigation between wizard's steps happens by clicking on Breadcrumb items (clickable steps), navigation buttons, or setting step's index (`activeIndex`) programmatically. The next screenshot shows how the wizard and the navigation could look like:

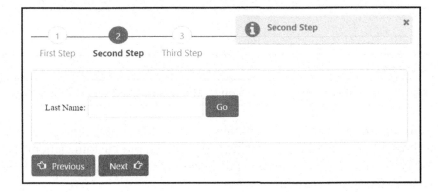

Before starting the implementation, let's specify the API. The `<pe-step>` component has the following:

Attributes:

Name	Type	Default	Description
styleClass	string	null	Style class of single Step component
label	string	null	Label of this Step shown earlier

Styling:

Name	Element
pe-step-container	Container element of a single Step component

The `<pe-steps>` component has:

Attributes:

Name	Type	Default	Description
activeIndex	number	0	Index of the active step (two way binding)
styleClass	string	null	Style class of wizard's container element
stepClass	string	null	Style class of each Step component

Events:

Name	Parameters	Description
change	label: Label of currently shown step	Callback invoked when switching steps

Equipped with this knowledge, we can implement `StepComponent` and `StepsComponent`. The first one has `ng-content` in the template to be able to put custom content. The component class has two specified inputs. Furthermore, there is a property `active`, which indicates whether the step is currently shown:

```
@Component({
    selector: 'pe-step',
    styles: ['.pe-step-container {padding: 45px 25px 45px 25px;
            margin-bottom: 20px;}'],
    template: `
```

```
    <div *ngIf="active" [ngClass]="'ui-widget-content ui-corner-all
        pe-step-container'" [class]="styleClass">
      <ng-content></ng-content>
    </div>
    `
})
export class StepComponent {
  @Input() styleClass: string;
  @Input() label: string;
  active: boolean = false;
}
```

The second component is more complicated. It iterates over child components of the type `StepComponent` and creates items in the life cycle method `ngAfterContentInit()`. The property `active` of the child component is set to `true` if it matches `activeIndex`. Otherwise, it is set to `false`. This allows to display exactly one step in the workflow. The complete listing would go beyond the size of this book. We will only show an excerpt:

```
@Component({
  selector: 'pe-steps',
  template: `
    <p-steps [model]="items" [(activeIndex)]="activeIndex"
      [class]="styleClass" [readonly]="false"></p-steps>
      <ng-content></ng-content>
      <button pButton type="text" *ngIf="activeIndex > 0"
        (click)="previous()" icon="fa-hand-o-left" label="Previous">
      </button>
      <button pButton type="text" *ngIf="activeIndex
        < items.length - 1"
        (click)="next()" icon="fa-hand-o-right"
          iconPos="right" label="Next">
      </button>
    `
})
export class StepsComponent implements AfterContentInit, OnChanges {
  @Input() activeIndex: number = 0;
  @Input() styleClass: string;
  @Input() stepClass: string;
  @Output() activeIndexChange: EventEmitter<any> = new EventEmitter();
  @Output() change = new EventEmitter();
  items: MenuItem[] = [];
  @ContentChildren(StepComponent) steps: QueryList<StepComponent>;

  ngAfterContentInit() {
    this.steps.toArray().forEach((step: StepComponent,
      index: number) =>
        {
```

```
    ...
    if (index === this.activeIndex) { step.active = true; }

    this.items[index] = {
      label: step.label,
      command: (event: any) => {
        // hide all steps
        this.steps.toArray().forEach((s: StepComponent) =>
          s.active = false);

        // show the step the user has clicked on.
        step.active = true;
        this.activeIndex = index;

        // emit currently selected index (two-way binding)
        this.activeIndexChange.emit(index);
        // emit currently selected label
        this.change.next(step.label);
      }
    };
  });
}

ngOnChanges(changes: SimpleChanges) {
  if (!this.steps) { return; }

  for (let prop in changes) {
    if (prop === 'activeIndex') {
      let curIndex = changes[prop].currentValue;
      this.steps.toArray().forEach((step: StepComponent,
        index: number) => {
        // show / hide the step
        let selected = index === curIndex;
        step.active = selected;
        if (selected) {
          // emit currently selected label
          this.change.next(step.label);
        }
      });
    }
  }
}

private next() {
  this.activeIndex++;
  // emit currently selected index (two-way binding)
  this.activeIndexChange.emit(this.activeIndex);
  // show / hide steps and emit selected label
```

```
      this.ngOnChanges({
        activeIndex: {
          currentValue: this.activeIndex,
          previousValue: this.activeIndex - 1,
          firstChange: false,
          isFirstChange: () => false
        }
      });
    }

    ...

  }
```

The fully implemented and documented components are available on GitHub at
`https://github.com/ova2/angular-development-with-primeng/tree` `/master/chapter9/primeng-extensions-wizard`.

To make the implemented wizard distributable, we need to create `WizardModule`:

```
import {NgModule} from '@angular/core';
import {CommonModule} from '@angular/common';
import {StepComponent} from './step.component';
import {StepsComponent} from './steps.component';
import {ButtonModule} from 'primeng/components/button/button';
import {StepsModule} from 'primeng/components/steps/steps';

@NgModule({
   imports: [CommonModule, ButtonModule, StepsModule],
   exports: [StepComponent, StepsComponent],
   declarations: [StepComponent, StepsComponent]
})
export class WizardModule { }
```

The `WizardModule` class can be imported in any PrimeNG application as usually with `imports` inside `@NgModule`. A concrete usage example to the shown picture looks like as follows:

```
<pe-steps [(activeIndex)]="activeIndex" (change)="onChange($event)">
  <pe-step label="First Step">
    <label for="firstname">First Name:</label>
    <input id="firstname" name="firstname" type="text"
      pInputText [(ngModel)]="firstName"/>
    <button pButton label="Go" (click)="next()"></button>
  </pe-step>
  <pe-step label="Second Step">
    <label for="lastname">Last Name:</label>
```

```
        <input id="lastname" name="lastname" type="text"
          pInputText [(ngModel)]="lastName"/>
        <button pButton label="Go" (click)="next()"></button>
      </pe-step>
      <pe-step label="Third Step">
        <label for="address">Address:</label>
        <input id="address" name="address" type="text"
          pInputText [(ngModel)]="address"/>
        <button pButton label="Ok" (click)="ok()"></button>
      </pe-step>
    </pe-steps>

    <p-growl [value]="msgs"></p-growl>
```

The corresponding component implements the `next()` and `ok()` methods, and the event callback `onChange()`. To go forwards, you can simple write `next()` `{this.activeIndex++;}`. Consult the GitHub project for more details.

 The wizard component can be published to the `npm` repository with `npm run update`. There is no running demo app and no `npm start` command in the project on GitHub.

Introduction to state management with @ngrx/store

State management in large Angular applications was a weak point over the last few years. In AngularJS 1, the state management is often done as a mix of services, events, and `$rootScope`. In Angular 2+, the application state and data flow are cleaner but there is still no unified state management in Angular core. Developers often use *Redux*--a predictable state container for JavaScript applications (`http://redux.js.org`). The Redux architecture is best known for its use with the *React* library (`https://facebook.github.io/react`), but it can be utilized with Angular too. One of the popular Redux-like state containers designed for Angular is *ngrx/store* (`https://github.com/ngrx/store`).

Redux principles

Redux follows three basic principles:

- The whole state of the application is stored in a single immutable state tree called *store*. No state management is allowed outside the store. A central immutable store has a lot of benefits. You can improve the performance by using `ChangeDetectionStrategy.OnPush` because with immutable data, Angular only needs to check object references to detect changes. Furthermore, the undo/redo functionality is easy done.
- *Actions* are used to send information from the application to the store. Only actions are source of information for the store. Actions are plain JavaScript objects having `type` and `payload` properties. The `type` property describes a kind of state change we want. The `payload` property is the data being sent to the store in order to update it.
- State changes are made through pure functions called *reducers*. Pure functions are functions that don't mutate objects, but return brand new objects instead. We can grasp reducers as processing steps in the store that allow state transitions. The reducer operates on the current state and returns a new state.

In general, the data flow is bi-directional. User inputs in one component can affect other components and vice versa. The data flow in Redux applications is uni-directional. Changes in the view trigger actions. Actions are dispatched to the store. Reducers perform state changes in response to actions by taking the previous state with the dispatched action and returning the next state as a new object.

> `Object.assign()` and the `spread` operator can help in returning new objects (`http://redux.js.org/docs/recipes/UsingObjectSpreadOpera tor.html`).

Several components can subscribe to the store to observe state changes over time and propagate them to the view. The following diagram memorizes described Redux principles:

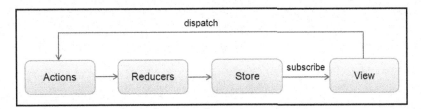

A classic Redux store provides two important APIs to:

- Dispatch actions using `store.dispatch(action)`
- Register listeners for change notification using `store.subscribe(callback)`

As you see, if you use a Redux store, you don't need to synchronize the state between components manually.

A predictable state management allows to debug applications with co, called time-travelling debugger. You need to install `store-devtools` (`ht tps://github.com/ngrx/store-devtools`) with an appropriate Chrome extension.

CRUD application with @ngrx/store

For a practical example, we will reuse the same CRUD sample implementation from the section *CRUD sample implementation with DataTable*. Start off by adding the `ngrx` dependencies for a Redux-based application:

```
npm install @ngrx/store @ngrx/core --save
```

First of all, we need to define a shape for the store. In real applications, most likely available employees and currently selected employee might be shared across several components. Hence the store could be defined as follows:

```
export interface AppStore {
  employees: Employee[];
  selectedEmployee: Employee;
}
```

Next, we need to define actions which consist of types and optional payloads.

The best practice is to create *Action Creator Services* encapsulating associated actions:
`https://github.com/ngrx/ngrx.github.io/blob/master/store/recip es/actions/action_services.md`

We will create the service `CrudActions` with four CRUD actions and associated action creators:

```
@Injectable()
export class CrudActions {
  static LOAD_EMPLOYEES = 'LOAD_EMPLOYEES';
  static CREATE_EMPLOYEE = 'CREATE_EMPLOYEE';
```

```
static UPDATE_EMPLOYEE = 'UPDATE_EMPLOYEE';
static DELETE_EMPLOYEE = 'DELETE_EMPLOYEE';

loadEmployees(employees: Employee[]): Action {
  return {type: CrudActions.LOAD_EMPLOYEES, payload: employees};
}

createEmployee(employee: Employee): Action {
  return {type: CrudActions.CREATE_EMPLOYEE, payload: employee};
}

updateEmployee(employee: Employee): Action {
  return {type: CrudActions.UPDATE_EMPLOYEE, payload: employee};
}

deleteEmployee(id: string): Action {
  return {type: CrudActions.DELETE_EMPLOYEE, payload: id};
}
}
```

The core part is the reducer. The reducer function takes a state and an action and then uses a `switch` statement to return a new state depending on the action type. The current state will not be mutated:

```
import {ActionReducer, Action} from '@ngrx/store';
import {AppStore} from './app.store';
import {CrudActions} from './crud.actions';
import {Employee} from '../model/employee';

const initialState: AppStore = {employees: [], selectedEmployee: null};

export const crudReducer: ActionReducer<AppStore> =
  (state: AppStore = initialState, action: Action): AppStore => {
    switch (action.type) {
    case CrudActions.LOAD_EMPLOYEES:
      return {
        employees: [...action.payload],
        selectedEmployee: null
      };

    case CrudActions.DELETE_EMPLOYEE:
      return {
        employees: state.employees.filter(
          (element: Employee) => element.id !== action.payload),
        selectedEmployee: null
      };

    case CrudActions.CREATE_EMPLOYEE:
```

```
        return {
          employees: [...state.employees, action.payload],
          selectedEmployee: null
        };

      case CrudActions.UPDATE_EMPLOYEE:
        let index = -1;
        // clone employees array with updated employee
        let employees = state.employees.map(
          (employee: Employee, idx: number) => {
          if (employee.id === action.payload.id) {
            index = idx;
            return Object.assign({}, action.payload);
          }
          return employee;
        });

        let selectedEmployee = index >= 0 ? employees[index] : null;
        return {employees, selectedEmployee};

      default:
        return state;
    }
  };
```

As you can see, there is also a `default` switch statement which just returns the current state in case the provided action doesn't match any of the predefined actions.

Now, we can configure `AppModule` with the `ngrx/store` module. It is done by importing the `StoreModule` that should call the `provideStore` method with the name of our reducer:

```
import {StoreModule} from '@ngrx/store';
import {CrudActions} from './redux/crud.actions';
import {crudReducer} from './redux/crud.reducer';

@NgModule({
  imports: [
    ...
    StoreModule.provideStore({crudReducer})
  ],
  providers: [
    ...
    CrudActions
  ],
  ...
})
export class AppModule { }
```

Generally, you can provide multiple reducers as well. An example is shown here:

```
let rootReducer = {
  reducerOne: reducerOne,
  reducerTwo: reducerTwo,
  reducerThree: reducerThree,
  ...
}

StoreModule.provideStore(rootReducer);
```

 Internally, @ngrx/store uses the combineReducers method to create a *meta-reducer* which calls the specified reducers with the correct state slice.

The last step is dispatching the actions and selecting the data. We can inject CrudActions into EmployeeService and create corresponding actions for every CRUD operation. Return values are of the type Observable<Action>:

```
constructor(private http: Http, private crudActions: CrudActions) { }

getEmployees(): Observable<Action> {
  return this.http.get('/fake-backend/employees')
    .map(response => response.json() as Employee[])
    .map(employees => this.crudActions.loadEmployees(employees))
    .catch(EmployeeService.handleError);
}

createEmployee(employee: Employee): Observable<Action> {
  return this.http.post('/fake-backend/employees', employee)
    .map(response => response.json() as Employee)
    .map(createdEmployee =>
      this.crudActions.createEmployee(createdEmployee))
    .catch(EmployeeService.handleError);
}

updateEmployee(employee: Employee): Observable<Action> {
  return this.http.put('/fake-backend/employees', employee)
    .map(() => this.crudActions.updateEmployee(employee))
    .catch(EmployeeService.handleError);
}

deleteEmployee(id: string): Observable<Action> {
  return this.http.delete('/fake-backend/employees/' + id)
    .map(() => this.crudActions.deleteEmployee(id))
```

```
      .catch(EmployeeService.handleError);
  }
```

In the component class, we receive actions and dispatch them by calling `store.dispatch(action)`. Dispatching the actions will only be demonstrated for two CRUD operations: loading all employees and removing one employee:

```
ngOnInit(): void {
  ...

  this.employeeService.getEmployees().subscribe(
    action => this.store.dispatch(action),
    error => this.showError(error)
  );
}

remove() {
  this.employeeService.deleteEmployee(this.selectedEmployee.id)
    .finally(() => {
      this.employeeForDialog = null;
    })
    .subscribe((action) => {
        this.store.dispatch(action);
        this.showSuccess('Employee was successfully removed');
      },
      error => this.showError(error)
    );
}
```

Selecting the data in @ngrx/store is achieved by calling `store.select()`. The `select` method expects a name of the reducer function to select slice(s) of state for displaying in view(s). The return value of the `select` method is `Observable`, which allows subscription to the store's data. The next code snippet demonstrates such subscription:

```
import {Store} from '@ngrx/store';
import {AppStore} from '../redux/app.store';
...

constructor(private store: Store<AppStore>,
  private employeeService: EmployeeService) { }

ngOnInit(): void {
  this.store.select('crudReducer').subscribe((store: AppStore) => {
    this.employees = store.employees;
    this.selectedEmployee = store.selectedEmployee;
  });
}
```

The lifecycle method `ngOnInit` is a good place for subscriptions.

 The complete demo application with instructions is available on GitHub at `https://github.com/ova2/angular-development-with-primeng/tree /master/chapter9/redux`.

Summary

In this chapter, you have learned more PrimeNG components and directives for various use cases. The chapter explained interesting features of FileUpload, Draggable, Droppable, Galleria, Defer, BlockUI, ProgressBar, and more. You have seen a real-world implementation of CRUD application with DataTable and mocked backend. A best practice with ConfirmationDialog and guarded routes was demonstrated as well. After reading this chapter, you are equipped with necessary knowledge to be able to create different custom components for the next few Angular and PrimeNG web applications. The Redux architecture is not a foreign concept anymore. You are best prepared for an advantageous state management in complex web applications.

The next chapter gives an introduction to the unit and e2e testing with modern frameworks. You will learn how to test and debug Angular applications. Tips on test-driven development will not be missing either.

10
Creating Robust Applications

Testing web applications is an important process to eliminate bugs. Tests ensure that the written code works as expected and the functionality is not broken on subsequent changes. They also help you to better understand the complex code you are working on. There are two main types of testing--**unit testing** and **end-to-end** (**e2e**) testing.

Unit testing is about testing isolated pieces of code. Unit tests normally use mocks for inputs and then assert that the expected results have occurred. The e2e approach executes tests against your application running in a real browser. Such tests assert that all pieces of code properly interact with each other. Standard test frameworks for Angular applications are Jasmine and Protractor. Jasmine is used for unit testing in combination with Karma-- a test runner for JavaScript. Protractor is an e2e test framework. This chapter describes two types of testing in a concise manner. You will learn how to set up and use the test frameworks efficiently. Testing and debugging tips round off the book.

In this chapter, we will cover the following topics:

- Setting up unit testing with Jasmine and Karma
- Unit testing of components and services
- Tips on how to speed up unit testing
- Setting up the e2e test environment with Protractor
- Writing automated UI tests at a glance
- Exploring an PrimeNG application with Augury and ng.probe

Setting up unit testing with Jasmine and Karma

This section will give a brief overview of Jasmine (`http://jasmine.github.io`) and Karma (`https://karma-runner.github.io`). We will set up a testing environment before writing concrete unit tests. For this purpose, the Webpack seed project introduced in the *Setting up PrimeNG project with Webpack* section of `Chapter 1`, *Getting Started with Angular and PrimeNG*, will be extended.

Brief introduction to Jasmine

Jasmine is a JavaScript testing framework with zero dependencies. With `npm`, you can install it as follows:

```
npm install jasmine-core --save-dev
```

You also need to install the Jasmine type definition file. Otherwise, the TypeScript compiler will not know about the Jasmine types.

```
npm install @types/jasmine --save-dev
```

Jasmine has four main concepts:

- **Specs**: In Jasmine terminology, unit tests are called specs. The `it(string, function)` function specifies a test. It takes a title and a function containing one or more expectations.
- **Suites**: Specs are wrapped in suites. The `describe(string, function)` function describes a test suite. It takes a title and a function containing one or more specs. Suit can contain other nested suites as well.
- **Expectations**: These are assertions which are specified using the `expect(actual)` function. The function gets one argument--the `actual` value.
- **Matchers**: Assertions are followed by matchers. Jasmine has a lot of matchers such as `toBe(expected)`, `toEqual(expected)`, `toBeLessThan(expected)`, and many more. The `expected` argument is the expected value. For example, `expect(2 + 3).toBeLessThan(6)`. Matchers implement a Boolean comparison between `actual` and `expected` values. If the matcher returns `true`, the spec passes; otherwise, an error is thrown. Any matcher can be negated with `not`; for example, `expect(array).not.toContain(member)`.

A full list of matchers is available on GitHub at `https://github.com/Jam ieMason/Jasmine-Matchers`.

An example of a simple test with Jasmine is shown here:

```
describe("Test matchers:", function() {
  it("Compare two values with 'toBe' matcher", function() {
    var a = 5;
    var b = 2 + 3;

    expect(a).toBe(b);
    expect(a).not.toBe(null);
  });
});
```

The titles in the functions `it()` and `describe()` serve the purpose of documentation. Tests should be self-described so that other developers can better understand what the test does.

Jasmine has some setup and teardown functions:

- `beforeAll()`: Executes some code before the suite runs.
- `beforeEach()`: Executes some code before each spec runs.
- `afterAll()`: Executes some code after the suite is finished.
- `afterEach()`: Executes some code after each spec is finished.

An example with `beforeEach()` and `afterAll()` is demonstrated here:

```
describe("Usage of beforeEach and afterAll", function() {
  var foo = 0;

  beforeEach(function() {
    foo += 1;
  });

  afterAll(function() {
    foo = 0;
  });

  it("Check if foo == 1", function() {
    expect(foo).toEqual(1);
  });
```

```
it("Check if foo == 2", function() {
    expect(foo).toEqual(2);
  });
});
```

Testing setup with Webpack and Karma

There are two runners to execute tests:

- **HTML runner from the Jasmine's standalone distribution** (https://github.co m/jasmine/jasmine/releases): Download the ZIP file, unzip it, and open the SpecRunner.html file in any text editor. This HTML file includes some base code that loads the test framework. You need to add regular Angular dependencies, an Angular testing library, and a SystemJS loader, which loads the .spec files. After that, you can open the HTML file in your web browser to see the test results.
- **Command-line runner Karma**: Karma can run tests in different browsers and report possible errors with various reporters. The runner can be integrated into the build process so that the unit tests get executed automatically as a part of the build.

In this book, we will only concentrate on the Karma runner. The Webpack-based project setup needs the following Karma dependencies:

```
"devDependencies": {
  ...
  "karma": "~1.7.0",
  "karma-chrome-launcher": "~2.1.1",
  "karma-jasmine": "~1.1.0",
  "karma-jasmine-matchers": "~3.7.0",
  "karma-mocha-reporter": "~2.2.3",
  "karma-phantomjs-launcher": "~1.0.4",
  "karma-sourcemap-loader": "~0.3.7",
  "karma-webpack": "~2.0.3",
  "phantomjs-prebuilt": "~2.1.14"
}
```

Attentive readers will notice that we want to run tests against Google Chrome and PhantomJS (http://phantomjs.org)--a headless browser, which is perfect for testing web applications.

The complete project with instructions is available on GitHub at `https://github.com/ova2/angular-development-with-primeng/tree` `/master/chapter10/unit-testing`.

The testing setup with Webpack and Karma requires three configuration files. First of all, we need a Karma configuration file: `karma.config.js`. This file will tell Karma where the tests are located, which browser(s) to use to execute the tests, which reporting mechanism to use, and so on. In the project on GitHub, this file has the following content:

```
let webpackConfig = require('./webpack.test.js');

module.exports = config => {
  config.set({
    autoWatch: false,
    singleRun: true,
    browsers: ['Chrome', 'PhantomJS'],
    basePath: '.',
    files: ['spec-bundle.js'],
    exclude: [],
    frameworks: ['jasmine', 'jasmine-matchers'],
    logLevel: config.LOG_INFO,
    phantomJsLauncher: {exitOnResourceError: true},
    port: 9876,
    colors: true,
    preprocessors: {
      'spec-bundle.js': ['webpack', 'sourcemap']
    },
    reporters: ['mocha'],
    webpack: webpackConfig,
    webpackServer: {noInfo: true}
  });
};
```

Two important points should be mentioned here. There is a special Webpack configuration for tests, which is located in the `webpack.test.js` file. Its content is simple:

```
var ContextReplacementPlugin =
require("webpack/lib/ContextReplacementPlugin");

module.exports = {
  devtool: 'inline-source-map',
  resolve: {extensions: ['.ts', '.js', '.json']},
  module: {
    rules: [
      {test: /\.ts$/, loaders: ['awesome-typescript-loader',
        'angular2-template-loader']},
```

```
        {test: /\.json$/, loader: 'json-loader'},
        {test: /\.(css|html)$/, loader: 'raw-loader'}
      ]
    },
    plugins: [
      new ContextReplacementPlugin(
        /angular(\\|\/)core(\\|\/)@angular/,
        path.resolve(__dirname, '../src')
      )
    ]
  };
```

The `webpack.test.js` doesn't specify entry points for files to be tested. The location and file extension for test files are defined in `spec-bundle.js`. This is another important file processed by Webpack. It loads Angular modules required for testing and initializes the test environment. At the end, all the test files are getting loaded in the browser. The content of the `spec-bundle.js` file is listed here:

```
require('core-js/es6');
require('core-js/es7/reflect');
require('zone.js/dist/zone');
require('zone.js/dist/long-stack-trace-zone');
require('zone.js/dist/proxy');
require('zone.js/dist/sync-test');
require('zone.js/dist/jasmine-patch');
require('zone.js/dist/async-test');
require('zone.js/dist/fake-async-test');
require('rxjs/Rx');

const coreTesting = require('@angular/core/testing');
const browserTesting = require('@angular/platform-browser-
dynamic/testing');

// Initialize the test environment
coreTesting.TestBed.resetTestEnvironment();
coreTesting.TestBed.initTestEnvironment(
  browserTesting.BrowserDynamicTestingModule,
  browserTesting.platformBrowserDynamicTesting()
);

// Let the browser show a full stack trace when an error happens
Error.stackTraceLimit = Infinity;
// Let's set the timeout for the async function calls to 3 sec.
// (default is 5 sec.)
jasmine.DEFAULT_TIMEOUT_INTERVAL = 3000;

// Find all files with .spec.ts extensions
```

```
const context = require.context('../src/', true, /\.spec\.ts$/);

// For each file, call the context function that will require
//the file and load it up here.
context.keys().forEach(context);
```

The convention is to name your test file the same as the file it is testing, but with the suffix .spec before the file extension. For example, header.component.spec.ts and language.service.spec.ts. It is also the best practice to keep each test file in the same directory as the corresponding file under test.

In package.json, we can configure three convenient commands.

```
"scripts": {
  ...
  "test": "karma start ./config/karma.conf.js",
  "test:headless": "karma start ./config/karma.conf.js
    --browsers PhantomJS",
  "test:chrome": "karma start ./config/karma.conf.js
    --browsers Chrome"
}
```

Now, we are ready to run our tests using one of the three commands. When we execute npm run test, Karma will open and close each configured browser and print the test results.

When using the Angular CLI, it handles the configuration for us. You don't need to write any configuration files and can quickly run all tests by typing ng test in our project root. This command watches for changes and reruns the tests automatically.

Unit testing of components and services

In this section, we will introduce Angular testing utilities and show how to test components and services. Testing of directives, pipes, router, and so on, will not be explained due to the limited size of the book.

Angular testing utilities

As you could see in the previous section, Angular comes with a testing library, `@angular/core/testing`, which offers the `TestBed` helper class and many other utilities. `TestBed` helps us to set up dependencies for tests--modules, components, providers, and so on. You can call `TestBed.configureTestingModule()` and pass the same metadata configuration object as used with `@NgModule`. The `configureTestingModule()` function should be called within a `beforeEach()` setup function.

Another useful function from the testing library is called `inject()`. It allows you to inject the specified objects into the tests. The following code snippet provides an example:

```
describe('MyService', () => {
  let service;

  beforeEach(() => TestBed.configureTestingModule({
    providers: [MyService]
  }));

  beforeEach(inject([MyService], s => {
    service = s;
  }));

  it('should return the city Bern', () => {
    expect(service.getCities()).toContain('Bern');
  });
});
```

The next useful function is the `async()` function. It may be used with asynchronous operations because it doesn't complete the test until all asynchronous operations in the test have been completed or the specified timeout occurs. The `async()` function wraps the second argument of the `it()` function:

```
it('do something', async(() => {
  // make asynchronous operation here, e.g. call a REST service
}), 3000));
```

The timeout parameter is optional. It is also possible to call `async()` in combination with `inject()`:

```
it('do something', async(inject([SomeService], s => {
  ...
})));
```

Note that if you change some component's property value and this property is bound to the view via the `ngModel` directive, you have to do this within `async()` as well. The reason: `ngModel` updates the value asynchronously. We will develop an appropriate example in this section.

The `fakeAsync()` function from the Angular testing utilities is similar to `async()`, but it enables a linear coding style by running the test body in a special *fakeAsync test zone*. The `fakeAsync()` method is used in combination with the `tick()` function, which simulates the passage of time until all pending asynchronous activities have been finished. There are no nested `then(...)` blocks anymore; the test appears to be synchronous:

```
changeSomethingAsync1();
...
tick();
expect(something).toBeDefined();

changeSomethingAsync2();
...
tick();
expect(something).toBeNull();
```

There is one limitation with `fakeAsync()`--you cannot make an XHR call from within `fakeAsync()`.

Testing a component

We want to test a component called `SectionComponent` with just one property `username`. The component has the following markup:

```
<label for="username">Username:</label>
<input id="username" name="username" type="text" pInputText
       [(ngModel)]="username"/>
```

In the test file `section.component.spec.ts`, we will assign the value `James Bond` to the property `username` and then check whether the value appears in the view. The full listing of the test code is shown here:

```
import {TestBed, async, ComponentFixture} from '@angular/core/testing';
import {By} from '@angular/platform-browser';
import {DebugElement} from '@angular/core';
import {SectionComponent} from './section.component';
import {FormsModule} from '@angular/forms';
```

```
describe('Component: SectionComponent', () => {
  let fixture: ComponentFixture<SectionComponent>;
  let sectionComponent: SectionComponent;
  let element: any;
  let debugElement: DebugElement;

  beforeEach(() => {
    TestBed.configureTestingModule({
      imports: [FormsModule],
      declarations: [SectionComponent]
    });

    fixture = TestBed.createComponent(SectionComponent);
    sectionComponent = fixture.componentInstance;
    element = fixture.nativeElement;
    debugElement = fixture.debugElement;
  });

  afterEach(() => {
    if (fixture) {fixture.destroy();}
  });

  it('should render `James Bond`', async(() => {
    sectionComponent.username = 'James Bond';

    // trigger change detection
    fixture.detectChanges();

    // wait until fixture is stable and check then the name
    fixture.whenStable().then(() => {
      // first approach shows one possible way to check the result
      expect(element.querySelector('input[name=username]').value)
        .toBe('James Bond');
      // second approach shows another possible way to check the result
      expect(debugElement.query(By.css('input[name=username]'))
        .nativeElement.value).toBe('James Bond');
    });
  }));
});
```

Let's explain the code. First of all, we need to configure the testing module with TestBed. It is done as usual within beforeEach(). The class TestBed has a static method createComponent(component), which we use to create ComponentFixture--a wrapper around the component instance on the test environment. The fixture provides an access to the component instance itself, to the native root element, and to DebugElement, which is a wrapper around the root element of this component. Furthermore, ComponentFixture has a lot of other useful methods:

```
class ComponentFixture<T> {
   componentInstance: T;
   nativeElement: any;
   debugElement: DebugElement;
   detectChanges(): void;
   whenStable(): Promise<any>;
   ...
}
```

The most important methods are detectChanges() and whenStable(). The first one triggers the change detection cycle for the component. This is necessary to propagate the changes to the UI. The second one returns Promise and can be used to resume testing when all asynchronous calls or asynchronous change detection have ended. We used two different APIs to check the expected result after Promise got resolved.

Jasmine has a concept of spies. A spy mocks any object or function and tracks calls to it and all of its arguments. The toHaveBeenCalled matcher will return true if the spy was called. The next code snippet creates a spy on the showDetails method. After some interactions, we can verify if the method was called:

```
const spy = spyOn(someComponent, 'showDetails');

// do some interactions
...
fixture.detectChanges();

fixture.whenStable().then(() => {
   expect(spy).toHaveBeenCalled();
});
```

We can also verify if the method was called with specific arguments, how many times it was called, and so on. Refer to the Jasmine documentation for more details.

Testing a service

The next example outlines how to test services. We want to test a service, which returns some countries from a remote backend:

```
@Injectable()
export class CountryService {
  constructor(private http: Http) { }

  getCountries(): Observable<Country[]> {
    return this.http.get('/assets/data/countries.json')
      .map(response => response.json().data as Country[]);
  }
}
```

The `Country` objects have the following shape:

```
interface Country {
  name: any;
  dial_code?: any;
  code?: any;
}
```

We don't want to make HTTP calls during the tests. To achieve that, we have to replace `XHRBackend` by `MockBackend`. The `MockBackend` allows us to catch outgoing HTTP requests and simulate incoming responses. We can just define a response as we want and then compare the result from the service with our expectations. The next code snippet shows how to build a mocked response, so when we finally make a call to our service, it gets the predefined array of countries:

```
import {TestBed, inject} from '@angular/core/testing';
import {HttpModule, XHRBackend, Response, ResponseOptions}
  from '@angular/http';
import {MockBackend, MockConnection} from '@angular/http/testing';
import {CountryService} from './country.service';
import Country from './country';

describe('CountryService (MockBackend)', () => {
  let mockbackend: MockBackend, service: CountryService;

  beforeEach(() => {
    TestBed.configureTestingModule({
      imports: [HttpModule],
      providers: [CountryService, MockBackend,
        {provide: XHRBackend, useClass: MockBackend}
      ]
    })
```

```
  });

  beforeEach(inject([CountryService, MockBackend],
    (cs: CountryService, mb: MockBackend) => {
    service = cs;
    mockbackend = mb;
  }));

  it('should return mocked response', () => {
    let israel: Country = {'name': 'Israel',
      'dial_code': '+972', 'code': 'IL'};
    let angola: Country = {'name': 'Angola',
      'dial_code': '+244', 'code': 'AO'};
    let response = [israel, angola];

    mockbackend.connections.subscribe((connection: MockConnection) => {
      connection.mockRespond(new Response(new ResponseOptions({
        status: 200, body: JSON.stringify(response)
      }))));
    });

    service.getCountries().subscribe(countries => {
      expect(countries.length).toBe(2);
      expect(countries).toContain(israel);
      expect(countries).toContain(angola);
    });
  });
});
```

Note, that we don't need the `async()` function here because `MockBackend` behaves synchronously. Now, when all the tests are successful, you will see the following output:

```
START:

[at-loader] Using typescript@2.3.3 from typescript and "tsconfig.json" from C:\Projects\angular-development-with-primeng\chapter10

[at-loader] Checking started in a separate process...

[at-loader] Ok, 0.536 sec.
04 06 2017 18:22:56.947:INFO [karma]: Karma v1.7.0 server started at http://0.0.0.0:9876/
04 06 2017 18:22:56.949:INFO [launcher]: Launching browser Chrome with unlimited concurrency
04 06 2017 18:22:56.957:INFO [launcher]: Starting browser Chrome
04 06 2017 18:22:58.701:INFO [Chrome 58.0.3029 (Windows 8.1 0.0.0)]: Connected on socket t9GRLNPbjWGh9K6yAAAA with id 76648885
  Component: SectionComponent
    √ should render `James Bond`
  CountryService (MockBackend)
    √ should return mocked response

Finished in 0.39 secs / 0.364 secs @ 18:23:00 GMT+0200 (Mitteleuropäische Sommerzeit)

SUMMARY:
√ 2 tests completed
```

The demonstrated test of the service class was not an *isolated unit test*. Isolated unit tests explore the inner logic of the tested class and don't require the Angular testing utilities. You don't need to prepare a testing module, call `inject()`, `async()`, and so on. A test instance of the class is created with `new`, supplying mock, spy, or fake objects for the constructor parameters. Generally, services and pipes are good candidates for isolated unit testing. Read the official Angular testing guide to learn more details (`https://angular.io/docs/ts/latest/guide/testing.html`).

 The complete project with instructions is available on GitHub at `https://github.com/ova2/angular-development-with-primeng/tree/master/chapter10/unit-testing`.

Tips on how to speed up unit testing

In a real web application, you can have a lot of test files. The bundling and running of all test files might take a while. Karma takes a while for the booting process as well. It is not satisfactory for rapid software development if you always have to run hundreds and more tests in order to test a small change in a single file. If you would like to narrow testing for files you are writing the tests for, one file or a specified collection of files should be tested, without rebooting Karma. How to do this?

This is the case where `karma-webpack-grep` (`https://www.npmjs.com/package/karma-webpack-grep`) can help you. It allows to limit files, which are bundled by `karma-webpack`. First, install it:

```
npm install karma-webpack-grep --save-dev
```

After that, we have to extend the `karma.conf.js` file. Put the new `karma-webpack-grep` plugin to the array of all Webpack's plugins. Everything else remains unchanged:

```
let grep = require('karma-webpack-grep');

module.exports = config => {
  webpackConfig.plugins = (webpackConfig.plugins || []).concat(grep({
    grep: config.grep,
    basePath: '.',
    testContext: '../src/'
  }));

  config.set({
    // the same settings as before
    ...
```

```
    });
  };
```

Note that the `testContext` option is exactly the same that as passed in `require.context(...)` (see `spec-bundle.js`). But, where the `config.grep` coming from? Karma parses command-line arguments. That means, if you execute the following command:

```
karma start ./config/karma.conf.js --grep some/path
```

The `config.grep` will be set to `some/path`. Let's extend the `npm` scripts:

```
"scripts": {
  ...
  "test:headless:grep": "karma start ./config/karma.conf.js
    --browsers PhantomJS --autoWatch true --singleRun false --grep",
  "test:chrome:grep": "karma start ./config/karma.conf.js
    --browsers Chrome --autoWatch true --singleRun false --grep"
}
```

Now, you are able to run concrete tests in watch mode. For Chrome browser, it looks as follows:

```
npm run test:chrome:grep -- app/section/section.component.spec.ts
npm run test:chrome:grep -- app/section/service/country.service.spec.ts
```

For PhantomJS, the tests start with `npm test test:headless:grep`. The test result looks like the following (here for `CountryService`):

```
START:
  CountryService (MockBackend)
    V should return mocked response

Finished in 0.014 secs / 0.331 secs @ 14:33:58 GMT+0200

SUMMARY:
V 1 test completed
```

The Karma runner continues to run and watches the file changes. Test results appear very fast on every file change. It is also possible to watch and execute test files in a certain folder. For that, you can simple pass this folder to the `npm` script. For instance:

```
npm run test:chrome:grep -- app/section
```

All tests under `src/app/section` will be watched and executed. Just concentrate on writing the code:

The complete project with instructions is available on GitHub at `https://github.com/ova2/angular-development-with-primeng/tree /master/chapter10/unit-testing`.

Setting up the e2e test environment with Protractor

Protractor (`http://www.protractortest.org`) is an open source e2e testing automation framework, designed specifically for Angular web applications. The Protractor is a Node.js tool built on the top of WebDriverJS--an official implementation of the W3C WebDriver API to interact with the browser.

Protractor has many advantages. You no longer need to add `waits` and `sleeps` to your test for pending tasks. Protractor can automatically execute the next step in your test at the moment the web page finishes asynchronous tasks (for example, AJAX updates). The framework also supports Angular's locator strategies, which allows you to find Angular-specific elements by binding, model, and so on, without much effort. This section gives a brief introduction to Protractor including the setup and specific testing constructs.

Installing and configuring Protractor

The preferred method is to install Protractor globally with the following command:

```
npm install protractor -g
```

Protractor will automatically download the *Selenium Standalone Server* and all the browser drivers.

The Selenium Standalone Server is normally needed if you want to connect to remote machine(s) and run tests against browser(s) on remote machine(s). It is often used with *Selenium-Grid* when you distribute your tests over multiple machines.

Execute this command to update the Selenium Standalone Server and the browser drivers:

```
webdriver-manager update
```

Ensure that you have installed the `jasmine-core` package locally as shown in the *Setting up unit testing with Jasmine and Karma* section . The tests will be written in Jasmine, but you can also use Mocha (`https://mochajs.org`)--another JavaScript test framework running on Node.js. In addition, a reporter implementation is required. Install `jasmine-spec-reporter`:

```
npm install jasmine-spec-reporter --save-dev
```

The Protractor configuration takes place in the `protractor.conf.js` file:

```js
var path = require('path');
var SpecReporter = require('jasmine-spec-reporter').SpecReporter;

exports.config = {
  allScriptsTimeout: 11000,
  specs: ['../e2e/**/*.e2e-spec.ts'],
  capabilities: {'browserName': 'chrome'},
  directConnect: true,
  baseUrl: 'http://localhost:3000/',
  framework: 'jasmine',
  jasmineNodeOpts: {
    showColors: true,
    defaultTimeoutInterval: 30000,
    print: function () { }
  },
  beforeLaunch: function () {
    require('ts-node').register({
      project: path.resolve(__dirname, '../e2e')
    });
  },
  onPrepare() {
    jasmine.getEnv().addReporter(new SpecReporter());
  }
};
```

The description of the most important configuration options is listed down here:

Option	Description
allScriptsTimeout	The timeout in milliseconds for each script running on the browser.
specs	Spec patterns are relative to the location of this config. The best practice is to place all e2e tests in the e2e folder. The sub-folder names correspond to the page names. For example, tests for the home page should be in the home sub-folder. The file names also correspond to the name of pages. We add the .e2e-spec.ts suffix to our spec files. For example, the spec file for the home page is home.e2e-spec.ts.
capabilities	Configuration object for the browser the tests run against. You can also run tests on more than one browser at once. For that, use the multiCapabilities option, which expects an array of capabilities.
seleniumAddress	Use this option to connect to a running Selenium Server started with webdriver-manager start. For example, seleniumAddress: 'http://localhost:4444/wd/hub'. Protractor will send requests to this server to control a browser. You can see information about the status of the server at http://localhost:4444/wd/hub.
directConnect	Use this option to connect to Chrome or Firefox directly (only two browsers are supported for direct connection). In this book, we use directConnect instead of seleniumAddress.
baseUrl	The base URL for the application under test.
framework	Test framework to use. Normally, Jasmine or Mocha are used.
beforeLaunch	A callback function called once configs are read but before any environment setup. This will only run once, and before onPrepare. In the preceding configuration, ts-node will be executed. The ts-node module takes care of transpiling TypeScript files to JavaScript ones. You must install it via npm as npm install ts-node --save-dev. Also, consider the project configuration option which points to the folder with a specific tsconfig.json file. Normally, we need different TypeScript compiler options for e2e tests.
onPrepare	A callback function called once Protractor is ready and available, and before the specs are executed. We can add some reporters there.

All preparations are done. Now, ensure that the application is running at
`http://localhost:3000/` and run the tests from the project root with:

```
protractor ./config/protractor.conf.js
```

For the sake of convenience, you can configure this command as the `npm` script and run
with `npm run e2e`:

```
"scripts": {
  ...
  "pree2e": "webdriver-manager update",
  "e2e": "protractor ./config/protractor.conf.js"
}
```

The `webdriver-manager update` command should be running first as a
pre-hook. This is why we need `"pree2e"` in the `scripts` section.

It is possible to separate e2e tests into various suites and run suite-related tests separately.
You can accomplish this task in the configuration file within the `suites` section. For
instance, let's define two suites, `homepage` and `payment`:

```
suites: {
  homepage: '../e2e/homepage/**/*.e2e-spec.ts',
  payment: '../e2e/payment/**/*.e2e-spec.ts'
}
```

The following command will only run the homepage-related tests:

```
protractor ./config/protractor.conf.js --suite homepage
```

When using the Angular CLI, it creates the configuration file for us. You
can execute e2e tests by running `ng serve` and `ng e2e` in two separate
consoles. If you need different settings, specific mocks, and so on for e2e
tests, you must create a new `environment.e2e.ts` file with the specific
environment variables, and register it in `.angular-cli.json` under
`environments` as `"e2e": "environments/environment.e2e.ts"`.
Now, you can import the `environment.ts` in the `app.module.ts`, check
the environment variables and perform custom logic where required; for
example, provide mocks, and so on. To make it work, the application
should be started as `ng serve --env=e2e`.

Writing automated UI tests at a glance

This section describes the syntax of Protractor tests as well as the *Page Object* and *Page Element* design patterns, which are the best practices for the e2e testing. Armed with this knowledge, we will write a complete e2e test for the demo application introduced in `Chapter 9`, *Miscellaneous Use Cases and Best Practices*, in the section *Displaying confirmation dialog with guarded routes*.

Browser object, element, and locators

The browser object is a globally created wrapper around an instance of `WebDriver`. It is used for navigation and page-wide information. With `browser.get()`, you can navigate to a page and then check the page's title as follows:

```
describe('Google page', function() {
  it('should have a title', function() {
    browser.get('https://www.google.com');
    expect(browser.getTitle()).toEqual('Google');
  });
});
```

The current URL is returned by `browser.getCurrentUrl()`. For example:

```
expect(browser.getCurrentUrl()).toContain('/admin');
```

Other global objects created by Protractor are `element` and `by`. `element` is a helper function for finding DOM elements on the page you are testing. It requires one parameter--a *locator* for locating the element. Locators are created using the `by` object. There is a range of locators. We will only mention a few of them. For a full list, read the official API documentation (`http://www.protractortest.org/#/api`).

The `by.css` selector locates elements using a CSS selector. For example:

```
element(by.css('h1'));
```

The `by.id` selector locates an element by its ID. For example:

```
element(by.id('id'))
```

The `by.tagName` selector locates elements with a given tag name. For example:

```
element(by.tagName('div'))
```

Note that for Angular 2+ apps, the `by.binding` and `by.model` locators are not supported. They are only supported for Angular 1.x.

The `element` function returns an `ElementFinder` object, which can be used to interact with the underlying DOM element or get information from it. The following table lists the most important methods of `ElementFinder`:

Method	Description
`getText()`	Returns the text of an element.
`click()`	Executes a click on an element.
`sendKeys(keys)`	Sends passed in characters to an element (useful for filling in forms).
`element(locator)`	Finds child elements within a parent (this element) by a given locator. It returns the first found child element as an object of type `ElementFinder`.
`all(locator)`	Finds child elements within a parent (this element) by a given locator. It returns an array of all found child elements as an object of type `ElementArrayFinder`. The `ElementArrayFinder` object has a lot of useful methods. For instance, `count()` provides a count of found elements, `get(index: number)` provides an element at a specified position in the array. For more information, read the API documentation.
`getId()`	Gets the ID of the DOM element.
`isDisplayed()`	Checks whether the DOM element is visible.
`isEnabled()`	Checks whether the DOM element is enabled.

Let's see two examples, and check if an element with the style class `info` is displayed (visible) as follows:

```
expect(element(by.css('.info')).isDisplayed()).toBe(true);
```

The next code snippet checks if a button is clickable:

```
expect(element(by.tagName('button')).isEnabled()).toBe(true);
```

Be careful with animations. When an element appears after some animation, it is reasonable to wait for an animation end. To achieve that, use `browser.wait()` as `browser.wait(element(by.id('id')).isDisplayed()).toBe(true)`.

Be aware that access operations for DOM elements return promises and not elements themselves. It concerns, for example, `getText()`, `count()`, and so on. Protractor patches Jasmine's `expect()` function so that it waits automatically until the promise gets resolved and the located DOM element is accessible. After that, the matcher will be applied. This is convenient, but there are some cases where you need an access to the value of the resolved promise. In these cases, you can use the promise's `then()` function explicitly. Assume you want to output the count of rows within a table. The next code snippet exemplifies the idea:

```
it('should display the correct row count', () => {
  const pcount = element.all(by.css('table tr')).count();
  pcount.then((count) => {
    console.log(`Table has ${count} rows`);
  });
  expect(pcount).toEqual(20);
});
```

Clean architecture with Page Objects

A Page Object encapsulates the behavior of a web page. In single-page applications, we have views. For the sake of convenience, if we say "web page," we will mean both full page and view. There is one Page Object per web page that abstracts the page's logic to the outside. That means the interaction with the web page is encapsulated in the Page Object. The e2e tests operate on Page Objects. Take an example from a web shop: the Page Objects could be written as classes: `ProductPage`, `ShoppingCartPage`, `PaymentPage`, and so on.

A Page Element (aka *HTML Wrapper*) is another subdivision of a web page. It represents an HTML element and encapsulates the logic for the interaction with this element. For instance, an HTML Wrapper for DatePicker can provide the API methods such as "set a date into the input field," "open the calendar popup," and "choose given day in the calendar popup". An HTML Wrapper can be composite; that means, it can consist of multiple small elements. For instance, a product catalog consists of products, a shopping cart consists of items, and so on.

Page Objects and HTML Wrappers as design patterns were described by Martin Fowler (ht tps://martinfowler.com/bliki/PageObject.html). There are a lot of advantages with this architecture:

- Clean separation between test code and page-specific code.
- The by locators to find elements on the page are not disclosed to the outside. The Page Object's caller never bothers with the by locators.
- If some UI changes for any page, you don't need to change the corresponding tests. We just need to change the code at one place--within the Page Object.
- Page Objects reduce the amount of duplicated code. If the tests share the same scenario, you don't need to copy/paste your code. Write once, share everywhere!
- The spec files are more readable and more compact--one glance at the code and we know what the test does.

The next code snippet demonstrates a simple Page Object for an imaginary login page:

```typescript
import {browser, element, by, ElementFinder} from 'protractor';
import {promise} from 'selenium-webdriver';

export class LoginPage {
  nameInput: ElementFinder;
  passwordInput: ElementFinder;
  submitButton: ElementFinder;

  constructor() {
    this.nameInput = element(by.css('.name'));
    this.passwordInput = element(by.css('.password'));
    this.submitButton = element(by.css('button[type="submit"]'));
  }

  navigateTo() {
    browser.get('http://www.mywebshop.com');
  };

  login(name: string, password: string) {
    this.nameInput.sendKeys(name);
    this.passwordInput.sendKeys(password);
    this.submitButton.click();
  };

  isUserLoggedIn(): promise.Promise<boolean> {
    return element(by.css('.userProfile')).isDisplayed();
  }
}
```

As you see, many steps were extracted into one method. The test code using `LoginPage` is concise:

```
describe('Web shop user', function() {
  it('should log in successfully', function() {
    let loginPage = new LoginPage();
    loginPage.navigateTo();
    loginPage.login('Max Mustermann', 'mysecret');

    expect(loginPage.isUserLoggedIn()).toBeTruthy();
  });
});
```

A spec file should be grouped with the corresponding Page Object in the same folder. It is a best practice to use the `.po.ts` suffix for the Page Object files. For example, the Page Object file for the login page is called `login.po.ts`. For Page Element files, we suggest to use the `.pe.ts` suffix; for example, `dialog.pe.ts`.

Writing complete the e2e test

We are going to write e2e specs testing the UI from *Displaying confirmation dialog with guarded routes* of `Chapter 9`, *Miscellaneous Use Cases and Best Practices*. Just to recap: the first view has an input field (username) with a submit button. The button triggers a navigation to the second view. Whenever the user changes the username, a confirmation dialog with the text **You have unsaved changes. Are you sure you want to leave this page?** will appear. The user can click on **Yes** or **No**. We want to write five test cases that verify:

- Whether the first page has a proper title displayed within the `h1` tag
- Whether the navigation happens when no input exists
- Whether a confirmation dialog gets displayed when an input exists
- Whether the user leaves the current view when clicking on **Yes**
- Whether the user stays on the current view when clicking on **No**

Before writing specs, we need a Page Object called `FirstViewPage`:

```
import {browser, element, by, ElementFinder} from 'protractor';
import {promise} from 'selenium-webdriver';

export class FirstViewPage {
  nameInput: ElementFinder;
  submitButton: ElementFinder;
```

```
  constructor() {
    this.nameInput = element(by.css('input[name="username"]'));
    this.submitButton = element(by.css('button[type="submit"]'));
  }

  navigateTo() {
    browser.get('http://localhost:3000/chapter9/first-view');
  };

  typeUsername(name: string) {
    this.nameInput.sendKeys(name);
  };

  confirm() {
    this.submitButton.click();
  };

  getTitle(): promise.Promise<string> {
    return element(by.css('h1')).getText();
  }
}
```

The Page Element `ConfirmDialogPageElement` encapsulates the internal structure details of the confirmation dialog. It offers three methods to ask for the dialog's visibility and to interact with the **Yes** and **No** buttons:

```
export class ConfirmDialogPageElement {
  element: ElementFinder;

  constructor(by: By) {
    this.element = element(by);
  }

  isDisplayed(): promise.Promise<boolean> {
    return this.element.isDisplayed();
  }

  confirm() {
    this.clickButton('fa-check');
  }

  cancel() {
    this.clickButton('fa-close');
  }

  private clickButton(icon: string) {
    let button = this.element.$('button .' +
      icon).element(by.xpath('..'));
```

```
      button.click();
   }
}
```

 $() is a handy shortcut notation for `element(by.css())`. The `by.xpath('..')` locator allows to select the parent element.

The specs themselves are clean--they invoke public APIs from `FirstViewPage` and `ConfirmDialogPageElement`:

```
describe('FirstView', () => {
  let page: FirstViewPage;

  beforeEach(() => {
    page = new FirstViewPage();
    page.navigateTo();
  });

  it('should contain proper title', () => {
    expect(page.getTitle()).toContain('first view');
  });

  it('should change the view when no input exists', () => {
    page.confirm();
    expect(browser.getCurrentUrl()).not.toMatch(/\/first-view$/);
  });

  it('should display confirmation dialog when input exists', () => {
    page.typeUsername('Admin');
    page.confirm();

    let confirmDialog = new ConfirmDialogPageElement(
        by.css('p-confirmdialog'));
    expect(confirmDialog.isDisplayed()).toBeTruthy();
  });

  it('should navigate to another view on confirm', () => {
    page.typeUsername('Admin');
    page.confirm();

    let confirmDialog = new ConfirmDialogPageElement(
        by.css('p-confirmdialog'));
    confirmDialog.confirm();
    expect(browser.getCurrentUrl()).not.toMatch(/\/first-view$/);
  });
```

```
it('should stay on the same view on cancel', () => {
    page.typeUsername('Admin');
    page.confirm();

    let confirmDialog = new ConfirmDialogPageElement(
        by.css('p-confirmdialog'));
    confirmDialog.cancel();
    expect(browser.getCurrentUrl()).toMatch(/\/first-view$/);
});
});
```

The next screenshot shows spec reports in IntelliJ/WebStorm:

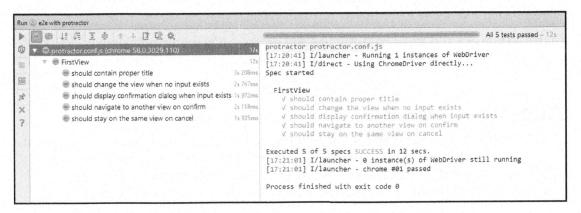

The complete project with instructions is available on GitHub at
`https://github.com/ova2/angular-development-with-primeng/tree`
`/master/chapter10/e2e-testing`.

Exploring a PrimeNG application with Augury and ng.probe

Augury is a Google Chrome browser extension for inspecting Angular 2+ applications (`http
s://augury.angular.io/`). The tool visualizes the application through a component tree,
router tree, module dependencies, and more. Developers immediately see the application
structure, change detection, and other useful characteristics. They can explore relationships
between several building blocks, such as components, services, routes, modules, injectors,
and so on. Augury is interactive. It allows for modifying application states and emitting
events.

You can install Augury from the Chrome Web Store: `https://chrome.goo gle.com/webstore/detail/augury/elgalmkoelokbchhkhacckoklkejnhc d`.

Once the plugin has been successfully installed, you will see a new **Augury** tab in the Chrome Developer Tools (DevTools). Shortcuts for opening the DevTools: *F12* (Windows), *Command + Option + I* (Mac).

There is another way to explore Angular 2+ applications. In the development mode, Angular exposes a global `ng.probe` function, which takes native DOM element and returns corresponding debug elements. With the debug element, you can inspect the current state of components, injectors, listeners, trigger events, and so on. The `ng.probe` function is accessible in the browser's console.

In this section, we will apply both Augury and `ng.probe` to the already known CRUD demo application from `Chapter 9`, *Miscellaneous Use Cases and Best Practices*.

Augury in action

The first visible view in Augury is the **Component Tree,** which shows loaded components. Selecting a component within the tree highlights the component's template within the browser. At the same time, additional information about the selected component is presented on the right side in the **Properties** tab. Let's select `DataTableCrudComponent`:

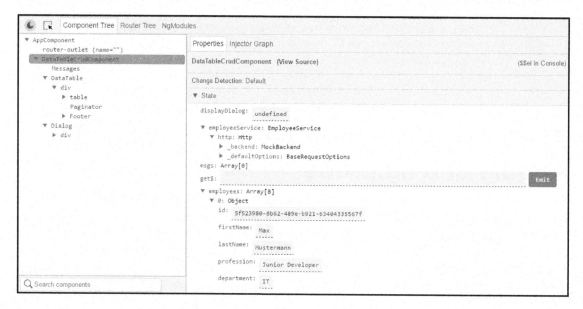

You see all the internal properties, inputs, and outputs. All the properties are editable. The next screenshot shows the properties of the Dialog component. The output property visibleChange is an event emitter. We can trigger the event emitter by setting the value to true and clicking on the button **Emit**. In response, the dialog becomes visible:

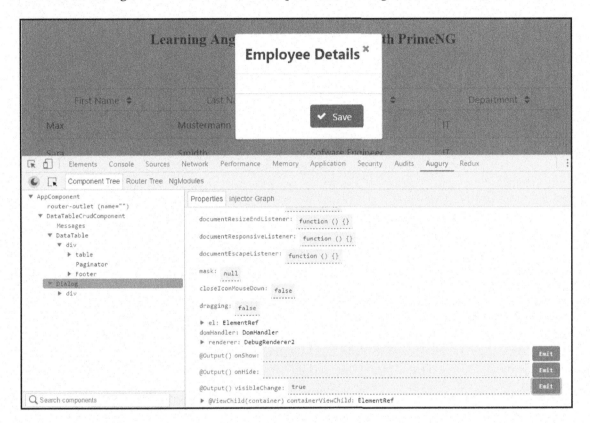

Next to the **Properties** tab is the **Injector Graph,** which displays the dependencies of components and services. If we select the DataTable component, the dependency of the DataTable and its ancestry chain to the root injector will be shown:

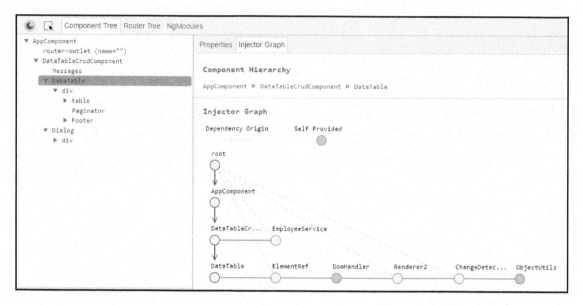

The circle symbols for services need to be clarified. The hollow red circle means the service is not provided by the component. It is provided from an ancestor in the dependency tree. A dashed blue line shows exactly where the service comes from. In our case, all services are provided by the root injector--the main module declaration in `app.module.ts`. The filled red circle means the service is being injected and registered in the same component.

The **Router Tree** gives you a tree view of all the routes in your application. You can explore which routes come from which parts of the application. We will skip the appropriate screenshot. The next tab, **NgModules,** lists all the modules in the application, along with the modules' imports, exports, providers, and declarations. An insight into **NgModules** gives the complexity and size of the available modules:

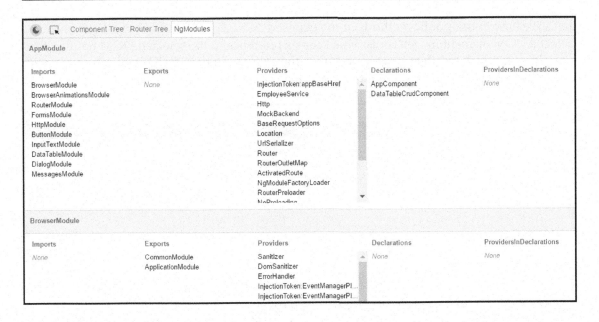

Debugging with ng.probe

By default, Angular runs in the development mode and builds a *debugging elements tree--*a tree, which has almost the same structure as a rendered DOM, but with objects of type `DebugElement`. Whenever `ng.probe(element)` is invoked in the browser console, a corresponding debug element is returned. The `DebugElement` class extends `DebugNode` (ht tps://angular.io/docs/ts/latest/api/core/index/DebugNode-class.html).

In the production mode, no debugging elements tree is available and you cannot debug an Angular application with `ng.probe`. The production mode is enabled with `enableProdMode()`, which is a function from Angular's package, `@angular/core`.

Let's see how to use public methods of the exposed `DebugElement`. First of all, we need to select a DOM element in DevTools. This keeps a reference to the selected DOM node in the variable `$0`, which can then be accessed from the console. In the CRUD application, we will select the **Add** button, as shown in the following screenshot:

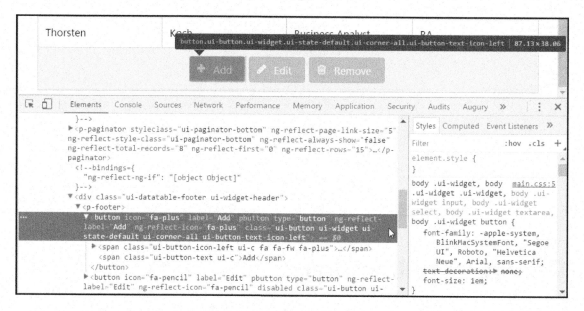

Now, we are able to get a reference to the component instance the button belongs to. Once we have that instance, we can interact with it; for example, we can change properties, and so on. Let's reset the array of `employees`:

```
ng.probe($0).componentInstance.employees = [];
```

 Selecting any element within the component template will always provide the same component instance.

There is one problem--the code explained didn't change anything in the UI. The reason is obvious--we need to invoke the change detector manually. The next line is a bit complicated, but does exactly what we need--it runs the change detection cycle. As a result, the table with employees becomes empty:

```
ng.probe($0).injector.get(ng.coreTokens.ApplicationRef).tick();
```

The `injector` property allows accessing all the providers on the component and its parents. For instance, assume there is the following provider definition:

```
providers: [{
  provide: 'PaymentEndpoint',
  useValue: 'http://someendpoint.com/v1/payment/'
}]
```

The value `http://someendpoint.com/v1/payment/` can be grabbed with the following code:

```
let element = document.querySelector('.some');
let endpoint = ng.probe(element).injector.get('PaymentEndpoint');
```

The DOM element with the `some` style class should be located within the component the defined provider is visible for.

One interesting use case is the triggering registered event handlers. In the demo application, we could select the **Add** button and trigger the click event on this button as follows:

```
ng.probe($0).triggerEventHandler('click');
```

This command will open the following dialog:

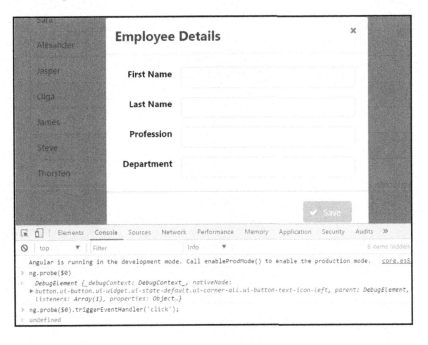

You might also be interested in a graphical analysis tool, *ngrev*, for reverse engineering of Angular projects (`https://github.com/mgechev/ngrev`). With this tool, you can explore the structure of your application, and the relationship between different modules, providers, and directives without running the application.

Summary

At the end of this chapter, you should be able to set up the test environment for unit and e2e testing. The *de facto* standard unit test framework and runner introduced in this chapter were Jasmine and Karma, respectively. You got skills in writing unit tests for most used constructs, as well as basic skills in writing the e2e test with the Protractor framework.

You are also equipped with useful tips for creating robust applications. The `karma-webpack-grep` plugin can give a huge performance boost when booting up Karma in development. The Augury tool, as well as `ng.probe`, enable debugging and profiling Angular 2+ applications. We hope that the last chapter and the entire book will contribute to a flawless development process of your next Angular and PrimeNG applications.

Index

CPSIA information can be obtained
at www.ICGtesting.com
Printed in the USA
BVOW04s0736121217
502545BV00007B/32/P